PRAISE FOR
UNLEASH YOUR INNER COMPANY

"Chisholm has written from his lifelong experience in business and created a wonderful book. Everyone should read it."

—Steve Mariotti, founder of the Network for Teaching
Entrepreneurship and author of *An Entrepreneur's Manifesto*

"Chisholm emerges as the Yoda of startups. He unleashes a rare combination of human insight and wisdom on the inner game of entrepreneurship."

—Rob Johnson, president of the Institute for New Economic Thinking

"John Chisholm not only offers an excellent practical guide to entrepreneurship but also helps you through the toughest personal decisions like what business to start and which cofounders to choose. A must-read for anyone considering starting a company, from an accomplished Silicon Valley entrepreneur."

—Mark Gorenberg, managing director of Zetta Venture Partners

"John Chisholm's successful example guides us on a fascinating journey. We learn not only how to create a company but how entrepreneurship drives economic growth and development and how it benefits the whole of society."

—Prince Michael of Liechtenstein, founder and
chairman of Geopolitical Information Service AG

"This book is jam packed with insights about the entrepreneurial journey: stories to inspire you, frameworks to guide you, and tactics to deploy during the inevitable ups and downs. Highly recommended."

—Ben Casnocha, coauthor of #1 *New York Times*
best seller *The Start-up of You*

"Full of good sense and great fun to read. If you're starting a business, this is like having a wise advisor whispering in your ear."

—W. Brian Arthur, author of *The Nature of Technology*

"Entrepreneurship is marked by the surprises of human creativity. John Chisholm has written a book that epitomizes the creativity it celebrates and surprises us with zero-to-one insights."

—George Gilder, author of *Wealth and Poverty*, *Microcosm*, and *Telecosm*

"Experienced and first-time entrepreneurs alike will find *Unleash Your Inner Company* invaluable for turning their ideas into a successful business."

—John S. Reed, former chairman of Citigroup
and New York Stock Exchange

"The definitive primer for entrepreneurs, filled with invaluable wisdom and uncommon insights."

—Joon Yun, MD, president of Palo Alto Investors
and creator of the $1 million Palo Alto Longevity Prize

"John Chisholm's achievements as an entrepreneur reflect signature MIT values—a passion for hands-on problem solving, an affinity for techno-logical solutions, and a commitment to making the world a better place. With *Unleash Your Inner Company*, he distills the lessons of a lifetime to give aspiring entrepreneurs a head start on success."

—L. Rafael Reif, president of MIT

"*Unleash Your Inner Company* shows people from all walks of life, step by step, how to do what they love, achieve financial independence, and make the world a better place through entrepreneurship. People across the nation and the world should embrace this book."

—Lorraine Hariton, former special representative
for Commercial and Business Affairs for the US
Department of State and senior vice president of Global
Partnerships for the New York Academy of Sciences

"This is a deceptive book. It can profitably be read as a business book but, much more fundamentally, it is an insightful and inspiring guide on how each of us can achieve far more of our potential and create environments where all parties are better off."

—John Hagel III, founder and cochairman of the Deloitte Center for the Edge and coauthor of *The Power of Pull*

"This practical and inspiring book will not only be an essential guide for budding entrepreneurs; it should be required reading for government regulators, who might wield their power more wisely if they understood the dampening effect of regulations on the passion and perseverance required to start a successful business."

—Susan E. Dudley, founder and director of the George Washington University Regulatory Studies Center and former administrator of the Office of Information and Regulatory Affairs of the US Office of Management and Budget

"Creating a successful startup may be an act of magic, but good magicians study the experts very closely; John Chisholm is an expert in startups, and he shares his wisdom in these pages."

—Alan Cooper, founder of Cooper and author of *About Face: The Essentials of Interaction Design*

"A unique combination of a personal memoir, a passionate defense of passion, and a lucid presentation of the strategies and tactics required to start and build a successful business. I love the fact that Chisholm is willing to argue for heart first, without ever compromising on experiments, analysis, or reason, and his insight that economic success builds on the deepest emotional commitments."

—David Krakauer, president of the Santa Fe Institute

"John Chisholm's awesome experience gives him the expertise to write this book—so you should listen."

—Adam Draper, CEO and founder of Boost

"A fascinating guide to how to be an entrepreneur—and thereby do the world a favor—from one who has done it."

—Matt Ridley, author of *Genome: The Autobiography of a Species in 23 Chapters*, *The Rational Optimist: How Prosperity Evolves*, and *The Evolution of Everything: How Ideas Emerge*

"Passion, Perseverance, and Purpose. John Chisholm shows how to take those core ingredients and turn them into a business that can change the world for the better."

—Ramez Naam, author of *Nexus*

"Before now, startups always seemed so distant, and I didn't know where to start. Now I realize that I have all the resources I need."

—Ben Potash, MIT class of 2014

"*Unleash Your Inner Company* reveals a path to success and is lined with lots of provocative prompts and practical guidance. John Chisholm has provided a valuable resource for anyone seeking to translate ideas into a thriving enterprise."

—Michael Mauboussin, head of Global Strategies, Credit Suisse

"A new entrepreneur may want to reinvent how business is done, but there is a lot to learn from someone who has done it before. Those with the ambition to launch a new company should read this book carefully. John Chisholm puts his years of experience and wisdom to work in a contemporary context."

—Jim Champy, coauthor of *Reengineering the Corporation*

"John Chisholm provides aspiring entrepreneurs with the mental models that most of us had to learn by making mistakes. An essential read for anybody trying to apply or build tomorrow's technology."

—Joe Lonsdale, cofounder of Formation 8, Palantir Technologies, Addepar, and OpenGov

Dear Alireza,
Congratulations & Best Wishes!
John Chisholm
5 August 2016

JOHN CHISHOLM

UNLEASH
YOUR
INNER
COMPANY

USE PASSION AND PERSEVERANCE
TO BUILD YOUR IDEAL BUSINESS

GREENLEAF
BOOK GROUP PRESS

Published by Greenleaf Book Group Press
Austin, Texas
www.gbgpress.com

Distributed by Greenleaf Book Group

For ordering information or special discounts for bulk purchases, please contact Greenleaf Book Group at PO Box 91869, Austin, TX 78709, 512-891-6100.

Design and composition by Greenleaf Book Group
Cover design by Greenleaf Book Group

Publisher's Cataloging Publication Data is available.

ISBN: 978-1-62634-211-8

Part of the Tree Neutral® program, which offsets the number of trees consumed in the production and printing of this book by taking proactive steps, such as planting trees in direct proportion to the number of trees used: www.treeneutral.com

TreeNeutral

Printed in the United States of America on acid-free paper

15 16 17 18 19 20   10 9 8 7 6 5 4 3 2 1

First Edition

Other Edition(s):
eBook ISBN: 978-1-62634-213-2

*To my friends and colleagues at MIT,
in Silicon Valley, at Dale Carnegie,
and the Santa Fe Institute;
and to the next generation of entrepreneurs*

The path is a spiral—upwards.
—Herman Hesse, Siddhartha

CONTENTS

1

PASSION AND PERSEVERANCE (STEP 1): A POSITIVE FEEDBACK LOOP

It doesn't get easier. You get stronger.
—Anonymous

In the first half of 2001, the dot-com bust, I would often wake up around 2 a.m. with sweat-soaked sheets sticking to my skin. CustomerSat's second round of financing, long planned for that January, had refused to come together despite a flurry of meetings as we ran out of cash. Those nights I would get up, shower off the sweat, and try to get back to sleep. When my executive team and I finally grasped that the Series B round was not going to close, we huddled to decide what to do. First, we cut our salaries, then several weeks later those of all our employees, by 10 percent; I cut my own salary and that of my CFO by 50 percent. Debating and agonizing over every individual, we laid off 40 percent of our workforce. In our all-hands meeting immediately after, as I explained to our remaining employees that this was the only way we could keep together and stay afloat, my composure collapsed and I broke down sobbing. Our employees stood stunned, sympathetic, and embarrassed.

After many consecutive quarters of profit and growth, our recurring revenues had dropped that first quarter of 2001 by a whopping 20 percent.[1] Our first customers to stop paying were themselves dot-com companies, like highflier Webvan, who would file for bankruptcy in July

2001 just sixteen months after their initial public offering (IPO). Later, even Fortune 500 companies discontinued our online survey services or simply stopped paying. To help us get through, one of our Series A investors lent me $300,000—*for* but not *to* the company—meaning that I, the CEO and founder, would be personally liable for repaying the loan. The cash would last us ninety days. Later I would pay back the investor—to whom, despite the arrangement, I was deeply grateful—by mortgaging my townhouse in Menlo Park, California.

The next quarter our revenues fell again. To make payroll this time, we factored receivables, a costly maneuver, and cut salaries by an additional 10 percent. I reduced my salary to minimum wage, the legal limit. Our company moved into the second floor of our building and rented out the more attractive ground floor to another start-up. That company quit paying us rent after three months, came in late one weekend night, cleaned out their offices, and vanished without notice. The nightmare would not end.

After those fitful nights and drastic actions of the first half of 2001, we could finally see profitability ahead in the third quarter. Then, on September 11, terrorists viciously attacked US targets including the World Trade Center. Enveloped in smoke, dust, and debris, the twin 110-floor towers crumpled and collapsed. With much of the US northeast communications grid down, just accounting for all our employees took hours of emailing, phone calling, and pleading to know who had heard from whom. Our VP Sales Russ Haswell was marooned in London, unable to get back to the United States; our client invited him to stay at their home. The next day I was finally able to broadcast the message, "All CustomerSat team members are safe." The US West Coast escaped the full brunt of the horror, but even in Silicon Valley, every company I knew had customers or suppliers who lost employees or family members in the attacks. Our client Akamai Technologies lost its brilliant cofounder Danny Lewin on American Airlines flight 11. Our salespeople were calling insurance and other firms in the World Trade Center; tragically, their phones just rang and rang. After the dot-com bust, September 11 was the final blow for many start-ups.

We broke even in the third quarter, a milestone and quiet relief. A very small profit followed in the fourth. The going stayed tough through all of 2002 and the first half of 2003, during which time we didn't hire a single new employee. But we made it through. CustomerSat stayed profitable and grew nearly every quarter until the company was acquired in March 2008. Only a fraction of Internet companies survived; even fewer went on to successful exits. Why did CustomerSat do so when others did not?

———

Unleash Your Inner Company distills three decades of real-world lessons I have learned about entrepreneurship. During that time I have founded, grown, and sold two online software companies; cofounded a third; invested in a dozen privately held companies, several of which have had successful initial public offerings (IPOs—also known as "going public"); started and run consultancies in strategic marketing and entrepreneurship; and mentored hundreds of entrepreneurs on five continents. My mission today and for the past five years is to help aspiring entrepreneurs achieve the freedom, independence, and ability to do what they love through entrepreneurship. This book is part of that mission.

Unleash Your Inner Company offers unique guidance and perspective for anyone who wants to start and grow a business:

- Entrepreneurs are not interchangeable like batteries or light bulbs; the best opportunity for you is unique to you.

- You have many more resources than you likely realize to start a company and make it successful.

- Positive feedback loops pervade multiple aspects of your start-up and life; find, nurture, and ride them.

- Psychology is an essential part of strategy.

- Any business, no matter how modest, can be evolved and scaled into a large business, if desired.

This book provides a proven, step-by-step process: (1) Identify/develop your passions, (2) Generate/refine customer needs in those areas, (3) Generate possible solutions to those needs, (4) Inventory your resources, (4a) Generate additional needs suggested by your resources, (5) Match needs with resources, (6) Acquire/develop additional resources, (7) Determine your advantages, (8) Match needs with advantages to select the best fit, (9) Launch, and (10) Scale up.

This ten-step process, explained in greater detail in chapter 2 figure 2.4 and the flowchart in figure 2.5, guides you in finding and creating the best start-up for you, whether you choose mobile apps, construction, robotics, hairdressing, management consulting, gourmet food, enterprise software, or any other field.

In *Unleash Your Inner Company*, you first discover the essential roles of passion and perseverance and how to develop them. You see how to identify dozens of unsatisfied customer needs among your passions, develop solutions and build the advantages as required to satisfy those needs, and determine which needs you can satisfy most successfully. It doesn't matter whether you have a product or service in mind or not; here we start with customer needs, which precede products and services. By following the steps in this book, you vastly improve the likelihood of your start-up's success.

This is the only book you need to start the *right* business for you. *Unleash Your Inner Company* shows you how you can take your future into your own hands, follow your passions, and spend the rest of your life contributing to the world in the way you love best.

Why did CustomerSat survive and thrive while others did not? More generally, why do some companies do so while others do not? I don't believe we were smarter than any other company execs. We did act very quickly to minimize damage to our company. But if I had to choose a single factor, I believe that underneath it all we *cared* more deeply about our business: about every customer, the coolness of our products and technology, each of our employees, and each other. Among our team members who went through the dot-com meltdown together, there was very little turnover—very strong employee loyalty—for many years. And we did not give up as quickly as others did. In my view, it was this combination of passion and perseverance that got us through.

We hear much more today about passion, which sounds easy and fun, than perseverance, which sounds hard. Your *passions* are what you care most deeply about, have the highest expectations for, have powerful and compelling feelings about, or that give your life meaning. They may include your job, team, company, family, sports, school, hobbies, communities, faith, travel, investing, gaming, gadgets, or virtually any other subject or activity. *Perseverance* is persistence in purpose, ideas, or tasks in the face of obstacles or discouragement. Passion (an attitude) and persistence (a behavior) usually go together. But you can have one without the other: passion can be fleeting; perseverance can be uninspired. Without passion, perseverance is drudgery; with it, working long hours becomes effortless. Successful founders and teams have both. Various terms have been applied to the combination of passion and perseverance: flourishing, grit, and the term that to me best captures how time flies and organizations click when the two qualities come together— *flow*.[2] Figure 1.1 illustrates perseverance, passion, and flow.

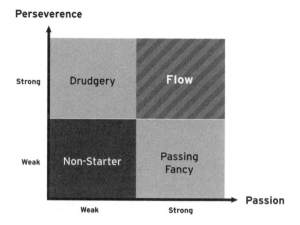

— *Figure 1.1* —

Perseverance, passion, and flow.

You and your start-up need passion and perseverance for several reasons. With passion and perseverance, the following are true:

- You are more likely to be first to reach or discover the limits of what is currently possible or convenient in your chosen field. This means you can recognize customer needs before others do. Passion and perseverance thus help you get your new venture off the ground.

- You're able to break through or find ways around obstacles. Layoffs, salary reductions, factoring receivables, and moving to downsized, more modest offices are hard and humbling actions to take. Passion and perseverance empower you to do whatever it takes for your venture to survive and grow.

- You're in it for the long haul and don't plan to quit. Ventures usually take longer than expected to reach their goals; the short term can turn into the long term very quickly. I ended up running CustomerSat for over a decade. Perseverance keeps you going for as long as it takes; passion makes the journey as important to you as the destination.

- You stay motivated. Perseverance and passion are contagious and motivate those around you, including coworkers, customers, suppliers, and partners.

- Your strengths and advantages are amplified.

CREATING POSITIVE FEEDBACK LOOPS

Passion and perseverance reinforce each other. Practicing the piano, designing circuits, or rock climbing until you are so good that you grow to love that activity are examples of perseverance driving passion. At the same time, your passion makes you want to spend time on that activity, driving you to ever greater proficiency and outstanding performance, further building your passion . . . and so on.

Similarly, being so deeply engaged by activities such as woodworking, cooking, or sailing that you become unaware of the passage of time demonstrates passion driving perseverance. As you spend more time in the activity, you refine your skills and deepen your knowledge, again further building your passion.

This reinforcement creates a *positive feedback loop*, just one of many you will seek or create in your new venture. Positive feedback makes magic happen. Whenever you see results or performance that is far above the norm—in sports, the arts, crafts, science, innovation, business, investing, or any other realm—positive feedback is working its magic.

Think of passion and perseverance as the north-south and east-west axes of a mountain. If you only move along one of these, your climbing options will be limited and difficult; reaching the top may be impossible. In contrast, if you can move along either axis, in any direction, you are much more likely to find a route that gets you to the top. Passion and perseverance together give you that flexibility and keep you going indefinitely. They positively reinforce each other.

Any number of initial motivations can get this positive feedback started: looking good in front of your peers; being an expert, named the leader, or the unnamed but de facto leader; achieving some specific milestone; winning her heart; providing for your family; making your first million; proving someone wrong; revenge; or surviving. Some of these motivations are more sustainable than others and some have undesirable side effects, but any or all of them can help you get started. I started both of my companies after being fired from previous companies—my first time was in high school while working for my hometown newspaper—and proving my former employers wrong was surely part of what motivated me. But if what drives you is not or does not fairly quickly become *doing good*—solving problems, addressing customer needs, or in some other way making the world a better place—it won't inspire others or be sustainable, in my experience.

If you are not passionate about your new venture, its chances of success are slim. Even with passion, starting a successful venture is hard. But it *is* achievable and you can do it. Yes, you. This book shows you how.

YOU CAN BECOME PASSIONATE

Your passions harbor your best opportunities for new ventures. For example, I've been a math geek since junior high school and both of the companies I started involved analyzing data. The following list offers a few such possible passions:

- **People:** Family, friends, coworkers, teammates, teachers/coaches, club members, neighbors, children, teens, and seniors

- **Activities:** Working, studying, reading, cooking, sports, fashion, gardening, hobbies, shopping, and travel

- **Things:** Home, food/health, electronics, home appliances, mobile devices, the Internet, sporting goods, vehicles, tools, money, and pets

- **Media:** Books, news, photos, maps, games, social networks, video, animation, and virtual reality

- **Arts:** Music, film, dance, theatre, painting, sculpture, literature, design, ceramics, and criticism

- **The sciences:** Research, analysis, discovery, math, physics, chemistry, life sciences, environmental sciences, astronomy, and cosmology

- **Engineering fields:** Civil, mechanical, electrical, computer science, materials, transportation, architecture, biotech, space, and nuclear

- **Business disciplines:** Marketing, sales, customers, planning, accounting, marketing, sales, manufacturing, purchasing, distribution, strategy, and communication

One or more of your passions may be listed, but please don't think yours have to be among these. Recently I became deeply interested in Africa after reading *Dark Star Safari* (Houghton Mifflin, 2003), Paul Theroux's detailed account of his overland trip from Cairo to Cape Town. The vivid picture of African life and landscape painted by Theroux has hooked me on visiting the continent. That could be the start of a new passion for me.

If nothing comes to you, that's okay. You can *become* passionate about something. In that case, the exercises at the end of this chapter under "If your passion is not well defined" are for you. *Warning*: they require perseverance. After a few hours of exploration and practice, you will have advanced a fair distance in a field of your choice. In a few weeks, you will have learned a great deal about it; in a few months, you will have become an expert. The more you learn and master the topic or activity, the more it engages you. Over time, the process becomes more like play than work. When it takes on a life of its own, so that you are drawn to it, it has become a passion—and a strong candidate in which to start your new venture.

UNPOPULAR IS GOOD

If your current field or the field you become passionate about isn't very popular, so much the better: *You will have less competition.* Few of the more than 100,000 health and fitness apps for the iPhone will survive. Conversely, I can't think of anything less sexy than *Municipal Sewer & Water.* That trade magazine is full of articles on automated flow control, remote monitoring, real-time alerts, hydraulic modeling, hydroxyl radical fogging (controls odors), and ultraviolet disinfection. The entrepreneurs applying these techniques and technologies in water and sewerage are doing good: improving water quality, sanitation, and public safety, while reducing manual labor costs and taxes.[3] So don't let what is merely popular blind you from other opportunities.

"Learning in Depth" is a secondary school teaching technique that assigns each first grader an everyday topic—such as apples, ants, water, dinosaurs, bridges, dust, or railroads—to study on their own, through grammar school and beyond. If the topic is apples, for example, the child may learn about varieties, agriculture, recipes, and genetics; make field trips to apple orchards; and bake apple pies. Very soon the students know more about the subject than their teachers do. By junior high school, each student is a real expert on the subject. Interestingly, the children become deeply passionate about their topics *even if they don't get to choose them.*

I don't suggest that you choose a field at random or ask someone to assign one to you. But realize that the more you learn about and practice something, the more engaging it becomes and the more passionate you will become about it. As Cal Newport, author of *So Good They Can't Ignore You* (Business Plus, 2012), says, "Don't follow your passions. Let them follow you."[4]

He did it with all his heart and prospered.
—*Second Chronicles 31:21*

GOOD QUESTION!

Q

My passions are not very business-oriented. They include long hot baths, kittens, and comic books. What should I do?

A

First, make certain that these passions provide the challenge, goal, and feedback that can sustain you as your life's work over the long term. Purely sensory pleasures typically lack one or more of these.

But if you believe they *can* sustain you, know that all passions, even sensory ones, contain an infinite number of opportunities. We see how to identify and create these later. For your three passions, for example, the following might be some opportunities:

- Waterproof, floating cases for mobile phones and tablets so people can read, text their friends, or listen to music while enjoying **long hot baths**.

- **Kittens** have different dietary requirements and preferences from full-grown cats and are near-universal symbols of cuteness and cuddliness. What new pet foods, toys, or other products might kittens need? Could the right diet or genetic therapy enable kittens to stay small, cute, and cuddly longer?

- The hugely popular and commercially successful tradeshow Comic-Con (www.comic-con.org) showcases **comic books**, science fiction/fantasy, and video games. It annually attracts over 130,000 attendees.

At this early stage of creating your business, consider several of your passions, if you have them. One will offer you better opportunities than others and it is hard to know which one it will be in advance. We'll also see that your path will be easier if what you do is not merely better, but different from what others are doing. So start thinking about how your approach to baths, kittens, comic books, and other topics can be unique.

Q

My passion is helping the poor, the handicapped, and victims of abuse. These seem more likely to be nonprofit than for-profit ventures. What do you suggest?

A

The principles and techniques in this book apply either way. Following are two important points:

- **To best sustain any activity long term, whether nonprofit or for-profit, make it** *self-funding.* Even nonprofits can earn income from operations and investments, as long as that income is used to further the mission of the nonprofit. By becoming self-funding, you won't have to rely indefinitely on funds from donors, whose interests and priorities can change. You will also be able to spend more time and resources helping the people and causes you care about, and less on fund-raising.

- **Whether your venture is nonprofit or for-profit, rather than give handouts to those in need, help them become** *self-sufficient.* This, too, is the most sustainable long term. Food and other supplies intended for the poor in low-income countries often end up in the hands of military strongmen or dictators. Despots keep the aid for themselves and their cronies or use it to further manipulate and oppress the poor. Dumping food and supplies in low-income cities and villages can put local farmers and entrepreneurs out of business, as vividly shown in the documentary *Poverty, Inc.* (www.povertyinc .org). Finally, aid given indefinitely reduces incentives for people to develop skills and income streams that lead to self-sufficiency. Instead, ask how can you help them grow their own food or earn enough to afford to live on their own. Making people self-sufficient will help your own venture sustain itself because the support you provide them will have a finite duration, rather than indefinite; put less strain on your resources; and let you help more people.

The Grameen Bank in Bangladesh makes small loans to the very poor. (The name *Grameen* is not a surname but comes from the Bengali word *gram* which means "rural" or "village."[5]) The bank helps people improve their lives and escape poverty through financing; new ways to generate income; and information about health, crops, and finances. This bank has done more sustained good around the world than aid programs many times its size. It is a for-profit that can serve as a role model for other for-profits and nonprofits alike.

Q

Should I rely on reports from leading market analysis and consulting firms—for example, McKinsey, Gartner Group, Boston Consulting Group, Forrester, Booz Allen, and Yankee Group—to choose an area or market in which to start a new business?

A

No. These firms address their clients' and analysts' interests, not what *you* are passionate about. Even if an area happens to coincide with your passions, the analysts typically use current and historical sales or production figures to project the sizes and growth rates of markets. Such historical extrapolations can help established companies justify their investment in or entry into those markets. But the opportunities you seek are specific, if not unique, to you; may result from innovations that are only now coming to market; and may have no history. In short, you and the analysts have different objectives. You will most likely recognize new opportunities that are right for you before they do.

Q

What about just being passionate about making money?

A

Be cautious about this. Steve Jobs at Apple and Bill Hewlett and Dave Packard at HP were passionate about building great products and great companies. Management teams whose primary motives were to make money succeeded them. Those companies lost their way.

The executives who acquired one of the companies I invested in cared more about creating an asset they could flip (sell) for financial gain than about building a great organization or serving customer needs. Employees quickly recognize such an attitude even if executives try to hide it. Their single-minded focus on short-term gain undermined employees' long-term commitments and dedication to customers that often extended far beyond normal working hours. The result was lost employee commitment, compromised customer relationships, and excessive turnover. Not only was value not created; it was destroyed. The parent firm ultimately sold the company at a loss.

In my experience, passion for making money alone fails to inspire people to design, build, and sell great products and services that drive growth. To accomplish that, you need passion to solve problems, address customer needs, and make the world a better place.

EXERCISES

IF YOU ARE ALREADY PASSIONATE ABOUT SOMETHING:

1. If your passion drives perseverance or vice versa in particular activities or subjects, list as many as you can think of. If you have more

than one, look for all the common threads among them. If you find more than one commonality, which ones are strongest or show up in more subjects?

2. Later we see how the *combinations* or *intersections* of things we are passionate about harbor particularly good opportunities for new ventures. Consider the combinations of activities or subjects on your list. Is any combination one you have not considered before? Is the combination something you could *become* passionate about?

   - **Fashion and multiplayer games:** Are you or could you become passionate about multiplayer games having to do with fashion?

   - **Travel and aerospace:** Could you become passionate about tourism to rocket-launching sites around the world, or about travel to space for tourists?

   - **Polymers and cooking:** Could polymers enhance the cooking process, health benefits, or flavor of food?

   - **Golf and scuba diving:** How about underwater golf?[6]

IF YOUR PASSIONS ARE NOT WELL DEFINED (OR TO BECOME MORE PASSIONATE ABOUT A SUBJECT OR ACTIVITY)

1. Becoming passionate about *something* is your first task. Make a list of a least a dozen subjects or activities that interest you or that you have spent time on. Mark the ones that are (a) most important to you, (b) that you have particularly mastered, or (c) that have special meaning for you. From these, choose one that you rate most highly overall, weighting these three criteria however you wish. If two or more are tied for most highly rated, still choose one—perhaps the one that is least common or popular.

2. Commit to spending at least ten hours a week or (preferably) ninety minutes a day for the next ten weeks learning about and developing skills in that field. Create your own routine and momentum to make certain you do this; no one other than you will do so. Make it a goal to learn, say, five times as much about your chosen field as you currently know. Perhaps start with Wikipedia, which will lead you to other references, which in turn will lead to still others. Talk to everyone you can find who shares your interest about those subjects. Perhaps take free courses on the subject offered by edX, MITx, Khan Academy, Coursera, or Udacity. Visit www.MeetUp.com to find others in your neighborhood interested in the same subject, or attend a Maker Faire (www.makerfaire.com) to experience and try out a huge array of crafts and meet their passionate advocates.

In addition to developing your skills and building relationships with people in your area of interest, learn about the field itself: its history, evolution, pioneers, leaders, schools of thought, and future trends—whichever are applicable and most engage you. If your chosen field is a

- **Sport:** Learn its teams, rules, players, owners, game schedules, and broadcast rights. Practice and play the sport, if possible.

- **Food or cuisine:** Learn its origins, nutrition, biology, ecology, which markets sell it, and which restaurants serve it. Cook, serve, and eat the food or cuisine.

- **Technology**: Learn the individuals and companies that developed it, the major milestones in its development, and its applications. Understand how it works or how to apply it.

- **Place:** Visit it and learn its geography, people, politics, history, and economics.

Follow your explorations in whatever direction they lead you *within* your area, but please don't change fields outright. After ten weeks, you will have spent one hundred hours on your chosen subject. Don't stop before you've reached one hundred hours or four weeks of elapsed time, whichever comes later.

During these weeks, weave your field into your day-to-day life. Find every opportunity to discuss what you've learned with friends and colleagues. Follow the local, national, and international news, if applicable, in your subject. Find others who are similarly interested; learn from them and share what you have learned. Savor the small moments when new knowledge clarifies your understanding. If you are able to share something interesting about the field, do so enthusiastically, even if doing so feels forced at first. Over time, your enthusiasm will become genuine.

If you have explored your topic diligently and enthusiastically, you will most likely recognize the field engaging you (passion growing), a willingness or desire to spend more and more time exploring it (perseverance becoming easier), and the two reinforcing each other. It may be subtle, especially at first. Even so, you'll be experiencing positive feedback between passion and perseverance.

3. If you don't experience passion growing and perseverance becoming easier by the end of the hundred-hour cycle, you have a choice: keep going or switch subject areas. I urge you to keep going, for at least one more hundred-hour cycle, for two reasons: (1) You may not be used to being diligent and enthusiastic. If so, commit yourself to being even more so on this second cycle. (2) You may have chosen a field that is harder and takes longer to penetrate than most. If so, good for you—you will have more of the potential market to yourself and it will be easier to be different. Please be patient and keep going.

4. If, after the second hundred-hour cycle, your chosen field still hasn't grabbed you, revisit your original list of subjects and activities that you created in exercise B.1. Because of the time you spent exploring your first chosen area, you may want to add new fields to your list. Again, choose one of these that you would rate highest overall.

If none ranks highest overall, choose the one that is least common or popular.

5. After you have discovered a passion, do the exercises under the A section of exercises, "If you are already passionate about something."

It may seem like a lot of work. It is—and, you can do it. If it were easy, everyone would have started their own company, rather than spending their lives in dull jobs or working for someone else. You're following these steps so you won't fall into that trap. Repeat the process and keep trying.

If you still can't find anything that grabs you, rather than lead a life without passion, try completely changing your routine. For example, quit your job or go part time, give away or sell many of your possessions, spend a month or more visiting new places, or dedicate a year to helping those less fortunate. You may discover a new passion—or one that was there all the time.

CORE LESSONS

- Passion and perseverance are strongly linked: Passion (an attitude) and perseverance (a behavior) form a positive feedback loop and reinforce each other.

- Passion without perseverance is a fleeting fancy; perseverance without passion is drudgery.

- Passion gives you the curiosity and desire to find solutions to problems; perseverance enables you to break through obstacles or find ways around them.

- If you are not passionate about your new venture, its chances of success are limited.

- Anyone can become passionate about something.

- To inspire others, you need passion for solving problems, satisfying customer needs, and making the world a better place. Passion for making money alone is not usually contagious or sustainable.

2

ALL YOU NEED IS A NEED AND ADVANTAGE: ROADMAP TO CREATING YOUR BUSINESS

Great things are not done by impulse,
but by a series of small things brought together.
  —Vincent Van Gogh

Now, let's turn your passion and perseverance into a business. If you don't have a particular business in mind, this book shows you how to find, create, and grow your best opportunity. If you do already have a business in mind, this book shows you how to test, validate, and refine that opportunity. The steps can take from a few days to multiple calendar quarters depending on you and your venture.[1]

Here's your road map. To create a new business, you need only two things:

- **A need:** A real, unsatisfied customer need in an area about which you are passionate

- **An advantage:** An advantage for satisfying that need

A REAL, UNSATISFIED CUSTOMER NEED

"Real, unsatisfied customer need" has four parts. First is the *need*—a desire, requirement, or most generally, a gap between a preferable and current state. To be very clear, the term *need* as we use it here does not mean something required for human survival (food, clothing, or shelter, especially in the developed world). This "need" may be as frivolous as a rubber duck with the face of your favorite sports figure.

Second is the set of *customers*—individuals, businesses, nonprofits, governments, or other groups of people—who have that need. I prefer the more concrete *customer* need to the more abstract *market* need: Customer need makes it harder to forget that the need belongs to a living, breathing person (or group of people, as with a corporate customer). The customers may not be aware of the need—the possibility of a preferable state; you may have to create that awareness. Preferable is in the mind of the customer.

Third is *unsatisfied*, meaning that the need is not addressed, at least fully, by currently available products and services.

Fourth is *real*, which means that the need is either shared by a sufficient number of customers, or is sufficiently intense in one or more customers to make it worthy of you to satisfy.

YOUR RESOURCES AND ADVANTAGES

In chapter 6, you inventory all your *resources* (skills, strengths, assets, etc.) that can help you satisfy needs. You will likely discover that you have many more resources than you thought. Of all your resources that can help you satisfy a particular need, your *advantages* are the subset that are different from or better than those of others—your current or potential competitors—who may satisfy the same need. Whether a resource is an advantage for a need may not be readily apparent and may require exploration and testing.

Your customer need (the one your business will satisfy) on the one hand, and your resources and advantages, on the other, are like puzzle pieces because they have to fit each other (as in figure 2.1). Here are a few examples. Your fluency in Basque may be a resource applicable to satisfying needs in Bilbao but not in Botswana. Your scuba instructor certification may be an advantage for providing underwater location services but not for mobile payment solutions. Even a sole proprietor can have a significant advantage— for example, Maria, if you refuse to let anyone but her clean your house. We will go step-by-step to find your best need-advantage fit, which is where you are most likely to be successful.

Customer Need

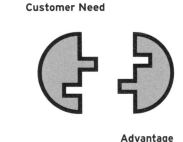

Advantage

Figure 2.1

Two puzzle pieces: A need and an advantage.

THE TEN-STEP PROCESS

Here are highlights of the *Unleash Your Inner Company* process. We've already seen the importance of passion and perseverance in chapter 1. In chapters 3 and 4, we generate dozens of potential needs in the areas you are passionate about. For those we identify as real and not already being served (unsatisfied; figure 2.2), we generate possible solutions (products and services).

In chapter 6, we inventory all your resources, using the acronym STARS—Skills; Technologies; Assets (knowledge, physical, and financial) & Accomplishments; Reputation & Relationships; and (Inner)

Strengths. After that, we explore what is quite possibly your most important resource—your mind—and the psychology of entrepreneurship (chapter 7).

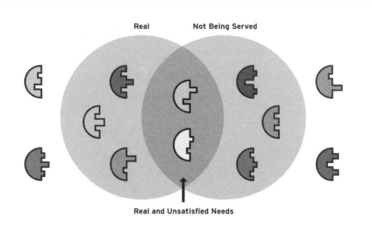

——— *Figure 2.2* ———

Potential, real, and unsatisfied customer needs in areas you are passionate about.

Your resources are the raw materials from which you conceive, design, and build your solutions. As you mature each possible solution, it becomes one of your resources. Even if your solutions fail, you still have your resources to fall back on.

Generally, existing businesses will have more and better resources than you, so your being different is usually more successful than trying to be better (chapter 9). Next, we see how you can combine the resources you have to create new resources (chapter 11) and how choosing the right cofounder hugely expands the range of customer needs and solutions you can consider addressing and offering (chapter 12). After that, we identify and examine your competitors to determine which of your resources, if any, are advantages for each of the real, unsatisfied needs you identified (chapters 16–17).

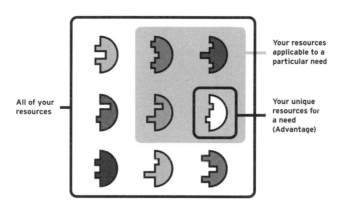

Your resources
applicable to a
particular need

All of your
resources

Your unique
resources for
a need
(Advantage)

───── *Figure 2.3* ───

Your advantages for a need are a subset of all of your resources.

Finally, we assess how well each need and your relevant advantages (figure 2.3) and solutions fit to choose your best opportunity (chapter 20). After that, it is a matter of designing, customer testing, pricing, launching and, if and when you achieve traction (customer acceptance), scaling up your business (chapters 21–24).

The process is not linear but *iterative*, meaning that you constantly experiment to learn what works and doesn't work, then loop back to refine and repeat steps based on what you have learned. Such experimental trial and error may seem haphazard or disorganized, but it is actually the most reliable form of learning in your new venture, and necessary for success.

The table of contents lists the steps next to the chapters that introduce each step. The exact order you follow will vary from case to case. The ten steps arc (see figure 2.4 also)

1. Identify/develop your passions.

2. Generate/refine customer needs in those areas; confirm that the needs are real and unsatisfied.

3. Generate possible solutions to those needs.

4. Inventory your resources (STARS).

4a. Generate additional needs suggested by your resources.

5. Match needs with resources and assess each fit.

6. Acquire/develop additional resources as necessary to strengthen each fit.

7. Identify competitors and determine your advantages for each need.

8. Match needs with advantages to determine the best fits overall. From these, choose your best opportunity.

9. Build, customer test, and launch your minimum viable solution (MVS).

10. Scale up.

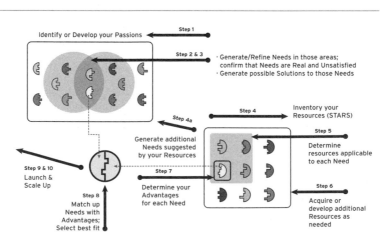

Figure 2.4

Unleash Your Inner Company: *The ten-step process.*

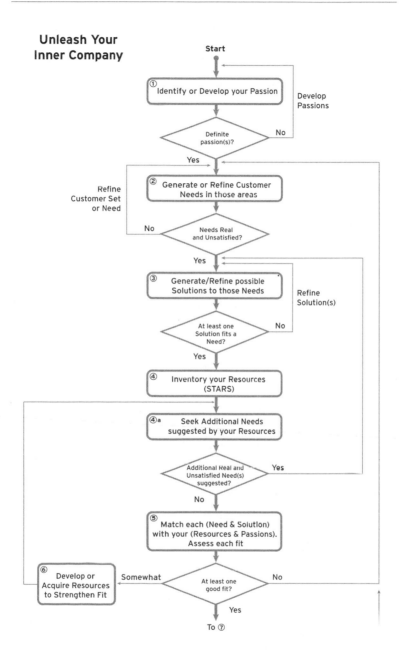

Figure 2.5a

Unleash Your Inner Company *ten-step process (flowchart). (Continued on next page)*

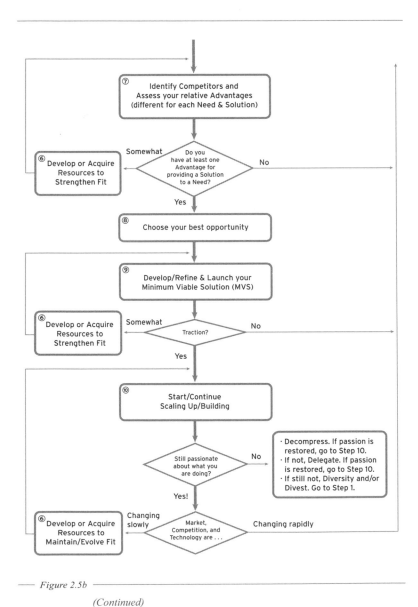

Figure 2.5b

(Continued)

As you develop and deliver your solution to satisfy a need, and ultimately create satisfied customers from it, your solution becomes one of your resources. As you refine the solution to better satisfy needs, add more customers, or both, and the solution surpasses what your competitors offer, the solution becomes one of your advantages. You create resources and advantages for your business—knowledge, expertise, solutions, name recognition, and retained earnings—as you satisfy customer needs. Over time, your venture becomes more self-sustaining. As it does, you will have more options for guiding the business to maximize its value to you (and to your cofounders or investors). Value may be income from or financial value of your business; its social impact; your freedom or financial independence; or some combination thereof. Maximizing value is optimizing your business to your objectives. If you follow the steps in this book, and persevere in applying your resources and developing advantages to satisfy a customer need in an area you are passionate about, the value of the resources you create will eventually surpass that of your initial resources (see figure 2.6).

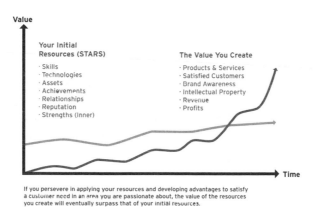

If you persevere in applying your resources and developing advantages to satisfy a customer need in an area you are passionate about, the value of the resources you create will eventually surpass that of your initial resources.

Figure 2.6

Creating value.

GOOD QUESTION!

Q

Why start with needs? Why not start with resources?

A

For two reasons. First, doing so ensures that your business really satisfies a need. It is easy to get so excited about a new idea, technology, or product that you overlook the need or don't confirm that it is real. Over 90 percent of seasoned technology execs I recently surveyed favored defining a new business by starting with needs rather than with technology (part of your resources).

Second, you have a near-infinite number of resources you can draw on—your knowledge of yoga techniques or of major league baseball stats; how to make crepes; the locations of all the McDonald's in your neighborhood; the lyrics to Lady Gaga hits; your fluency in Basque; and your friendship with your cousin in Toledo. It is impossible to list them all, and the overwhelming majority of them are irrelevant to the needs that you will possibly satisfy. Identifying needs first guides you in specifying which of those resources are relevant.

However, your resources also suggest needs (Step 4a); so, we include any of your resources you think may satisfy some need you could address, even if those resources don't apply to the needs you listed in Step 2. If you definitely confirm that a possible need suggested by your resources is real—you will see how to confirm that a need is real in chapter 4—then it is okay to start with resources, if you wish.

Q

As you hone a need and your advantages to better fit each other, does the need generally move toward your advantages or vice versa?

A

Often, the need or advantage you are less confident about or that is less well defined is the one that will gravitate toward the other. If you are very confident about a need, you tend to find a way to satisfy it, even if it means acquiring or developing advantages you don't currently have. If you are very confident about certain advantages, you tend to find needs to which they can be applied. So be alert to needs and advantages that are either ill defined or that you might be overly confident about. Define needs and advantages crisply and test their validity to get the best results. Let's dive in.

3

LET A THOUSAND NEEDS BLOOM (STEPS 2 & 3)

To innovate, live in the world of what might be,
not in the world of what is.
   —*Alan Cooper*

I started my first company, Decisive Technology, with a really cool technology: conditional voting.[1] Our team spent much time and money designing and prototyping this collaboration software. We gradually realized that few wanted or needed it. To make the software more sale-able, we added features to let users conduct surveys. After several more months, we dropped conditional voting entirely and launched Decisive Survey, the first software to automate surveys via email, which became a hit.[2] Was conditional voting a passion that ultimately led us to a real customer need, or an obstacle that distracted us from recognizing the need and delivering a solution sooner? Some of both. In any event, to create a viable business, identify a real customer need in an area you are passionate about and create a solution that satisfies that need as soon as possible.

Countless unsatisfied customer needs surround us. If you have ever waited in line, were dissatisfied with a product or service, or couldn't buy something you wanted, you have experienced an unsatisfied customer need. You could use any of the adjectives in the following list to describe a possible customer need for any product or service:

More accurate	More durable	Larger
More adjustable	Easier	Lighter
More beautiful	More economical	More powerful
More biodegradable	Faster	More responsive
Cheaper	More flexible	Safer
Cleaner	Healthier	Smaller
Clearer	More intelligent	Sturdier
More compatible	More intuitive	Tastier

Finding real, unsatisfied customer needs and solutions is a process of generation and selection. *Generation* combines your research, brainstorming, and imagination to envision how to make the world better for a customer set. Your research includes customers, current solutions, and competitors; may be conducted by phone, in person, as face-to-face interviews, online, or by test or experiment; and helps you understand both possibilities and limitations of current solutions. The word "research" might suggest something you mainly do alone, but well over half of your research should be with other people: prospective customers, other entrepreneurs, competitors, or experts in your field. As serial entrepreneur Steve Blank says, "Get the heck outside."[3] Brainstorming and imagining what *might* be, as in the quote from noted software designer Alan Cooper at the beginning of this chapter, lets you visualize preferable states and unsatisfied customer needs.

Selection uses research to either confirm that customer needs and solutions are real or to eliminate customer needs and solutions that are not real. A customer need is real only if significant numbers of customers have that need or if a few large customers have the need sufficiently intensely. A solution is real only if significant numbers of customers (or a few large customers) use or are likely to use that solution.

Generation and selection may use the same research. In this chapter, you'll see examples of generation and selection, and in chapter 4, specific research and brainstorming techniques.

Here is one way—the first of several that we will discover—to generate many customer needs and solutions. Start with any product or service you currently use, say, running shoes.

Now work backward from "running shoes." What need are running shoes a solution for, and who are the customers? That's easy: The need is something like "comfortable footwear" and we'll say the customers, to keep it simple, are runners and walkers.

What are *limitations* of that solution? You can probably think of several for the shoes you use. I can think of three for my running shoes:

- Shoes smell after many wearings.

- Shoes don't tell me how far or fast I have run.

- Changing shoelaces to match outfit is cumbersome.

Simply restate these limitations positively to get possible customer needs, for example, "Shoes that smell fresh after many runs." You still must validate limitations, needs, customers, and solutions. Let's say your research satisfies you that the three customer needs are indeed real (figure 3.1).

Need	Customers	Solution		Limitation	Need	Customers	Solutions
				Shoes smell after many wearings	Shoes that smell fresh after many runs.	· Frequent runners · Heavy perspirers	
Comfortable footwear while running	Runners	Running shoes		Shoes don't tell me how far or fast I have run	Shoes that report how fast and far I have run	Serious runners	
				Changing shoelaces to match outfit is cumbersome	Easily change shoelaces to match outfit	Fashion-conscious wearers of running shoes	

—— *Figure 3.1* ——

Next, you research solutions for these needs. You find that each of the first and second needs has two solutions currently available (see figure 3.2). However, a solution itself may not be real—purchased or used by a significant number of customers—for either of two reasons:

- The need it satisfies isn't real.

- The solution isn't attractive or effective.

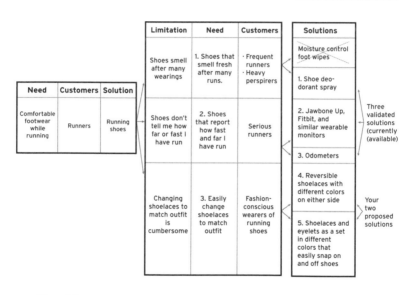

Figure 3.2

Confirming that existing solutions are real for needs 1 and 2 and proposing solutions for need 3.

You've already established that the needs are real, but let's say you learn that customers think using foot wipes is inconvenient for keeping shoes smelling fresh. Rather than further explore foot wipes, you've eliminated (crossed out) that possible solution in figure 3.2. Furthermore, say your research validates that the other three existing solutions for the first two needs *are* real.

The third need, easily change shoelaces to match outfits, has no current solution that you can find. Great—this is an opportunity. You brainstorm with friends and colleagues and wonder if two possible solutions would work: (1) reversible shoelaces with different colors on front and back that could be twisted to use either side, or (2) shoelaces and eyelets of different colors that snap on and off the shoes as a set.

For the three validated, existing solutions and your two proposed solutions, you repeat the process: research and validate their strengths and limitations, needs corresponding to those limitations, and possible customers for each need.

The shoe deodorant spray, an existing solution, has to be reapplied every few days. Would a shoe with more air vents, or inserts with time-release deodorants, work for weeks or months? With Fitbit, Jawbone UP, and odometers, customers have to remember to put them on and take them off. Instead, could similar devices be built into or attached to running shoes?

At the same time, you test and refine your two proposed solutions. To explore and address their limitations, you may build prototypes and try them out with prospective customers. In general, limitations can be addressed either by enhancing your solutions or by narrowing your customer set to those who aren't affected by a particular limitation.

Now you have six proposed solutions: shoes with air vents; freshener inserts; speed and distance monitors built into shoes; speed and distance monitors that attach to shoes; shoelaces consisting of flat segments that swivel to display the different colored sides; and colored shoelaces and eyelets that snap into a frame that attaches to existing eyelets. Researching these, you conclude the following:

- Shoes with the necessary air vents don't protect the feet from cold and rain.

- Speed and distance monitors built into shoes are less practical than those that attach to shoes.

- Fashion-conscious wearers of running shoes want many color choices in shoelaces, not just two different colors on the front and back of shoelaces.

So you eliminate those three solutions, leaving you with these three:

- Freshener inserts

- Speed and distance monitors that attach to shoes

- Colored shoelaces and eyelets that snap into a frame that attaches to the existing eyelets

You can continue generating, researching, and eliminating needs, customers, and solutions, giving rise to a virtually unlimited number of possible new needs and solutions, all from a single product or service that you currently use! As we draw, we create a tree like figure 3.3. The needs and proposed solutions at the far right of figure 3.3 are the ones you are actively evaluating.

Imagine how large the tree would be if you included *a dozen* of the products and services you currently use—easily a thousand needs would be blooming! With so many possibilities, you can see why I urge you to start with areas you are passionate about, where you have natural advantages.

In summary, if based on your research

- **A customer need is real and solutions already exist for it:** Seek limitations of those solutions or seek out different needs.

- **A customer need is not real today (whether or not "solutions" exist for it):** Seek different needs or check whether a different set of customers has that need.

- **Your proposed solution does not satisfy the customer need:** Find ways to address the solution's limitations; seek different solutions that satisfy the customer need; or seek different needs or customers for that solution.

- **A customer need is real and *no* real solutions exist for it:** Great! Brainstorm, develop, test, and refine your solution(s) to that need.

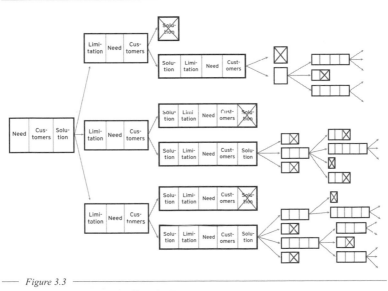

——— *Figure 3.3* ———

Your needs tree.

Some people get so carried away generating needs and solutions that they divide their precious time among too many to do any of them justice. Others latch on to the first need and solution that comes along without fully exploring the landscape in the area they are passionate about. In figure 3.4, you explore up to six different solutions for different needs at one time, probably as many as is reasonable. Balance your generation and selection of needs and solutions so you can both explore the landscape and narrow down to just one need and solution in a reasonable amount of time.

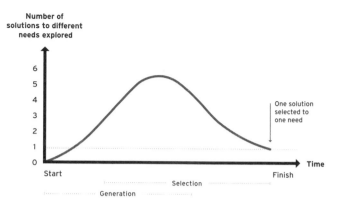

Number of
solutions to different
needs explored

6
5
4
3
2
1
0

One solution
selected to
one need

Start   Finish

Time

Selection

Generation

Figure 3.4

Generate many solutions, then narrow them down.

Note: Dozens of different needs and solutions may be considered and rejected between Start and Finish, of which six is just the maximum explored at any one time in this example. The peak of the curve is the point at which your rate of eliminating possible solutions exceeds your rate of generating possible solutions. Your curve may have multiple peaks before getting down to a single solution. Or if you explore just one possible solution at a time, one after another, your curve is a flat line.

The customer needs we have identified so far—those based on limitations of products and services you currently use—are an important subset but by no means the entire set of customer needs that surround you. Later we generate even more customer needs using other techniques.

Also, we have already eliminated many customer needs that either did not seem real or that are adequately being satisfied by solutions currently available. Later, we further eliminate customer needs for which you don't have advantages.

The customer needs that are real (exist for a significant number of customers, or for a few sufficiently important customers); that are not adequately satisfied by currently available solutions; and for which you have the strongest advantages will be the best needs for you to satisfy.

EXERCISE

As in the running shoe example, choose a product or service that you use, ideally in an area you are passionate about. Create a needs tree of at least a half a dozen possible needs and solutions from that product or service.

CORE LESSONS

- When thinking about your new venture, start with one or more real customer needs, ideally in areas you are passionate about.

- A *customer need* is a gap between a preferable state and a current state for the customer. It has two parts: the need and the set of customers who have that need. Your customers might be individuals, businesses, or other organizations. A *solution* is a product or service that satisfies a customer need. To find unsatisfied customer needs and solutions for them, imagine possibilities: what might be.

- Countless unsatisfied customer needs surround us all the time. Creating a needs tree is one technique to generate and validate or eliminate (i.e., select) dozens of unsatisfied customer needs and solutions.

4

DON'T LISTEN TO YOUR CUSTOMERS: DISCOVER THEIR GOALS

It's not the customer's job to know what they want.
—*Steve Jobs*

Mice keep Mrs. Havisham awake in her nightgown and pin curlers at night. Her companion, Mr. Finnkin, grumbles that he cannot possibly relax in a bubble bath in the clawfoot tub with a mouse scurrying across the bathroom floor. They both need *a safe, convenient, clean way to catch, kill, and dispose of household mice,* they tell you.

Seated on the piano stool in Mrs. Havisham's parlor, you look at them across the porcelain tea set. The flicker of scattered bulbs dimly reveals a spider scooting across a web between the arms of the chandelier drooping above you. Raised by your grandparents, one of your passions has long been helping the elderly. "You mean . . . a better mousetrap?" you ask. "Precisely," says Mr. Finnkin, taking a sip from a floral teacup. Tiny Mrs. Havisham nods in agreement, engulfed by her overstuffed wingback chair.

That's what they tell you.

You rotate slightly on the stool. "What if you could keep mice out of the home in the first place?" you ask. "Impossible," says Mr. Finnkin, grimacing behind his bifocals. Mrs. Havisham nods in agreement again and insists that her house has had mice since she and her late husband, Percival, moved there fifty years ago. "And sometimes rats, too," she whispers.

You politely acknowledge and record their comments on your iPad Air. But you're the entrepreneur, so you think further out of the box—more broadly and creatively—than your potential customers do. You wonder if you could find or invent a safe, convenient, clean, and cost-effective barrier to keep rodents out of the house or even the yard. Such a barrier might use physical, chemical, electronic, mechanical, ultrasonic, or optical means, or a combination thereof.[1] Might ultrasound, imperceptible to humans and pets, be used to repel mice? If necessary, might food pellets with tiny transmitters let GPS track mice and assist in targeting the ultrasound? You would completely eliminate the mousetrap and the need to dispose of dead mice, too.

With effort, Mrs. Havisham gets on her feet, gently taps her cane against the mouse hole in the wall, and has you get down on all fours to peer inside. You suddenly know that neither she nor Mr. Finnkin will ever be early adopters of anything. You wonder if seniors are more likely than other groups of people to live in older homes with rodent infestations. If so, any solution you develop would have to be extremely simple for the elderly to install and maintain. You wonder if pest exterminators might distribute, install, and maintain whatever solution you develop; how long seniors would continue to buy familiar mousetraps even if superior solutions were available; and whether the best initial customers for a high-tech rodent barrier might be young, affluent households rather than the elderly.

It has been an informative session, as much for the questions it has prompted you to think about as for Mrs. Havisham's and Mr. Finnkin's responses. You thank them for their time and the tea. Mr. Finnkin has fallen asleep on the sofa, snoring, clutching a lace handkerchief; Mrs. Havisham takes your arm as you walk to the door. You promise her that you will come back and meet her granddaughter, a noted transsexual linebacker.

This story illustrates three points about customer needs:

- Seek out, listen to, talk with, and observe prospective customers in person.

- Discover what they want to achieve or accomplish—their goals—to understand their true needs.

- Don't accept stated needs as the real needs.

SEEK OUT, LISTEN, TALK, AND OBSERVE IN PERSON

Meet and talk to prospective customers either individually or in a group, to understand

- their goals, desires, or dreams,

- their current states, and

- gaps between the two.

Perhaps invite prospective customers for coffee or a meal; listen and take notes. If your customer is a type of organization (e.g., call center, bakery, or manufacturing firm), talk to the staff, managers, and leadership of several organizations of that type, if possible, to get different perspectives. These meetings will enable you to confirm or reject some or all of the needs you have in mind, suggest other needs, or both.

Needs you have experienced personally are an excellent place to start, but don't assume that they are necessarily shared by many others. Make certain the need(s) you identify are experienced by a significant number of individuals or organizations, in the near future if not right now.

Try splitting a research session into two parts: green-light brainstorming and critical red-light thinking. The first half generates ideas for possible needs; the second half eliminates those that exist only among a very small group of people or businesses or not at all. Seek out positive, open-minded people for the first half, and critical ones for the second. Some time after that first session, you may want to have additional sessions starting with the ideas that survived the earlier session. Distilling needs is a journey, not a one-time exercise.

Customers are often not consciously aware of their needs, so also try to *observe* prospective customers firsthand in the current state or engaged in the activity for which they have a desire, goal, or dream. Observing may include recording a video with the prospective customer's permission. For example, to enable or help

- Homemakers and caterers prepare food more cleanly and rapidly, watch how dozens of them work in their kitchens

- Party throwers, event planners, and fund-raisers more easily create announcements and registration forms online for their events, watch as they use existing online tools and see where they have difficulties

- Retail stores better distinguish between real shoppers and shoplifters from their security camera video streams, watch how dozens of companies use and analyze such data

- DJs to access any song instantly from anywhere and automatically synchronize lighting with music, go to dozens of nightclubs and dance clubs and watch how DJs perform these tasks

> *If I had asked what people wanted,*
> *they would have said faster horses.*
> *—Henry Ford*

DISCOVER THEIR GOALS

In the earlier story, Mrs. Havisham and Mr. Finnkin's real goal was not a better mousetrap or even catching mice, but to rid the home of mice in the first place.

Prospective customers are often uninformed about ways their needs *might* be satisfied. My mother recently bought a staticky portable AM/FM radio because she wanted music for her living room. She didn't know that she could stream music static-free from the Internet, which she now enjoys. Knowing goals opens up the widest range of possible ways for you to satisfy needs.

IBM's account execs, once hailed as the most professional sales force in the world, recited this mantra with their customers: "How much, by when?" That is, how much in the way of benefits (e.g., productivity gains or cost savings) do you want to achieve by when? They were asking for their customer's objectives and goals. Armed with that knowledge, account execs could propose IT solutions that (at least arguably) delivered those benefits within that time. Similarly, knowing your prospective customers' goals, desires, or dreams (preferred states), together with their current states, tells you their needs.

> *You can have everything in life you want, if you'll just help*
> *enough other people get what they want.*
> —Zig Ziglar

STATED NEED MAY NOT BE REAL NEED

While the *stated* need (e.g., catching and killing mice) may have an existing solution (a better mousetrap), the *real* need based on objectives or goals (ridding the home of mice) may not. If so, that's an opportunity for you. Test each need: For each one, ask yourself, "Is this the real need?" and "What probing questions could I ask to determine the real need?"

Table 4.1 contains examples of customer needs that you might hear from your prospective customers (or think of yourself), and questions you might ask to validate them. For #4, for example, you might ask how the pebbles got into the grass in the first place. You might discover that "Keep lawn mowers from throwing pebbles into the yard" is the real need. For #5, you might ask whether satisfying the need requires using fresh fruit. If it is just the ends (tea flavor) rather than the means (fresh fruit) that is important, you might consider many means other than fresh fruit (such as a liquid additive, gel, or crystals) to achieve the ends. For #10, what exactly are the scuba divers trying to accomplish with underwater GPS? Do they want to know their absolute location, or relative location to the dive boat, coral reef, or both? What about depth? For #11, what are the Bitcoin users trying to accomplish that requires better security? Maybe there is a way to satisfy the need without using Bitcoin.

Table 4.1. Validating customer needs.				
Stated Need/desire	Prospective customer	Sample probing question(s)	Possible Goal/ objective	Possible actual need(s)/ desire(s)
1. Fresh, hot gourmet meals ready for your neighbors when then get home from work or school	Your neighbors	Do meals liter- ally have to be ready? What if they take only five minutes to heat up?	More free time, either with family or alone? Desire to impress friends?	Impress friends/ family and/or enjoy bragging rights among foodies
2. Make kite boarding easy and safe enough that your grandpar- ents can experi- ence and enjoy it	Seniors; their grandchildren*	How many hours of practice, if any, allowed?	Spend more time doing fun things with elders?	Activities both cool for young people and fun for elders
3. A game that combines the teamwork of *World of Warcraft* with the long- term cultivation of *Farmville*	Multiplayer online game players	Who would you want to play the game with?	Play with dif- ferent friends than my current WoW guild	Games I can play with anyone; fun way to engage and get to know new friends

Stated Need/desire	Prospective customer	Sample probing question(s)	Possible Goal/ objective	Pos- sible actual need(s)/ desire(s)
4. An easier way to remove pebbles from grass in your yard	Home dwellers with yards	How did the pebbles get there?	Cleaner yard, healthier grass	Keep lawn mower from throwing pebbles into yard
5. A way to use fresh fruit to infuse stronger citrus flavors in home-brewed tea	Tea drinkers	Is fresh fruit or just fresh fruit flavor important?	New and/or better tasting home-brewed tea	New ways for infusing citrus (and other?) flavors in home-brewed tea
6. An easier way to convert software applications from Adobe Flash to HTML 5	IT departments; independent software developers	What's objective of conversion: new platforms, performance, functionality, or ease of use?	How can I easily add extensive new function to Flash apps?	Easily convert Flash apps to HTML 5; easily extend functionality of existing Flash apps
7. A better way to clear cobwebs out of your attic	Home dwellers with attics	What if cobwebs didn't arise at all?	Cleaner attic	Stop cobwebs from appearing
8. A way to monitor activity on high-rise roofs from anywhere	Security companies; high-rise property management companies	What does "monitor" mean? A visual view? Detect movement? Detect access?	Deter and detect intruders on high-rise roofs	Means of deterring and detecting (from anywhere) intruders on high-rise roofs
9. A way on a plane to see your laptop screen clearly even if partly folded down because the seat in front is retracted	Airline passenger laptop users	Could solution be an accessory for any laptop, a specially designed laptop for frequent fliers, or either?	See your laptop screen clearly even if partly folded down on a plane	No change to proposed need
10. GPS for scuba divers	Scuba divers	Is need to know location absolutely; relative to dive boat, reef, or other divers; depth; or combo?	Safely return to dive boat	Means of knowing direction and distance back to dive boat while underwater
11. Better security for Bitcoin	Bitcoin users	Does objective require Bitcoin?	Secure online investments	More secure online investments

*Sometimes the purchaser, user, and/or decision maker are different. If so, list both or all to keep this visible.

NEEDS GROW INFINITELY

Occasionally I hear people say that all the best opportunities have already been addressed. Utter nonsense, as Mr. Finnkin from the mouse story would say. As the needs tree we saw in chapter 3 (figure 3.2) makes clear, *satisfying needs creates new needs*. New solutions create new needs in three ways:

- The solutions themselves have limitations that need to be satisfied.

- The people and organizations that provide those solutions have needs (e.g., sales and marketing).

- New solutions create needs around them (e.g., data centers create needs for uninterruptible power supplies and security services).

With technology advancing at an ever-increasing pace, new customer needs are being created at a similar pace. For some of these needs, you are the best person in the world to satisfy them.[2]

EXERCISES

For the needs tree you created in chapter 3

1. **Choose one possible need.** To validate, eliminate, or refine that possible need, do research both online and in person with prospective customers.

2. **Choose one possible solution.** To validate, eliminate, or refine that possible solution, do research both online and in person with prospective customers.

CORE LESSONS

- Think further out of the box—that is, more broadly and creatively— than your prospective customers do. Don't limit your thinking to the solutions they suggest.

- Understand what your prospective customers are trying to accomplish or achieve—their goals, desires, and dreams—not necessarily what they tell you. Then consider how you can help them get there (i.e., close the gap from where they are today).

- Test each need that prospective customers mention to you. To pinpoint real needs, ask, "Is this the real need?" and ask yourself, "What probing questions could I ask to determine the real need?"

5

THINK BIG; START FOCUSED

Not failure, but low aim, is crime.
  —James Russell Lowell

Next, make sure you are thinking big enough. Very deliberately upsize and supersize the customer needs and solutions you have identified. For example, if you are thinking of providing

- **Healthy snacks in a kiosk at your neighborhood mall:** Consider a chain of kiosks for those snacks at many malls across your city.

- **Plumbing, electrical, or Internet connectivity services for single-unit homes in your town:** Consider providing these services or a combination of them for homes, retail stores, and office, condominium, and apartment buildings.

- **Software that speeds up downloading of a popular mobile application:** Consider software that speeds up downloading of *any* mobile application.

Your upsized customer needs will help guide your venture as you grow. If you think you can satisfy your upsized needs immediately, you are not thinking big enough. Satisfying your upsized needs ideally requires applying the new advantages (knowledge, experience, relationships, brand awareness, and more) that you will gain by first satisfying your narrower set of customer needs.

HOW TO THINK BIG

To think big, upsize your customer need. You can upsize your customer set for a particular need, or the need you satisfy for a particular customer set, or both.

Expanding from your neighborhood mall to many malls while offering the same solution (healthy snacks while shopping) is an example of upsizing your customer set for a particular need. Your customer set (health-conscious shoppers in one mall) expands (to shoppers in many malls) but the need you satisfy (healthy satisfaction of hunger) for those customers stays the same.

In contrast, adding Internet connectivity to electrical installation services for single-unit homes is an example of upsizing the need you satisfy for a particular customer set. Your customer set (single-unit homes) stays the same but the needs you satisfy for those customers now include Internet connectivity.

Customer set and needs are intertwined. If, at your same neighborhood mall kiosk, you start offering mineral water with your healthy snacks, that both expands your customer set (to new customers for mineral water) and expands the need you address (thirst as well as hunger) for your existing customers (upsizing both needs and customer set). If you start providing Internet connectivity in addition to electrical installation services to single-unit homes, you may find that small businesses and restaurants want your new services, too, thus expanding your customer set as well (upsizing both again). Consider upsizing customer set and need separately first, then together. Doing so ensures that you don't overlook either approach to upsizing your overall customer need and that, if you need to, you choose one or the other rather than both.

BOWLING PINS LEAD YOU TO YOUR BEST PATH

You can upsize a customer need in many ways. For example, figure 5.1 shows possible paths from "Enhance home-brewed tea with orange flavor" to "Enhance any food or beverage with any flavor." The fewer the qualifiers (orange, citrus, home-brewed, tea), the broader the customer need. In this example, over a dozen paths could take you from your focused starting point to your "Think Big" goal. How do you choose which path to take?

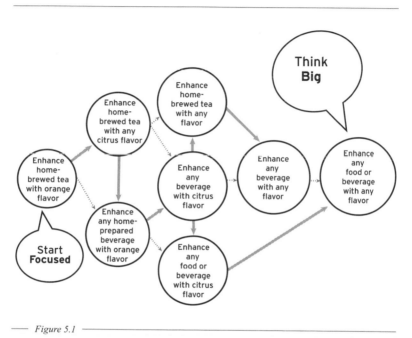

Figure 5.1

Upsizing a customer need.

Think of each customer need as a bowling pin that helps you knock down the next one.[1] Each customer need that you satisfy strengthens your resources—through increased knowledge, experience, field-proven technology, distribution channels, and satisfied customers—to help you satisfy a larger customer need. Seek the overall path that has the highest chance of success for you at every step.

Your likelihood of success is greatest if you grow along a single path at a time. But if two customer needs are closely adjacent to ones you are already serving, and you have strong advantages in each case, then you might follow two paths in parallel, as in the paths following "Enhance any beverage with citrus flavor" in figure 5.1.

The largest customer need you envision your venture satisfying is your *vision* for your business. In this example, it might be: *Enable homes and businesses worldwide to enhance the flavor of any food or beverage.*

Notice that your vision is more about the needs you satisfy and less about specific solutions, or even resources and advantages. Solutions tend to change rapidly; the largest customer need you satisfy will evolve slowly.

In the flavored beverage example, we primarily upsized (generalized) the need. Alternatively, we can upsize the customer set. Figure 5.2 shows possible paths for upsizing your customer set from San Francisco to the entire globe.

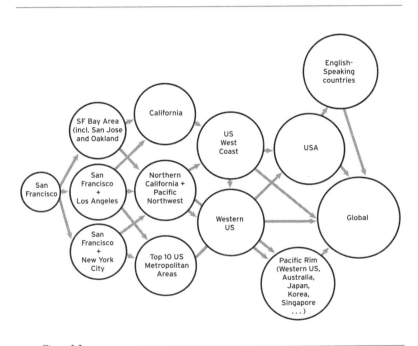

Figure 5.2

Upsizing your customer set.

Later in this chapter, we consider upsizing customer set and need at the same time.

Silicon Valley–based Singularity University asks its student entrepreneurs, "How can you improve the lives of *one billion people* on earth?" This is a great exercise in thinking big. One of its incubated companies, Getaround, took this challenge to heart. Getaround recognized that hundreds of millions of cars around the world are used only a small fraction of the time and asked what if there were an easy, secure way for any car owner to rent their car to anyone? Fewer cars would clutter our roads and parking lots, and many more people could enjoy transportation who otherwise might not be able to, either because of cost or access. Car owners could benefit from a new income stream. Getaround's novel solution combines mobile, GPS, and other technologies. The world's population is approximately seven billion individuals. I don't know if Getaround will actually achieve the goal of improving the lives of about 15 percent of the world's population, which one billion individuals would represent, but I *am* certain that thinking big will help them serve more people and make a greater positive impact in the world than they would otherwise.

START FOCUSED

The more you upsize the customer need you satisfy, the greater your venture's potential, but the more resources you will generally require. The initial customer need you satisfy should be sufficiently bounded, focused, or specific—choose whichever adjective you wish—so that you can satisfy it with the resources (and advantages) you have at the outset. In case you already think big (congratulations!), I want you also to *downsize* your "original" customer need by one notch. For example, if your original customer set was residents in your city, a downsized (smaller) set might be residents in your neighborhood. If the original need was to satisfy cravings for a range of healthy snacks, a downsized (more targeted) need might be doing so for just low-carb snacks. Table 5.1 and table 5.2 offer examples of "original" customer sets and needs with three upsized levels and one downsized level for each.

Table 5.1. Customer sets.				
Downsized	**Original**	**Upsized**	**Supersized**	**Gigasized**
Neighborhood residents	City-wide residents	State-wide residents	Country-wide inhabitants	Global inhabitants
San Francisco Giants fans	National League baseball fans	Major league baseball fans	Major league sports fans	Sports fans
Seniors (age 65+) in assisted living	Seniors (age 65+)	Adults (age 55+)	Adults (age 40+)	Adults (age 21+)
BMW SUV owners	BMW owners	Luxury vehicle owners	Auto owners	Vehicle owners
Japanese tourists sightseeing in NYC	Asian tourists sightseeing in NYC	Tourists sightseeing in NYC	Tourists visiting the US	Tourists
Android users	Android or iPhone users	Smartphone users	Cell phone users	Personal electronic device users (cell phone, iPad, Kindle, MP3 player)

Table 5.2. Needs.				
Downsized	**Original**	**Upsized**	**Supersized**	**Gigasized**
Orange flavor for home-brewed tea	Any citrus flavor for home-brewed tea	Any citrus flavor for any beverage	Any flavor for any beverage	Any flavor for any food or beverage
Rid single-family dwellings of mice	Rid single-family dwellings of rodents (mice and rats)	Rid single-family dwellings of pests (rodents and insects)	Rid any residential building (incl. condos and apartments) of pests	Rid any commercial or residential structure of pests
Low-carb snacks	Range of healthy snacks	Healthy snacks and beverages	Healthy, balanced meals	Healthy meals, yoga, and aerobics
Facilitate (make faster or easier) purchases at Amazon.com	Facilitate online purchases at any site	Facilitate, budget, and track all online purchases	Facilitate, budget, and manage all purchases	Optimize personal spending and savings

ENVISION YOUR PATH IN TWO DIMENSIONS

Next, to get even greater clarity, envision the most likely path you will take to upsize customer set and needs *together.* Create a chart like figure 5.3, in which you move step-by-step from the lower left to the upper right of the chart. On the vertical axis, list your customer sets, and on the horizontal axis, your upsized needs, in order from easiest to hardest for you to address, as best you can determine.

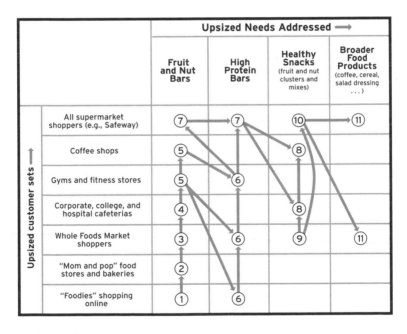

—— *Figure 5.3* ——

Upsizing customer set and need.

Two Degrees Food cofounders Lauren Walters and Will Hauser are passionate about helping address world hunger (see www .twodegreesfood.com). They make fruit and nut bars with a unique twist: For every bar purchased, the company donates a meal to a hungry child.

In 2010, they began selling all natural, vegan, gluten free, and low-sodium bars online (1 in figure 5.3), and in 2011 expanded to "mom and pop" food stores and bakeries (2). Their big breaks came from Whole Foods Market when first thirty-five northern California stores and then 300 stores nationwide started selling the bars (3). The credibility that Whole Foods provided enabled Two Degrees to expand into corporate, college, and hospital cafeterias (4)—the point that Two Degrees has reached as of this writing. Every channel, they discovered, has pros and cons. While Whole Foods brought credibility and volume sales, Two Degrees is just one of some fifty food bar brands crowded onto their shelves; while in corporate, college and hospital cafeterias, Two Degrees is often the only bar offered, meaning less competition and discounting.

The paths from 5 to 11 indicate Two Degrees' vision for expanding their business. They are now targeting customers at gyms, fitness stores, and coffee shops (5). They plan to offer high protein bars online (6) and through Whole Foods, gyms, and fitness stores. Only then do they plan to take on mainstream supermarkets (7). Further product expansion will take them into healthy snacks and beyond (8 through 11), offered through selected channels. They plan to gradually phase out mom and pop food stores and bakeries.

Draw a similar path leading to your vision, as you see it today. This exercise should be fun. Whatever path you chart, this is certain: you will not follow it very far. *It cannot be known very far in advance.* Even allowing for the most advanced forecasting and planning tools and techniques available today, growing your venture is not like driving on interstates from New York to Los Angeles; it's more like finding your way through a thick, steep, dark, rocky jungle with only a compass and not even knowing the distance. You climb up many rocks and scramble across many ledges before being dead-ended by twenty-foot chasms and thirty-foot drops. The terrain very gradually opens up and becomes more accessible as you progress. So your vision "guides" you only in the broadest sense: It doesn't tell you how to get there, or even how far you have to go, but *it keeps attracting you*. The more tangible you make your vision, the more strongly it attracts you. The path helps make your vision more tangible, and it also tells you what to work on next and why.

WORK BACKWARD FROM YOUR VISION

As a sales and marketing associate at Google, Shireen Yates often had to dine out with clients, suppliers, and partners. There was just one problem: She had celiac disease, an immune reaction to eating gluten that can cause inflammation of the small intestine, weight loss, bloating, and diarrhea. Many foods are commonly prepared with gluten, a protein found in wheat, barley, and rye. But few restaurants have gluten-free menus, and restaurant staff often don't know whether the food they serve contains gluten. Stomach pain, especially after meals, became part of Shireen's daily work life. And she was not alone. She surveyed hundreds of people and found that those with celiac disease thought they got sick about one out of three times when dining out, even when ordering from gluten-free menus. Her parents had been bakers, so she decided to start a bakery that sold only gluten-free foods, from which consumers with celiac disease or similar allergies could buy with confidence.

But to satisfy her upsized and supersized customer sets—three million people in the United States with celiac disease, and many millions more worldwide—she would have to grow the bakery from a single outlet, to a regional chain, to a national chain, to a global brand. This endeavor would require lots of capital and face much competition and regulation. Most importantly, it would not squarely address the need: A consumer would still not know whether foods served by most *restaurants* contained gluten or not. She wanted to find a solution that was at once more tightly focused on the need and more readily scalable to millions of consumers. At a wedding, Shireen wondered if she could safely eat the hors d'oeuvres. That was when she had the idea of a portable device to test food for gluten.

The only such solution she could find on the market was, in effect, a special-purpose chemistry set: test tubes, pipettes, liquid solutions, test strips, and a mortar and pestle to grind food. Apart from the impracticality of bringing all that equipment into a restaurant, it would take about twenty minutes to set it up and conduct the test. That meant an opportunity for Shireen.

Unlike gluten-free foods, a compact, battery-powered tester could be produced in one location and economically shipped around the world. Shireen recognized that she did not have the technical skills herself to create the device. So she teamed up with a chemical engineer and a mechanical engineer, and together they designed and built a device about the size of a pack of cigarettes that tests for gluten in less than two minutes. Now cofounder and CEO of 6SensorLabs in San Francisco (see www.6sensorlabs.com), Shireen and her team expect to launch their product in 2016.

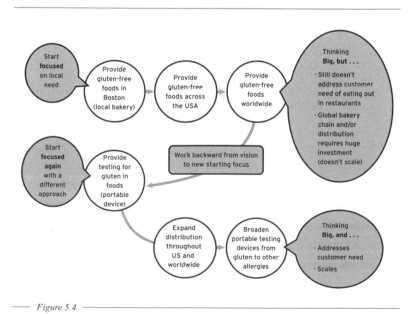

—— *Figure 5.4* ——

Work backward from your vision to find a path to it.

In short: if your planned solution doesn't *scale*—that is, it requires an impractical amount of capital or other resources to satisfy your upsized and supersized customer need—*work backward* from that vision to seek a solution that will (figure 5.4). Your new approach supersized will require fewer but *different* resources than your original approach supersized. For further information on being different, see chapter 9; for more on scalability, see chapter 24.

Finally, be inspired by and learn from your parents, but don't necessarily follow in their footsteps.

EXERCISES

For each of your "original" customer needs (the ones you came up with in chapter 3)

1. Think of three corresponding upsized, supersized, and gigasized customer needs, and one downsized customer need.

2. For one or more of the original needs of your choice, write down your vision and draw a diagram like the ones earlier showing possible paths from your original need to your vision.

3. Highlight the path that seems to you to be the most natural way to grow your venture.

CORE LESSONS

- Thinking big—upsizing the customer need you will satisfy—helps guide your business as you grow. You can upsize the customer set, the need, or both.

- Downsize your initial customer need, if necessary, so you can satisfy it with your initial resources or those that you can readily acquire.

- Project the best path from your initial customer need toward your vision. Your vision should be tangible enough to guide you and draw you through the path. But know that the path cannot be known very far ahead and that you will need to update it frequently.

- If you can't visualize a path leading from your initial need and solution to your vision, *work backward* from that vision to find a new initial need and solution that *do* offer a path leading to your vision.

6

THE FUTURE IS IN YOUR STARS (STEP 4):
SKILLS, TECHNOLOGIES, ASSETS AND ACCOMPLISHMENTS, RELATIONSHIPS AND REPUTATION, (INNER) STRENGTHS

I've missed more than 9000 shots in my career.
I've lost almost 300 games. Twenty-six times I have
been trusted to take the game-winning shot and have
missed. I've failed over and over and over again in
my life. And that is why I succeed.
   —Michael Jordan

YOU HAVE ACRES OF DIAMONDS

Centuries ago near what is now Hyderabad, India, an ancient Buddhist priest told Ali Hafed, a successful Persian farmer, that mining diamonds could make him the richest man in the world.[1] Excited by the prospect, and not satisfied with the considerable wealth that he already enjoyed, Hafed sold his farm, abandoned his family, and for the next two decades traveled throughout Asia, the Mideast, and Europe in search of diamonds. He found none. When all his money was gone, he found himself, starving and afflicted, on a steep cliff above the Mediterranean Sea. In his rags, wretchedness, and despair, he threw himself into a great wave. He "sank beneath its foaming crest, never to rise in this life again."

Shortly after Hafed sold his farm, the man who bought it noticed something shiny in a stream on the property while his camels were drinking. The man rolled up his sleeve, reached into the stream, and pulled out a curious black stone with a small round "eye" that reflected all the hues of the rainbow. He brought it home, put it on the mantel over the fireplace, and forgot about it.

A few weeks later, the same Buddhist priest returned to the farm. When he saw the stone on the mantel, he recognized it as a diamond in its natural, unpolished state, and shouted out to the farmer. Together the two men rushed out to the fields and with a bit of digging unearthed thousands of the black stones. The fields were literally covered with them. The farm would become Golconda, the greatest diamond mine not just in India but also the world, where the crown jewels of England and Russia, among many others, were mined. Had Ali Hafed remained at home and worked his own fields instead of seeking greater riches elsewhere, he would have had—literally—acres of diamonds.

You, too, have resources you may not recognize, that can help make your new venture a success. In this chapter, we are going not merely to discover but catalogue and inventory *your* acres of diamonds.

STARS = DIAMONDS

Your diamonds are your resources (and those of your cofounder(s), if applicable). They fall into five categories:

- **S**kills

- **T**echnologies

- **A**ssets (knowledge, physical, and financial) and Accomplishments

- **R**elationships and Reputation

- **S**trengths (as in *inner* strengths).

These are not in order of importance—that varies from case to case—but ordered to spell "STARS" so they are easy to remember. As you satisfy customer needs, you will create new resources for you and your business, and these will eventually exceed in importance the resources you started out with. But for the moment, we'll focus on your starting resources.

SKILLS

Your skills include abilities you have developed or acquired though study, practice, exposure, or application. The following are examples:

- Chemistry bachelor's degree and lab skills

- Scuba certification

- Microsoft Office proficiency

- Making gourmet desserts

- Conversational Spanish skill

- Three years of work experience in medical services

- Played guitar in a rock band for four years

TECHNOLOGIES

These are technologies for which you have acquired significant firsthand knowledge and experience, either by using the technologies directly, working on or with the technologies, or worked closely with others who know them well. Most of us think first of consumer technologies such as cell phones and microwave ovens, but these are only a fraction of all technologies that you probably know something about. Here are a few of the millions of examples you might know or aspire to know something about:

- **Transportation:** Automotive mechanics, avionics, Global Positioning System (GPS) tools, self-driving cars, highway paving, snow removal, traffic management, logistics

- **Energy/Power:** Heating, ventilation, air-conditioning, hydraulic fracturing, photo voltaics, power transmission and distribution, refrigeration

- **Life Sciences/Health:** Genomics, microfluidics, pharmaceutics, polymerase chain reactions (PCR), prosthetics, radiology, sonography, wearable devices

- **Construction and manufacturing:** Brazing, ceramics, fire protection, home building, robotics, packaging, power tools, synthetic fibers, 3-D printing, welding

- **Computers and telecom:** Circuit design, memory, storage, sensors, routers, batteries, data transmission, video compression

- **Information:** Software development, data security, analytics, infographics, user experience, machine learning, virtual reality

New technologies deserve a special place among your technologies and your STARS overall. The Internet, social networks, and mobile technologies are making it easier to share, mix and match ideas, and are accelerating the pace of change. As a result, old technologies are being replaced by new technologies and becoming obsolete even more rapidly. Twitter and fax are both used for marketing communications, but knowing all about Twitter will help you better satisfy such customer needs today than knowing all about fax.

The same resource (e.g., circuit design) can sometimes be categorized in multiple ways: as a skill, a technology, or a knowledge asset. That's okay. Just make certain to list it at least once. The categories are there to remind you of all your considerable resources. For our purposes, it matters less how you categorize them and more that you not overlook any of them.

ASSETS AND ACCOMPLISHMENTS

Assets

Your assets may be knowledge/information, physical, or financial.

Knowledge/Information Assets

- Practical knowledge that you possess—recipes, clothing or furniture design, electrical circuits, or algorithms—that is not widely known by others

- Knowledge of "a machine not fully employed, or somebody's skill which could be better utilized, or . . . surplus stock which can be drawn on during an interruption of supplies" in the words of Nobel prize winning economist Friedrich von Hayek

- Recognizing a real, unsatisfied customer need before anyone else

- A software design or prototype

- Firsthand knowledge of your hometown or the town where you currently live

- A failed previous company that you founded

Your intimate knowledge of your hometown may well deserve to be listed. Your knowledge of its streets, merchants, civic leaders, buildings, businesses, and neighborhoods could give you an advantage in starting your new venture there. Nathan Labenz and Jay Gierak, cofounders of Stik. com, a provider of customer-reviews-based marketing services, moved from Silicon Valley back to their hometown of Detroit. Their extensive family and professional connections there helped them get Stik off the ground rapidly and contributed to their winning the $100,000 "Rise of the Rest" challenge in 2014. This prize from AOL cofounder Steve Case is awarded to the most promising start-ups in four mid-American cities.

And yes, even your failed previous company may deserve to be listed. As we will see later, every concerted attempt you make, whether it succeeds or fails, imparts valuable learning that increases your likelihood of success next time.

Physical Assets

- A bedroom or garage in your home that you can use as an office, research lab, showroom, or production facility

- Computers, servers, software, Internet access, and smartphones

- Equipment, machinery, and supplies relevant to your venture

I started both of my companies from a large master bedroom that I turned into an office in my townhouse in Menlo Park, California. With CustomerSat, our programmers, desks, computers, servers, and peripherals gradually outgrew that "office" into my living room and dining room. When I received a threatening letter from my homeowner's association complaining that our employees' cars were taking up all available parking on Sand Hill Circle and reminding me that residents were not allowed to run commercial enterprises out of their homes, we finally had to move to commercial offices.

Financial Assets

- Funds you can invest from your savings

- Your history of fastidiousness in paying back borrowed money as quickly as possible, whether the amounts are large or small, and your resulting good credit and impeccable reputation for trustworthiness, thus making friends and family receptive to lending you money or investing in your business

- Your ability to generate funds through services

In my second company, CustomerSat, we funded software development for our first three years by providing services: designing, implementing, and managing online surveys for corporations.

Accomplishments

We list your accomplishments to remind you of the strong foundation you have to build on and to build your self-confidence. Examples might include the following:

- Completing a project on time and under budget

- Making a down payment on a home

- Paying off a debt

- Earning a college degree

- Putting a child through college

- Taking first place in a competition important to you

If you have overcome challenges before, you can do so again in your new venture.

RELATIONSHIPS AND REPUTATION

Relationships

Your relationships might include the following:

- Family, friends, and mentors who can provide advice, help, recruitment, funding, or encouragement

- Coworkers or others in your field who are potential cofounders, employees, customers, or partners

- Your social network and professional and alumni associations

- A loyal and loving spouse or domestic partner who will help support you (and potentially your family) emotionally, financially, or both while you are getting your new venture off the ground

Reputation

Your reputation includes what people know, think, and say about you; the extent to which they trust you; and what is generally recognized about what you have accomplished. How you treat people every day is a major determinant of reputation.

Think of your reputation as a reflection and summary of all your thoughts, words, and deeds. It is tempting to try to build that reflection and summary directly—through self-promotion and exaggeration of your accomplishments—rather than by focusing on the thoughts, words, and deeds that they reflect and summarize. Succumbing to these temptations may help build your reputation in the short term but not the long term.

Among the most significant reputation resources (and profound satisfactions) a serial entrepreneur can create and enjoy are stakeholders from previous ventures—employees, customers, investors, suppliers, or business partners—who are eager or willing to be part of his or her next venture. That says, in a nutshell, "our previous experience with you was good and we trust that it will be good again." If no one at all follows you from one venture to the next, something is wrong.

STRENGTHS (INNER)

Finally, your strengths—here we use the term to mean *inner* strengths—include personal qualities such as courage, loyalty, health, integrity, perseverance, peace of mind, friendliness, intelligence, knowledge, convictions, physical strength and coordination, thoughtfulness, courtesy, vision, self-confidence, humility, and empathy.

Inner strengths are so important that we devote the entire, very next chapter "Growing Your Mind from the Inside Out" to them.

YOUR STARS CHART

Create a chart like the example shown in table 6.1 and stand back and realize how many resources you have to work with. Table 6.1 is representative only; please make your chart specific to you and your personal

Table 6.1. STARS: Your resources (an example).		
Letter	**Category**	**Resource**
S	Skills	–Chemistry (bachelor's degree) –Three years' work experience in medical services –Scuba certification –Conversational Spanish
T	Technologies	–Social networking (Facebook, LinkedIn, Twitter) –Online search (e.g., Google) –Natural language processing (NLP) –Global Positioning System (GPS) tools
A	Assets and Accomplishments	**Assets** *Physical* –Laptop, printer, and high-speed Internet access –Hardware prototype *Financial* –Savings –Full-time job and income (medical services) *Knowledge* –Software design and prototype –Know my hometown well (born and raised here) **Accomplishments** –Earning a college degree –Completing a project on time and under budget
R	Relationships and Reputation	**Relationships** –Family who can provide help and encouragement –Mentors who can provide advice –Coworkers as potential cofounders, employees, customers –Alumni association **Reputation** –Friends I trust and who trust me –Recommendations –Strong credit score
S	Strengths (Inner)	–Leadership (led soccer team to regional championship) –Diligence/perseverance (got a raise or made honor role this quarter despite broken foot) –Compassion (helped neighbors after their house flooded) –Entrepreneurship (bought up friends' DVDs and sold them online for a profit) –Excellent health

resources. Your skills, technologies, knowledge-based assets, and (business) relationships will most help you determine which customer need or needs you are best equipped to satisfy. Your other resources— financial and physical assets, accomplishments, (personal) relationships, reputation, and (inner) strengths—are more generally applicable to, and increase your likelihood of success in satisfying, any customer needs. Listing your accomplishments, personal relationships, and inner strengths builds your self-confidence.

THE ADVANTAGE OF LIMITED RESOURCES

If your resources seem modest to you, don't be discouraged. First, we are generally our own worst critics. Second, limited resources can be an *advantage*. How so? Consider this: immigrants to a new country generally have little in the way of assets and other resources, yet they account for a very high percentage of new companies started. In the United States, a report from the Partnership for a New American Economy found that immigrants or their children founded more than 40 percent of Fortune 500 companies.[2]

Entrepreneurs starting with less personal liquidity may be more resourceful, cautious, and ultimately successful, according to finance professors Jarle Møen of the Norwegian School of Economics and Hans K. Hvide of the University of Aberdeen. They found that Norwegian entrepreneurs in the *top* quartile of personal wealth fared *worse* in terms of profit than those with fewer assets. Less wealthy entrepreneurs, they theorize, work with less room for error, and may be more receptive to financial advice from investors and lenders.[3]

"Great wealth can do more harm than good for entrepreneurs," said Møen. "It has been normal to see a lack of capital as an obstacle to entrepreneurship and innovation. Our findings nuance this picture. If new businesses are not disciplined by a certain scarcity of capital, both the entrepreneur and investors should be very much on the alert."

CustomerSat survived the dot-com bust of 2000–2002 in part because we had no venture capital investors who would bail us out if we didn't make it on our own.[4] Knowing this, we had no choice but to cut spending immediately as market conditions deteriorated. Meanwhile, our better-financed competitors, confident their investors would bail them out, kept spending and unwittingly wasting money. Some of these competitors were not bailed out and went out of business; others were indeed bailed out and survived. However, the resulting dilution reduced their investors' and employees' interest in the business, both financially and psychologically, dulling their competitive edge. CustomerSat went on to grow profitably without dilution until the company was acquired. Passion gives you curiosity to find new solutions and enables you to break through obstacles, which has the effect of multiplying your resources, so if you are deeply passionate about your venture, your resources are both greater than they appear and than you may realize.

Start-ups even have an advantage over well-established businesses. As Clayton Christensen explains in *The Innovator's Dilemma* (HarperBusiness Essentials, 2003), the demands of existing customers, and natural flow of capital to address those customers' needs, constrain and disadvantage established companies from addressing opportunities that disrupt their current businesses. Your start-up thus has an advantage over established companies in addressing such opportunities.

EXPERIMENTS, BOTH SUCCESSES AND FAILURES, GROW YOUR KNOWLEDGE AND CONFIDENCE

Your successes and failures together endow you with two invaluable resources:

- Knowledge of what *you* can achieve with a given set of resources

- Knowledge of what *others* can achieve with a given set of resources

KNOWLEDGE OF WHAT YOU CAN ACHIEVE

Figure 6.1 starts with what you know you can do successfully (#1). It could be anything you are passionate about, for example, cleaning or selling houses, completing engineering projects on time and under budget, becoming an expert on the Python programming language, or winning a loyal following for your monthly blog. From that base, you try something new—think of it as an experiment—and complete it successfully (#2). Congratulations!

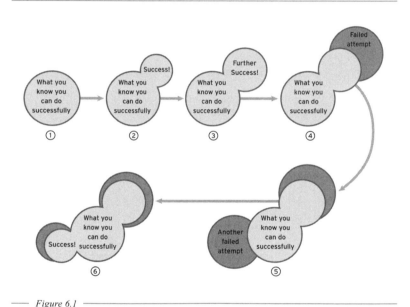

Figure 6.1

Success and failure together expand your knowledge.

The region enclosed by the heavy gray line, which traces the boundaries of what you know you can do successfully, expands accordingly. Emboldened, you try something new of a similar type—another experiment—only larger or more ambitious (#3), and again you succeed! The lightly shaded region expands again. You try again, but this time you fail (#4). You decide you have pushed as hard and far as you reasonably can in that direction, so you try a different direction you are passionate about (#5), and again you fail (#5). But this time, you are confident that success is still waiting to be yours in this direction, and plus, you learned something important in step #5. You try again with a slightly downsized objective than before, and this time, you are successful (#6). What you know you can do successfully—the lightly shaded region—is now about three times the size of what it was originally. Your success and failure together enable you to trace out and extend the boundaries of your potential and better sense how much can be achieved with a given set of resources.

From your five tries in #2 through #6, you have learned a great deal: not only what you can achieve—the light gray region—but also what you could not achieve given your resources (skills, technologies, assets, etc.) at the time. This is represented by the white space directly beyond the outer edge of the dark gray region. The dark gray region itself represents uncertainty: Had you set your sights somewhere in between the inner and outer edges of the dark gray regions, rather than right at the outer edge, you might have been successful. Each time you succeed you directly enlarge where you know you can succeed; each time you fail you learn what did not work and can better judge what will work next time.

If you are too conservative given your resources each time you try something new, your chances of success will be high, but you won't learn much or extend what you know you can do. If you are too ambitious, your chances of failure will be high, in which case you again won't learn much about what is possible for you. So there is an optimal level of risk taking for you and your resources. If you have tried several new things in a row and been successful each time, chances are you can and should stretch significantly further next time than you did last time. If you have failed each time, chances are you should set a more modest goal.

KNOWLEDGE OF WHAT OTHERS CAN ACHIEVE

Each of your experiments gives you a better sense of what *you* can accomplish. Beyond that, each one also gives you a better sense of what *anyone* can achieve with a given set of resources. This real-world experience improves your judgment as entrepreneur, executive, and future investor in others' start-ups. The more experiments, whether successes or failures, you can compress early on in your life and career, the better.

Eric Jacobus and his colleagues at The Stunt People produced the martial arts film *Death Grip* on a budget of $100,000. They now have a very good idea of how much work it takes to produce a film of that quality with that budget and can better advise other filmmakers and evaluate other projects. Building on their learning from and success of *Death Grip*, they expect to raise many times that amount for their next film.

In the next two chapters, we dive more deeply into two of your STARS—inner Strengths (chapter 7) and Technologies (chapter 8).

GOOD QUESTION!

Q

Should I get work experience at an existing company before starting my own business, and if so, for what length of time?

A

Consider doing whatever you believe will most strengthen your STARS overall the fastest. That will depend on how much weight you place on each of your STARS, the existing company, and your position there. Following are five thoughts on the matter:

1. If, at the existing company, you will be working with and learning from capable people, developing skills and acquiring knowledge that will directly benefit your start-up, and saving money that will help fund your start-up, go for it. Choose the company and position carefully to make sure they best satisfy these conditions, however you weigh them. The earlier stage the company, the better.

2. The longer you remain an employee, the less likely you are to start your own business. Be wary of becoming too comfortable, too specialized, or too dependent on staff. You will probably learn less each passing year as an employee than the year before. Don't stay too long.

3. Working at an established company teaches you firsthand the customer needs that businesses have. Most new entrepreneurs with little or no work experience consider only consumer customer needs, not business customer needs, of which they have little knowledge. Satisfying a business need generally means you will have fewer competitors. Perhaps consider it your mission at the established company to discover and validate an unsatisfied business need for your start-up to satisfy, and as soon as you start to develop a solution for it, plan to leave the company. If any concern might later arise as to the ownership of intellectual property—yours or the established company's—leave sooner rather than later. Leaving before you start to develop your solution generally avoids this concern.

4. The year I learned the most about management, business, and life was 2001, the year CustomerSat survived the dot-com bust that I recounted in chapter 1. It was tough. All of my STARS got stronger. In my view, I first earned my executive stripes that year. I was in my forties. It's better for you to have that intensity of learning and experience sooner in life. So again, don't wait too long.

5. Even if you have worked at established companies for many years, don't despair. It is never too late to venture out on your own.

Q

Should I get an MBA before starting my own business? What about joining a start-up accelerator?

A

An MBA offers three potential benefits. First is an education encompassing business, commerce, and economics. Much of this won't be immediately or directly applicable to your start-up. It will broaden you if you can afford the time and money. As I mentioned in the fourth point of the previous question, for me the best way to learn about starting and building a company was to do it. When you learn what you need when you need it, in order to do it, learning becomes part of your knowledge and skill set more completely than it ever could through classroom assignments. You further learn by hiring people who know what needs to be done and how to do it, and by doing your own research as needed.

A second benefit of an MBA is your ready-made professional network of classmates, probably representing a diverse range of functional areas, industries, and geographies. Some networks are better than others; let this be part of your MBA program evaluation. Here again, you can also do your own networking without an MBA, by going to meetups, helping people, and introducing people to each other. Seek out the professional, civic, and business networking organizations in your area.

A third benefit is a marketable credential—your MBA—mainly valuable for getting a job with an established organization. Your start-up's customers likely care more about the quality of your products and services than whether you have an MBA. For many angel investors, myself included, a degree in engineering or science that you can apply to your start-up counts more heavily than an MBA. Beyond that, the importance of any credential is quickly eclipsed by what you have or have not accomplished in the past few years. An MBA from a top business school, if it demonstrates that you have made it through a tough selection, retention, and completion process, will have more lasting marketable value.

But it, too, will eventually be eclipsed in importance by what you have or have not recently accomplished.

On the cost side, getting an MBA will likely burden you with tens of thousands of dollars of debt, which will detract from funds you have to invest in your new venture.

Given all these factors, an MBA is not an ideal fit for most entrepreneurs. If you think an MBA is right for you, here are several questions that can help you assess specific programs:

- Is entrepreneurship a concentration, and if so, what percent of the students enroll in it? This will determine how many of your classmates are aspiring entrepreneurs and how focused the overall program is on entrepreneurship.

- Is the entrepreneurship curriculum more classroom- and lecture-based or experiential (learning by doing)? To the extent the program is experiential, who are the coaches and mentors? Ideally, they are current or recent successful entrepreneurs.[5]

- What percent of grads go on to start companies?

- How strong is, and what is the composition of, the alumni network?

- How much does the program cost?

If you are considering an MBA to postpone the scary step of starting your own business, please reconsider. Better to just take that first step.

In contrast to MBA programs, I strongly recommend considering start-up accelerators. These programs do not grant degrees, but typically provide mentoring by successful entrepreneurs and angel investors and space in an incubator (offices housing many start-ups) for an intensive ninety days or longer, in exchange for a small percentage of ownership in your company. In Silicon Valley, the best known accelerators include Y Combinator, TechStars, 500 Startups, Draper University, and the Thiel

20under20 Fellowships. The other participants are fellow entrepreneurs who share your single-minded focus on starting their companies. Accelerators accept you based on the potential and scalability they see in your start-up. Rather than your paying tens of thousands of dollars in tuition, many accelerators provide seed capital, convertible notes, or a combination of the two. Acceptance rates at some of the best-known accelerators are lower than those for leading business schools; you may have a better chance of getting into Harvard. Fortunately, many such accelerators are now appearing across the United States and around the world.

Q

I know a particular technology at multiple levels, for example, an overall system, the subassemblies that comprise it, and the components of those subassemblies. In my STARS chart, should I list them all among my technology resources?

A

List any and all skills and technologies that you think might either increase your likelihood of success in addressing customer needs, or suggest new customer needs for you to address, either alone or in combination with other skills and technologies.

For example, if you are an experienced automotive mechanic, your list of technologies might include power train, cooling, suspension, braking, steering, lighting, and dashboard subsystems. Could any of these subsystems be applied to bicycles, skateboards, skis, all-terrain vehicles, sailboats, sailplanes, or self-driving cars?

If you are experienced in customer satisfaction measurement and enterprise feedback management, the skills you list might include authoring questionnaires, analyzing and reporting on survey results, designing enterprise-wide feedback systems that map to the organization's business processes, and linking customer satisfaction to management compensation. Many surveys composed by nonexperts with do-it-yourself tools like SurveyMonkey produce meaningless results. Could you use your skills to design an automated interactive dialogue that would empower anyone, not just a trained market researcher, to create professional, actionable surveys?

EXERCISE

Make a STARS chart like the one in table 6.1 of your resources by category. Include as many resources as you can think of and reasonably list in each category, even if they don't seem applicable to your identified customer needs. You may later discover a way that they can be applied after all, or you may end up addressing a different need to which those other resources *are* applicable. If you think a resource could give you an advantage over others (your competitors) satisfying a possible customer need, or help you determine whether to satisfy one need versus another, you should include it. List at least six to eight resources in each category, then put them in order, starting with the one or ones you consider most significant.

CORE LESSONS

- You and your cofounder(s), if applicable, have resources—"acres of diamonds"—you may not even realize you have.

- Inventory (list) your resources in five categories: Skills, Technologies, Assets and Accomplishments, Relationships and Reputation, and Strengths (STARS).

- Virtually every successful entrepreneur and company starts out with limited resources. Limited resources can be an advantage: They force you to focus and act quickly.

7

GROWING YOUR MIND FROM THE INSIDE OUT

We cannot become what we need to be
by remaining what we are.
   —Max De Pree

SEE WHAT YOU CANNOT CHANGE AS AN ASSET

In my midthirties, I accepted the fact that I'm gay. Many folks don't see that as an asset. I disagree. It has been an asset for me in at least five ways:

- People routinely assume that others are attracted to the opposite sex. I have long known—definitely—that those assumptions can be wrong. Being gay has thus made me more willing to challenge routine assumptions and the status quo, making me a better entrepreneur.

- Being gay has sensitized me to the discrimination faced by women, blacks, and other minorities (not to mention gays themselves).

- It wasn't socially acceptable to be openly gay when I was growing up, so at least some and possibly much of the time and energy that I would otherwise have put into dating, I put into school, sports, and career instead. Today, I tremendously enjoy the benefits of that early investment.

- By being openly gay today, others recognize that I'm comfortable with and don't try to hide who I am, which builds trust between us.

- More broadly, being openly gay signals that I am confident enough in myself that it doesn't matter to me whether or not people know that I'm gay.

Similarly, if you genuinely cannot change some aspect of yourself— height, ethnicity, accent, childhood, or that you or one of your parents were incarcerated—find a way to view it as an asset. Please set your bar very high. If you would like to change something about yourself that you indeed can change—you smoke, are overweight, or haven't finished a degree—please don't use this as an excuse not to make the change.

But if it is genuinely out of your control, finding a way to view it as a strength will be hugely liberating and empowering for you and it will become one of your assets, as it was and has for me.

Some years ago I shared these ideas in a talk in Guatemala. A young man sitting several rows back in the auditorium slowly raised his fist and gently pressed it against his chest. At first I thought it was a small gesture of agreement or support. Then, when I looked again, I saw that he was not making a fist at all. His hand had no fingers. I imagine he was saying, "This I cannot change. This is my strength."

Starting a new venture demands every resource and advantage you can bring to bear to increase its likelihood of success. One of those key resources is your mind. Your mindset can easily make or break your start-up. This chapter explores eight ways to protect, develop, and leverage your key resource—your mind.

Courage is in much shorter supply than genius.
—Peter Thiel

NEVER SAY ANYTHING NEGATIVE ABOUT YOURSELF

In December 2010, I boarded the *Plancius,* a polar expedition ship, and crossed the Drake Passage from Tierra del Fuego to explore the Antarctic Peninsula. Icebergs floated by us, crawling with penguins.

Only about 10 percent of an iceberg is above water; 90 percent is below. Our minds are similar to that iceberg: We are consciously aware of around 10 percent of the comments, observations, signals, sounds, smells, and touches that we experience. Our minds register the remaining 90 percent without our even being aware of them. Some of these messages and signals, especially any that are repeated again and again, our minds accept as truths, which affect our self-confidence, attitudes, and behaviors. The most dangerous messages are negative ones we repeat either aloud or to ourselves:

I'm ill at ease socially.

I'm forgetful.

I'm not good at math.

I have no sense of direction.

I'm bad at sports.

I'm a slow learner.

No one listens to me.

I can't manage people.

Such messages can become self-fulfilling prophecies. Tell yourself you are socially inept, and you will become (or remain) socially inept. Constantly reinforce to your unconscious mind that you are bad at sports, and you will become (or remain) bad at sports. Don't let messages like these become lodged in your mind as truths. *Never say anything negative about yourself.* If you must, use the past tense: This is the way I used to be.

To be very clear, this is not to avoid negatively impressing others. We are not concerned about what they think; we are concerned about what your unconscious mind thinks. Avoid negatively impressing your unconscious mind—your most important audience.

Similarly, do not dwell in your mind on the times you were socially inept or bad at sports. How do you avoid doing this? There is only one way: *Think of something else.*

For all the negative things you have recently said about yourself, or negative thoughts that have recently crept into your mind, make a list of the moments your behavior, performance, or actions—no matter how small—have demonstrated the opposite of those negative thoughts:

Negative Thoughts	Positive Moments
I'm ill at ease socially.	At the party, I put everyone at ease.
I'm forgetful.	I remembered where everything was filed.
I'm no good at math.	I did the math in my head.
No sense of direction.	I got us there without getting lost.
I'm bad at sports.	I was the star of that game.
I'm a slow learner.	I knew how to do it before he explained it.
No one listens to me.	I held everyone's rapt attention for an hour.
I can't manage people.	My team did it under budget and on time.

Make your positive moments as detailed and graphical as possible with photos, videos, articles, awards, and other artifacts. The primary beneficiary of posting diplomas and trophies is *you*. Josh Lamour, our star account exec at CustomerSat, displayed his dozens of sales awards in his office. There was almost not enough room for them all. Seeing these awards every day reinforced to Josh's unconscious mind that he was a top achiever and helped propel him to further achievement. You can do the same. Think of it as feeding your mind, just as you would feed your body, a nutritious diet.

As MIT professor Ann Graybiel says, "The only way to break a habit is to create a new habit."

DON'T COMPLAIN OR CRITICIZE OTHERS

Who benefits when you complain or criticize others? You do. But not in a good way.

Carnegie Mellon professor Randy Pausch was dying of pancreatic cancer in 2007. He gave a powerful talk, now known as "The Last Lecture," that went viral and became a best-selling book. In it he said, "Complaining does not work as a strategy. We all have finite time and energy. Any time we spend whining is unlikely to help us achieve our goals. And it won't make us happier."[1]

When we criticize others, endorphins flow to our brains, which for five seconds give us a sense of well-being and superiority. But at the end of five seconds, the endorphins go away, we go back to the way we were before, and the criticized individual or individuals are discouraged and demoralized. By any measure, the net outcome is negative.

I used to say that positive feedback should exceed negative feedback by a factor of 10:1. That is true. But over time, the optimal ratio to my mind has grown to 25:1 to 50:1 to 100:1 and beyond.

Many other approaches are better than complaining or criticizing. Ask questions that help others discover the implications of their behavior or actions. Factually articulate the consequences of the behavior or action you would like to change. Invite the other person to offer specific suggestions. Celebrate the good in what somebody else has done. Try these instead.

LOOK FOR AND FIND THE GOOD IN OTHERS

We saw how reminding ourselves of our strengths makes us stronger. Similarly, reminding those around us of their strengths helps make them stronger. Even if we detect just a glimmer of courage, good judgment, or perseverance in someone, letting them know we see this (being as specific as possible) helps build those strengths in them. People are drawn to those who build them up. Practicing this attracts good people to you and elevates you to a position of leadership.

Think of a point on a carpet. Try to grab the carpet at that spot and lift it up. We can't lift up that point very high unless all the other spots around it are lifted up, can we? We are all like the points on that carpet.

SHORT TERM BECOMES LONG TERM VERY RAPIDLY

Long ago, in high school, I was klutzy and in the bottom 10 percent in physical fitness in high school. In flag football, I tagged the opposing team's ball carrier only once. The handsome and charismatic cocaptain of the Jupiter High football team, Buddy Smallwood, was there and said it should not count. No one could have expected that I would tag someone.

That was in high school. Over the years I worked to get in shape and maintain a healthy diet. Not obsessively, just consistently. By my forties, I was in the top 10 percent of physical fitness for my age group.

You can do the same. For most aspects of life—athletic, professional, scholarly, managerial, diplomatic, romantic—you can move from any starting point to any level that you wish simply by earnestly persisting. As you do so, gauge your performance, gather and act on feedback, and refine your approach.

The same is true of entrepreneurship. Assuming you learn from each experience, every new venture that you start is more likely to succeed than the previous one. If you have passion and perseverance, the odds add up rapidly in your favor. Let's say for example, that your first venture has only a 30 percent chance of success. Your second venture might have a 50 percent chance; your third venture, 70 percent; and your fourth venture, 85 percent. The probability that at least one of these four ventures is successful is over 98 percent.[2]

BE HUMBLE ABOUT YOUR "ORIGINAL" IDEAS

In my midtwenties, I came up with a catchy melody for cello, wrote it out on music paper, and proudly played it for my teacher, Cheryl Fippen. She agreed that it was catchy but thought it sounded familiar.

Impossible, I insisted—this was an original creation, coming straight from my heart and soul.

A few months later, I was out driving and my song came on the radio! Not only was it exactly the same melody; the composer had had the audacity to write it over a century before I was born! Turns out my theme was from Borodin's *Prince Igor* overture, a popular piece of classical music I had surely heard but forgotten.

Similarly, the idea of doing surveys via email, which seemed so fresh in the early '90s, was also no doubt originally inspired by a forgotten person or source. My point is that whenever you (think that you) have an original idea, be humble: You never know when another person or event may have smuggled it into your mind.

FIND AN ANCESTOR THAT YOU ADMIRE

Everything I ever heard or learned about my father's grandfather, Captain William Chisholm (1819–1903), was impressive. Born in Antigonish, Nova Scotia, Captain Chisholm was one of over a dozen children and became a master mariner and seaman. He visited nearly all the principal ports of the world, served as governor of a Pacific island and as officer on the *Great Eastern*, the ship that laid the first trans-Atlantic telegraph cable. He was physically imposing: My father's mother said that his enormous hands hung at his sides like a couple of hams. And he was highly regarded in his community. His death was listed in a historical booklet as one of fourteen most significant events of 1903 in Marblehead, Massachusetts.[3]

Overall, my family tree is not particularly distinguished. My great-grandparents, Luigi Digiuni and Maria Beltrami, could neither read nor write, and I was the first male in my family to earn a bachelor's degree. But everyone is related to someone accomplished or admirable—you just need to find that person. Captain William Chisholm provides a fine reputation for me to live up to. I'm proud to be his great-grandson and know that my genes are similar to his. Find one or more ancestors of yours in your family tree that you admire; know that you have much in common with them; and let them inspire you.

CONNECTING PEOPLE: THE EASIEST WAY TO MAKE THE WORLD A BETTER PLACE

Think of a person who introduced you to your best friend, cofounder, significant other, or spouse. That person did you a great service, didn't they? They made the world a better place. Probably you feel deeply grateful to that person. You can do the same thing for someone else.

If a week goes by that you or I haven't introduced two people who share a common interest or passion, whether it's a sport, hobby, industry, technology, book, skill, or academic interest, we've missed an opportunity to enrich people's lives. Email makes it easy. If it is a professional introduction, my subject line will invariably be something like, "Mary, meet John Smith of XYZ; John, meet Mary Jones of ABC"; if it is personal, I omit the "of XYZ" and "of ABC." Make certain to mention at least one common interest of the two people. Otherwise, they may not be motivated to meet. Here are some real examples.

———————

Hi Marsha and Martin, you two fellow entrepreneurs based in Buenos Aires should know each other! Marsha runs a for-profit secondary school; Martin runs a music streaming start-up. Google Maps says you are less than five miles apart—practically neighbors!

John

———————

Hey Joe,
Greetings—hope all is well! Meet Danny Trujillo. He is a serious bodybuilder, studies real estate, and trains people at gyms in San Francisco and Hayward.

Hey Danny,

Meet Joe Carrero, former California State Light Heavyweight Champion. He keeps in great shape even many years later. I trained with him at Gold's in Mountain View when I lived in Menlo Park. He is now in real estate.

Joe: I told Danny you'd be great to talk to about professional and competitive bodybuilding, and he was eager to meet you. If you guys are free in the next month, I'll treat you to lunch so you get to meet each other and I get to see both of you.

Let me know what works for you. See you both soon.

John

Dear Bruce,

Greetings from San Francisco! Hope all is well with you and your family in Cedar Rapids. Please meet David Wu of the China Nuclear Power Design Corporation, LTD in Shenzhen, China. David manages the nuclear security system design office. In this role, he designs nuclear security systems for clients, including project design, working design, equipment selection, and related consulting services. His team has already designed security systems for five nuclear power plants (1000MW), two of which are currently in operation.

Dear David,

It was a pleasure meeting you on a recent flight from San Francisco to Albuquerque. Please meet my longtime friend and classmate Bruce Lacy. Bruce served for four years as an officer in the US Army; worked for the noted Dr. Sol Levy in San Jose, CA, who previously ran GE's Nuclear Operations there; and went on to become superintendent of maintenance at the Duane Arnold nuclear power plant in Cedar Rapids, Iowa. Later he was in charge of strategy for Alliant Energy, and now consults to nuclear industry through Lacy Consulting Group (www .lacyconsultinggroup.com).

Gentlemen, I am confident you will discover many interests in common and will mutually benefit by knowing each other. Hope to see both of you again soon, either in the US or China.

John

The cost of making an introduction? Just your thoughtful support of their interests and passions. Priceless.

EXERCISE

Think of two or three negative thoughts you might have had about yourself. What are specific instances when you disproved and demolished the negativity that those thoughts represent?

CORE LESSONS

- If you genuinely cannot change some aspect of yourself, find a way to view it as an asset.

- Never say anything negative about yourself.

- Don't criticize or complain.

- Look for and find the good in others.

- The short term becomes long term very rapidly.

- Be suspicious of your "original" ideas.

- Find an ancestor that you admire. Know that some of him or her is in you.

- Connect people; make the world a better place.

8

YOU'RE A TECHNOLOGIST. KNOW IT.

We're still in the first minutes of the first day
of the Internet revolution.
    —*Scott Cook*

I was raised in Jupiter, Florida, in the 1960s, amid sea turtles and fishing tackle and surf shops. For over a century, the brick red Jupiter Lighthouse had been our best known and loved landmark. Every night, we kids looked up and saw the Light's silent beacon sweep out a protective shield a hundred feet over our front yards every ninety seconds. On weekends they let you go inside and climb up the 105 steps to the lantern. You could admire the huge Fresnel lenses and lamp that had beamed every night since 1860 and look down on Evinrudes, Chris Crafts, and sloops navigating the Loxahatchee River and Jupiter Inlet.

In 1979, Burt Reynolds, our most famous citizen, opened his Dinner Theatre with much fanfare. The star-studded tourist attraction quickly eclipsed the Light as Jupiter's most famous landmark. After a few short years, Burt sold the theatre and in 1996 it was abruptly shut down. The Light again became our most famous landmark, unaware of and unchanged by the fuss.

When I was seven, a truck swerved around the corner and scattered hundreds of pebbles all over our front yard and into the sea grape. Dad and I were picking them out of the grass and sandy topsoil one by one, when I said, "Let's use a rake!" Dad praised me for thinking of this; I was proud of my idea. I ran to the utility room in the carport and grabbed the bamboo rake; with it, we finished the job in no time. That's the first time I can remember having a useful idea. Maybe Dad actually thought of it first and somehow planted it in my mind, launching a passion for innovation in me. If so, I am grateful to him. Half a century later, I still see innovation occurring the same way: a new tool, technique, or solution driven by a need.

Whether or not you remember them, you also have come up with many tools, techniques, and solutions to problems. You found a way to

- Get into your house, car, or apartment after locking yourself out

- Repair a shirt or pair of slacks in a pinch

- Turn leftovers into a new recipe, or salvage one gone wrong

- Get tickets to a sold-out concert

- Remember a list of numbers or items

- Use Facebook with Twitter or Google with LinkedIn

- Use a Band-Aid as Scotch tape, or Scotch tape as a Band-Aid

You are an innovator. Entrepreneurship is in large part a stream of one such idea put into action after another. You don't have to be the first person to think of an idea; others may have had the same ideas but never put them to work; and your application of the idea may be different from anyone else's. Some of your innovations you will use again and again.

Apart from innovating, you use technology every day: a smartphone, instant messaging, Instagram, Skype, Facebook, an iPod, PayPal, or iPad. These have been around for at most a decade. If we add technologies that have been in general use for a couple decades or so, they include email, color printers, Microsoft Windows, laptops, PC projectors, and digital cameras. If we add technologies that have been in general use for the past fifty years or so, they include color TV, oral contraceptives, wireless garage door openers, microwave ovens, commercial jetliners, and soft contact lenses. You also likely use one or more of these every day.

If we add technologies that have been around for a century or more, they include automobiles, elevators, electric lights, bifocals, flush toilets, photography, sewing machines, and aspirin. If we go back a thousand years or more, they include cooking pots, oil lamps, and written language. If we go back 10,000 years or more, they include agriculture, the wheel, footwear, cosmetics, and various hunting and fishing tools. Even that shirt or pair of slacks that you repaired in a pinch was a new technology if you go back far enough. Anthropologists tell us that man's first technology may have been a hand-held stone used over two million years ago for cutting or chopping. You come from a long line of technologists, whose innovations have accumulated to our benefit.

So you are an innovator, use technology daily, and come from a long line of technologists. Despite what you may think, the fact is that you are a technologist!

TECHNOLOGIES THAT BENEFIT ANY BUSINESS

Any new venture can benefit from thoughtfully applying technology. Doing so can let you make your business more efficient, productive, and effective; and favorably differentiate yourself from others who are satisfying the same or similar needs as you—that is, give you an advantage.

Some technologies can be effectively applied to virtually any business, such as

- A website

- A customer and prospect database and email address manager

- Tools enabling customers to schedule or order your product or service online

- Online surveys for customer feedback

- Online communities where customers and prospects can share tips (and hopefully rave about) your product or service

- Tools that enable sharing of all kinds of data—such as team members' locations, contact info, and schedules; upcoming events; customer information; the status of projects; and available resources— throughout your company

- Software to help automate payments, accounting, inventory, forecasting, payroll, and shipping

These technologies make your business more efficient, productive, and effective. Plan to apply them as you ramp up delivery of your product or service. But because of their widespread use, they probably won't differentiate you. They will simply put you on equal footing with your competitors.

TECHNOLOGIES THAT BENEFIT YOUR BUSINESS SPECIFICALLY

Now let's take the next step and seek technologies that give you an advantage. This requires work to discover the right ones and how to incorporate them. Any business can benefit from technology and gain an advantage by using it. For very traditional businesses like winemaking, homemade basketry, and stamp collecting, technology may seem irrelevant, if not antithetical. But even in these cases, new technologies can most assuredly give you an advantage:

- **Winemaking**: Using chemical testing to recognize every bad bottle before it leaves the winery, or to finely tailor each bottle's contents to precisely match the winemaker's intended bouquet and flavor.

- **Homemade basketry:** Using optical fibers to create baskets that glow in the dark and whose patterns change and are programmable.

Lasers might also be used to guide weavers' fingers quickly and reliably through complex patterns.

- **Stamp collecting:** Using a smartphone camera to scan stamps, identify them using image processing and a stamp database, assess their conditions, and instantly determine their values based on current market prices.

If even these very traditional businesses can gain an advantage from using technology, so can yours.

> *The best way to predict the future is to invent it.*
> *—Alan Kay*

NEW TECHNOLOGIES ARE LEAST LIKELY TO HAVE BEEN APPLIED ALREADY

While any technologies you know about might meaningfully be applied to differentiate you, *new* technologies are the ones least likely to have already been applied by others. My first company, Decisive Technology, was first to automate surveys online twenty-five years ago. Most practitioners and especially our competitors—companies that did conventional paper and phone surveys—dismissed us. They insisted we would never achieve representative samples of respondents using the Internet. LOL (laugh out loud). Today, far more survey data is collected online than by any other means. Similarly, few would have guessed a decade ago that today we would distribute books wirelessly, read them on tablets, or use Twitter for customer service. So don't listen to those who say a new technology doesn't apply or something can't be done. Stay informed about, experience firsthand, and experiment with as many new technologies as you can.

You are likely most familiar with consumer technologies such as smartphones, iPads, Facebook, Twitter, Skype, the Global Positioning

System (GPS), Bluetooth, and PayPal. John Doerr of Kleiner Perkins, the Silicon Valley venture capital firm, characterizes these online technologies as *SoLoMo*: social, local, and mobile. But there are just as many if not more new business technologies:

- New **materials** that enable products ranging from soft drink cans to SUVs to be lighter, stronger, and shipped more economically

- New **batteries** that make electric and hybrid vehicles more practical and affordable and enable households to go off-grid

- High-precision **genome duplication** processes for use by pharmaceutical firms

- **Lasers** that clear near-earth orbits of space trash, making them safe for satellites

Still other technologies blur the lines between consumer and business:

- **Wearables** for tracking body temperature, blood sugar, perspiration, heart rate, and more—part of the Quantified Self and personalized medicine movements

- **Programming languages** and environments that allow virtually anyone to develop applications for mobile devices

- **Gene sequencing equipment** for do-it-yourself (DIY) hobbyists

- **Autonomous aerial vehicles** (drones) for both commercial and personal use

And there are thousands more in almost any category—far too many to name here. Check out this partial categorized list.

Energy

Biofuels

Fusion

Geothermal energy

Horizontal drilling

Hybrid vehicles

Hydraulic fracturing (fracking)

Solar cells

Wind

Information Technology (IT)

Analytics

Case management

Correlation

Crowdsourcing

Global Positioning System tools

Image recognition

Natural language processing

Network security

Online search

Optimization

User interface design

User-generated content

Materials

3-D printing

Batteries

Ceramics

Composites

Genetically modified materials

Magnetics

Membranes

Memory/data storage

Metallurgy

Nanodevices

Polymers

Semiconductors

Medicine, Pharmaceuticals, and Medical Devices

Bio-absorbable polymers

Blood substitutes

Computer-assisted drug design

Drug delivery

Genomic pharmacology

Haptics

Implants

Intelligent prosthetics

Life extension

Micropumps

Nuclear magnetic resonance

Nutraceuticals

Smartphone-based diagnostics

Ultrasonics

HOW TO LEARN ABOUT TECHNOLOGIES

With thousands of technologies to choose from, you have to be selective. Here are two criteria:

- Which ones are you or can you become most passionate about?

- Which ones seem most likely to help you satisfy your customer need better and differently?

Wikipedia (www.wikipedia.org.) stands out for me among all other learning sources; I use it many times every week. HowStuffWorks.com explains how things as varied as electric guitars, real estate bubbles, and wireless radios in major league football helmets work; Quora.com provides crowdsourced answers to questions. Other things I do to stay apprised of new technologies include the following:

- Make, hang out with, and invite over technology-savvy friends

- Watch TED videos and attend local TEDx conferences

- Read *Wired, Technology Review,* and *Scientific American*

- Go to technology trade shows:

  - Consumer Electronics Show (CES) in Las Vegas

  - South by Southwest (SxSW) Interactive in Austin, Texas

  - MakerFaire (locations around the world)

Many of the world's best universities—MIT, Harvard, Stanford, and others—make science and engineering courses available to anyone for free online. Still others teach computer programming for free. Check out

- www.edx.org

- www.coursera.org

- www.udacity.com

- www.codecademy.com

Khan Academy (www.khanacademy.org) offers thousands of free online minicourses at high school and college levels.

If you were previously blocked from getting a first-rate education by exorbitant tuition fees, rafts of qualifying exams, or wretched public schools, now you are no longer. Increasingly, with free online courses available to anyone, all you need is passion and perseverance.

To the extent that you can, follow trends in adjacent technologies. At CustomerSat, we noticed that case management—the ability to document, categorize, assign, and escalate customer concerns—was central to software for customer relationship management, a space adjacent to ours. Members of our product team proactively explored how case management would benefit and could be integrated into our software.[2] As a result, when one of our major clients, Honeywell, proposed that we add cases to our system, we were able to respond very quickly. This feature would become a key CustomerSat advantage.

GOOD QUESTION!

Q

I'm a poetry major. I have never even downloaded an app. My humanities professor insists that I am not a technologist and never will be.

A

You go right back to that "professor" and beg to differ with him. Are you human? Yes. For all the reasons given earlier in this chapter, you are a technologist.

EXERCISES

1. List three innovations, no matter how small, in any area of life, you have made in the past thirty days.

2. Identify a technology that you believe might give you an advantage in satisfying one or more of the customer needs you have targeted. Find an online course, ideally free, covering that technology. Take the course, not merely watching the lectures but taking and passing the exams. Master the material. Add that technology to your list of resources if you haven't done so already.

3. Contribute your knowledge to others. Create or edit a Wikipedia entry.

CORE LESSONS

- You are a technologist and come from a long line of technologists.

- Virtually any business can benefit from the thoughtful application of one or more technologies. Beyond merely making you more efficient, technologies can make you unique and give you an advantage.

- New technologies are least likely to have been applied to your customer need already. Do your best to stay apprised of as many as you can.

- Consider both consumer and business technologies.

- To the extent that you are able, also keep abreast of technologies adjacent to the areas you are passionate about.

9

DIFFERENT IS BETTER
THAN BETTER

Strategy is about making choices, trade-offs;
it's about deliberately choosing to be different . . .
A strategy delineates a territory in which a company
seeks to be unique.
   —*Michael Porter, Harvard Business School*

HP, Lenovo, Dell, and others sell laptops that run Microsoft Windows. Each company's products are incrementally *better* than the others' along some dimension—one or another runs Windows 20 percent faster, offers 30 percent more favorable price/performance, 20 percent more compact packaging, 25 percent longer battery life, or a 20 percent larger display.

In contrast, Apple is *different* (see figure 9.1): more user friendly, more graphical, more unique tools and applications for publishing, photos, music, and video than Windows. Unlike HP, Lenovo, and Dell, Apple developed both the hardware and the operating system and tightly integrated them. Not coincidentally, Apple's slogan for many years was "Think Different." Over the years, Apple steadily took market share away from Windows. In 2010, for the first time, the market cap of Apple exceeded that of Microsoft. In 2011, Apple became the most valuable company in the world.

Different is better than better.

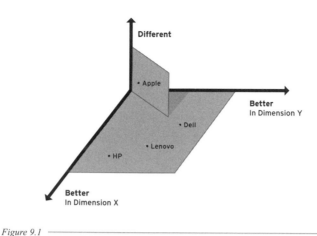

Figure 9.1

Being different places you on a different dimension.

What do I mean by that? When I say "better"—the second "better" in "Different is better than better"—I mean *quantitatively* better than what is currently available. Your battery lasts 25 percent longer. Your algorithm or software downloads are twice as fast. Your cupcakes or knitwear or storage devices are 20 percent cheaper than comparable competitors. For a start-up, such a quantitative advantage is at best tenuous. Your competitors likely include companies that are larger, better established, and more well-known than you, and in most industries, quantitative improvements in performance and cost happen continually. A purely quantitative advantage is hard for a start-up to sustain. CustomerSat increased speeds of computation for enterprise feedback analytics in a single release by a factor of ten. A competitor whose only advantage over CustomerSat were double or even triple our processing speed would be in a tough spot.

When I say "different," I mean a *qualitative* advantage using a different approach, design, or technologies that make your product or service the best choice for some important customer set. Being different places you on one or more different dimensions from your competitors, whether the dimensions are customer needs or product features. For example

- Other dentists require limited-mobility patients to come into their dental offices. But you make house calls.

- Other electricians and carpenters recommend each other. But you know that so many jobs involve both skills that the two of you use online tools to integrate your scheduling, service delivery, and billing.

- Other call centers allow customers to complete satisfaction surveys after the call. But you ask permission to record calls and use audio processing to measure tension or anger in the customer's voice, track whether it trended up or down in the course of the call with your agent, and flag outliers.

Your different product or service will not be for every customer, whether consumer or business. That's okay. If you can earn the loyalty of a small but sufficiently strong set of customers, they will become repeat customers for your product or service; will buy more of your product or service over time; and recommend you to their friends or colleagues, so you will further benefit from word of mouth.

It is possible, with a sufficiently large advantage, to be different along the same dimensions as established competitors, but that is much harder than being different along dimensions without such competitors. A tablet with twenty times the memory of other tablets at a comparable price would enable wholly new usage patterns and applications that exploit the voluminous memory. That's truly different. Maybe you use a novel memory technology to achieve it. But since memory size is one of the primary dimensions along which established tablet makers compete, watch out: They will work hard to catch and surpass you as quickly as possible. (Make sure one or more patents, licenses, or trade secrets adequately protect your novel technology.)

Better means your start-up has to fight larger competitors head-on. Different means finding a dimension without competitors that is valued by some set of customers and excelling along that dimension. If you can identify and excel along two such dimensions, even better. You won't be competing directly with the established competitors, and you'll have more time and room to become established yourself.

HEALTHIER SWIMMING POOLS

Tall and willowy Carol McKenna has spent a lifetime eating whole grains and many years doing yoga, so when she acquired West Hawaii Pool and Spa in Waikoloa in 2004, she brought a holistic perspective to what had been a commodity service business. Pure chlorine evaporates rapidly in hot climates, so pool services in Hawaii add cyanuric acid, which slows evaporation and keeps pools adequately chlorinated for a week. Most services simply add tablets that combine chlorine and acid to the pool every week. But while the chlorine evaporates, the acid does not, creating a buildup in the pool that burns the eyes, dries the skin, and etches plaster. Worse, at the higher concentrations of acid, the chlorine can't kill algae.

All of this disturbed Carol. Other pool servicers dealt with the buildup by draining pools yearly and refilling them with fresh water, but Carol did not want her clients and their families swimming and bathing for a whole year in increasingly unhealthy water. Finally, she hit on a simple solution: Each week, besides adding tablets to the pool, she drained the pool by two inches and added fresh water. That reduced the acid by just the right amount so it would not build up. It meant extra time and work for the pool service, but a healthier pool for her clients. Carol did the extra work each week gladly.

Today, West Hawaii Pool and Spa is known throughout Waikoloa for its all-natural pool maintenance. Carol has further expanded her services to add minerals that kill algae, soften water, and reduce or eliminate the need for not just acid but also chlorine. Her pool services are significantly different from others in Waikoloa. For Carol, different is better than better.

LIGHTER AIRCRAFT; SHRINKABLE POLYMERS

A chance assignment to work on a study for the Atomic Energy Commission introduced MIT-trained chemical engineer Paul Cook to the then-nascent industrial applications of high-energy radiation. Working at the Stanford Research Institute (now SRI International), Cook discovered that exposing polymers to ionizing radiation would create insulations with a variety of properties: lightweight, heat resistant, and even heat shrinkable. After much experimentation and development, he was able to turn these insulations into useful commercial products. The insulations could be used to cover electrical wiring, and because they were lightweight, could significantly reduce weight on aircraft and missiles, especially important for extending their range. Other polymers were heat shrinkable and could be formed into tubes to join two pipes, wires, or cables together. A polymer tube, slipped over their two adjacent ends and heated with a hot air gun, shrunk to provide a sealed, waterproof, and dustproof connection.

Cook cofounded Raychem, the first company to commercialize such products using radiation chemistry. Raychem deliberately developed and sold products that were sufficiently different that they could avoid direct competition. In its earliest years, 100 percent of its revenues came from products for which Raychem was the sole-source supplier. Even after twenty years, 50 percent of the products sold were sole source. The company grew rapidly, averaging 25 percent per year over its first twenty years, became a Fortune 500 company, and reached $2 billion in revenues before it was acquired. For Raychem, different was better than better.[1]

Being different not only gives you a unique customer set, it also makes it harder for established competitors to respond to you. As Clayton Christensen meticulously documents in his classic *The Innovator's*

Dilemma (HarperBusiness Essentials, 2003), established hard disk drive vendors in the 1980s and '90s found it very hard to shift to new, smaller form factors—first 5.25", then 3", then 2", then 1.8"—even though the smaller form factor drives were better suited for each new generation of smaller, more portable computers. The established vendors' existing customers—mainframe and minicomputer manufacturers—wanted high storage capacity and low price per megabyte. In contrast, the new form factors (initially) had both lower capacity and higher price per megabyte. In each case, one or more upstart disk manufacturers who did not compete in larger form factors won the market for the smaller form factor drives. Different was better than better.

EXERCISE

List the top three to four reasons customers choose among existing companies that address similar needs to the ones you plan to address. Now think of reasons those customers would pick you instead; only list reasons that don't apply to the other companies. These reasons differentiate you.

CORE LESSONS

- "Better" means your start-up has to fight larger competitors head-on.

- Instead, be different in a way that is deeply valued by some set of customers. You won't have to compete directly, and you'll have more time and room to get established.

- Your differentiation may be either core or supporting the need you address; either could be key to your success.

- As your customers buy from you again and again, and tell others about you, you will grow with them.

10

LISTEN TO YOUR RESOURCES (STEP 4A): WHAT ADDITIONAL NEEDS DO THEY SUGGEST?

Start where you are.
Use what you have.
Do what you can.
    —Arthur Ashe, American World top-ranked pro tennis player

In tiny Columbus, seventy-four miles west of Houston, strapping Ray Daley turned fourteen, got his learner's permit, and began driving the family truck around their farm. Soon after that, he used his life's savings to acquire his prized possession: a 1965 fire engine red Ford Thunderbird.

The two-door convertible with V8 engine and dual headlights was Ray's pride, and driving it around Columbus, his joy. Everyone in the mining and cattle ranching town knew the boy and his car. Then one night, Ray's older brother, Lonny, borrowed the T-bird. Lonny ran a stop sign, collided with a silver Oldsmobile Delta 98, totaled it, and smashed up the T-bird's front end. Ray was furious.

As was the boys' father. To get the matter behind them quickly, he had Lonny buy the Olds from its owner for the amount the owner had paid for it. A disgruntled Ray wanted Lonny to pay for repairs to his T-bird as well, but their father wouldn't allow it: Instead, he had Lonny give Ray the wrecked Olds that Lonny had bought. Ray would have to sell the Oldsmobile's parts for cash to repair or replace his T-bird's bumper, grill, and hood. What a hassle. He placed an ad to sell the Olds' salvageable engine, and started searching for a junked 1965 T-bird whose front end he could salvage. Then an opportunity fell into his lap.

An elderly Cuban widow in town wanted to get rid of an old, engine-less Thunderbird in her yard. It perfectly fit Ray's needs. There was just one hitch: She had four other junked cars that she wanted to get rid of as well. Ray could have the T-bird only if he hauled away all five cars, but if he did so, all five were his free of charge. Ray protested that he had no use for and no place to store five junked cars, but the lady was adamant. So Ray and a friend borrowed a pickup truck and a chain and made five trips to haul the cars, one by one, back to the Daley's farm.

Now Ray had seven wrecked cars: the totaled Olds, his original Thunderbird with the smashed up front end, the engineless T-bird from the Cuban lady, and the four other cars. He found a buyer for the Olds engine and ended up doing most of the restoration of his T-bird him-self, using parts from the other T-bird. Then something else happened: Word of his junked cars got around and neighbors started calling him for spare parts. Though only in junior high school at the time, Ray real-ized he had the makings of a business. Those seven junked cars became Daley Salvage, which over the years turned into Daley Iron and Metal, a million-dollar business that has had as many as nine employees.

In this case, Ray Daley did not first identify the customer need and then look for resources to satisfy it. Just the opposite. His seven junked cars suggested a need he could satisfy.

Similarly, as we saw in the last chapter, Paul Cook discovered a new class of insulators that could be used in aircraft and other commercial applications. That discovery led Cook to cofound Raychem, which grew into a $2 billion enterprise. In this case, Cook did not first identify the customer need and then look for a technology that could address it. Just the opposite. The unusual properties of the technology suggested the need it could satisfy.

RESOURCES SUGGEST NEEDS

Some of history's most significant inventions did not originate as a response to a specific need. Instead, the inventor started with a technology or other novel resource and stumbled by accident on the need it could satisfy. Such accidental inventions include anesthesia, corn flakes, dynamite, fireworks, the microwave oven, the pacemaker, penicillin, Post-it Notes, potato chips, saccharin, Silly Putty, the Slinky, Velcro, and Viagra.[1] In this and the next chapter, we turn "starting with resources and finding needs they can satisfy" into a systematic process.

Needs rather than resources do indeed suggest and drive most innovations. But resources suggest enough needs and innovations that it is worth deliberately searching for needs that your resources might satisfy, especially if the resources are unusual, like seven wrecked cars or a new type of insulation. Here are five tips to keep in mind:

1. **Consider lots of possible needs** that your resources might satisfy, because most of these possible needs won't be valid. The people who made the accidental inventions listed earlier were no smarter than you. In many cases, they were merely lucky. But it is a fair bet that they *tried* more possibilities than other people, because the vast majority of trials don't pan out. You will want to do the same.

2. **Focus on technologies**, and new technologies in particular, among your resources. The newer the technology, the more likely it is that you can find uses (needs it will satisfy) that others haven't considered yet.

3. **Be open-minded** to recognizing valid resource-need matchups when you find them. Customer needs are often hard to recognize until a means of satisfying them moves into your general proximity. In the early nineteenth century, people didn't think about talking to others who were long distances away because it just seemed impossible, not unlike how most people might view *Star Trek*–style teleporting today. Even shortly after the telephone was first demonstrated, a

Western Union memo stated, "This 'telephone' has too many short-comings to be seriously considered as a means of communication. The device is inherently of no value to us."[2] So don't make the same mistake: Be open-minded to possibilities.

4. **Be cautious:** Using resources to suggest needs is risky. Plan to work extra hard to confirm, through discussions with prospective customers and other research, that needs suggested by resources are indeed real.

   Recently a pair of young entrepreneurs briefed me on an interesting new technology: their "browser-based," "interactive," and "network aware" software. But they couldn't tell me what need it satisfied. After an extended discussion, we finally concluded that their technology could help distributed project teams share information. But virtually every major IT supplier—including Apple, Google, Microsoft, Oracle, Salesforce, and SAP—has workgroup productivity software that addresses this need. Their new software may have been slightly better, but it wasn't appreciably different from what these major IT suppliers offered.

   To avoid going up against IT industry giants directly, the entrepreneurs might identify a more specific need—perhaps installing or upgrading workgroup productivity systems for businesses in their home city, where the entrepreneurs had local-knowledge advantages, and where their competitors would be smaller systems integrators rather than major IT suppliers. Alternatively, perhaps their software could be adapted to enhance major workgroup productivity offerings, in which case the entrepreneurs would be collaborating with the existing IT giants, not competing with them.

5. **Systematically consider all combinations** of your resources to use your time most efficiently. We'll do this in the next chapter, "Look, Mom . . . I'm Inventing!"

EXAMPLE

Let's say the following STARS chart shows your resources. Now, think about needs to which those resources might be applied. By making the associations and links shown in figure 10.1, you come up with two possible needs you had not previously considered:

- Automatic English-Spanish translation between patient and doctor

- Same-day home delivery of prescription drugs throughout your hometown

Again, it is vitally important to validate these possible needs with potential customers.

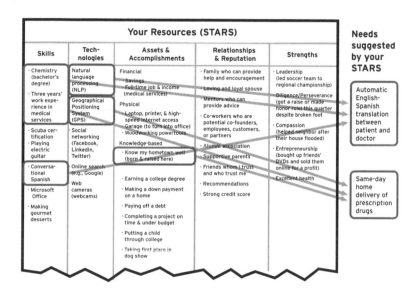

— *Figure 10.1* —

Your resources suggest customer needs.

EXERCISE

If you haven't done so already, make a STARS chart of your resources like figure 10.1. Find at least three needs they suggest that you might be able to use your resources to satisfy.

CORE LESSONS

- Your resources alone can suggest needs to satisfy and their solutions. Many significant innovations have originated this way.

- Consider lots of possible needs that your resources might satisfy, because most of these possible needs won't be valid.

- Focus on the new technologies among your resources.

- Be open-minded to recognizing valid resource-need matchups when you find them.

- Beware: using your resources to suggest needs is risky. Plan to work extra hard to confirm that the needs really exist.

11

LOOK, MOM . . . I'M INVENTING!
MIXING AND MATCHING TECHNOLOGIES

There are more things in heaven and earth, Horatio,
Than are dreamt of in your philosophy.
  —*Hamlet*

We usually think of a light bulb as a single unit. But it is actually a combination of several technologies. If it is a compact fluorescent lamp (CFL), it consists of a glass enclosure with a fluorescent coating, argon and mercury vapor, and integrated ballast. If it is a conventional incandescent light bulb, it consists of glass enclosure, filament, vacuum, inert gas, and base. Most innovations, including a majority of patents, similarly represent combinations—often new combinations—of existing technologies.[1]

If two technologies are both very new, the chances are that they do not intersect—that is, that no one has yet noticed or found a need or solution that combines those technologies. But if the use of those technologies is growing, one or more needs and solutions are likely to be noticed or found. The *intersection* between (combination of) the two technologies will be smaller but faster growing than either technology individually. The intersection of three or more growing technologies will be still smaller but will grow even faster. These intersections harbor good opportunities for business creation and advantage (see figure 11.1).

See appendix B for more complete details about the number of combinations of technologies.

"If you combine mobile phones, online maps, GPS, restaurant reviews, and online reservations, you can instantly find the closest Thai restaurants to you and their Zagat ratings, and reserve a table. Only by combining technologies do these novel solutions become possible,"[2] notes Erik Brynjolfsson, director of the MIT Center for Digital Business.

In this chapter, we systematically combine technologies that you know about. We look for and test combinations that might satisfy new customer needs or give your business an advantage. While our focus is on technologies, the same technique can be applied to skills, or for that matter, to any of your resources. But you are most likely to find useful combinations if the technologies, skills, and other resources are themselves specialized.

Because the number of combinations increases *exponentially* with the number of technologies, if you have even slightly more passion and perseverance in exploring combinations, you have a big advantage. Your passion and perseverance together enable you to explore more combinations faster and more thoroughly, and thus discover promising ones that others overlook.

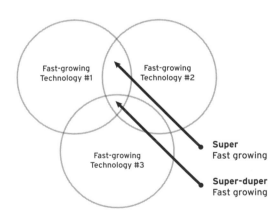

—— Figure 11.1 ——

Combine technologies to find new opportunities.

COMBINING TECHNOLOGIES THAT YOU KNOW ABOUT

In combining technologies, we'll follow four steps:

1. **List the technologies** that you (and your cofounder, if applicable) know about.

2. **List the *combinations*** of those technologies.

3. **Think of needs** that those combinations could satisfy and solutions they could enable.

4. **Confirm** that the needs are real and not already being satisfied, through research and discussions with prospective customers.

First, let's say that you and your cofounder are most familiar with six technologies:

- Natural language processing (NLP)[3]

- Global Positioning System (GPS) tools

- Social networking

- Online search

- Webcams

- Solar cells

Second, make a table like the one here with those technologies listed both horizontally and vertically. The numbered cells in the table represent different pairs of your technologies; the blank cells are duplicate combinations, which we ignore. We number the fifteen different pairs of our six technologies from 1 to 15. Number 1 is natural language processing (NLP) and Global Positioning System (GPS) tools; number 2 is NLP and social networking, and so on.

	NLP	GPS	Social networking	Search	Webcam	Solar
NLP		1	2	3	4	5
GPS			6	7	8	9
Social				10	11	12
Search					13	14
Webcam						15
Solar						

Third, consider each of the fifteen pairs one at a time as in the next list. Is the combination novel? For example, has NLP been combined with GPS? Without being constrained by the customer needs you have already identified, can you think of any need each combination might satisfy? This deserves plenty of time for brainstorming and reflection.

Combinations and Customer Needs

1. **NLP + GPS:** Might be used for a mobile app that alerts me when I am close to a location (e.g., store, friend's home) where I need to do an errand. I tell the app the number of days within which I'd like to complete the errand. The app optimizes my time by suggesting I do the errand only when I am sufficiently close to the location. As the app tracks my daily travel around town and the deadline draws closer, the app constantly updates whether I should do the errand now or later. *Note:* this combination is already used in GPS devices that announce directions to a vehicle driver.

2. **NLP + social networking:** Automate the chat exchange between you and people you are interested in meeting online. NLP interprets their text, responds intelligently, finds and discusses topics of mutual interest, checks your calendar, and suggests mutually

convenient places to meet for lunch or a drink. All with minimal involvement from you.

3. **NLP + search:** Ask.com and others already have NLP front ends to search: Type in a sentence in English and it searches for the answer.

4. **NLP + webcam:** A wearable webcam could use NLP to read and interpret signs that you pass while walking, driving, or window-shopping; and look for and act on special deals or other information that interest you.

5. **NLP + solar:** NLP reads and interprets weather forecasts to control geographically dispersed networks of solar panels, helping to optimize distribution and storage of solar-generated power.

6. **GPS + social networking:** (a) Combination already being used by online dating, meetup, and other services to let you know when your friends are, or who is, in your vicinity. (b) A mobile app alerts you when a friend of a friend whom you haven't met yet is in your close proximity. (c) Alerts you when your kids go outside your yard or neighborhood. (d) Alerts you when your ex-spouse is within x feet of you (e.g., at the same party).

7. **GPS + search:** (a) Already available: when you search online for a product or service, app tells you closest store, restaurant, hotel, gas station, or other retail outlet that can provide it. (b) Instead of a commercial retail outlet, source of product or service could be another individual who has room, car, or other item for rent; or library with the book in stock.

8. **GPS + webcam:** A global, crowdsourced network of real-time webcam feeds gives you the closest instantaneous view of a location you specify; especially useful for news reporting.

9. **GPS + solar:** Solar panels mounted on car, bus, and truck roofs use GPS to optimally orient themselves toward the sun (although local

optimization might not even require GPS). Any benefit to panels on different vehicle roofs being able to communicate with each other?

10. **Social networking + search:** Google and Facebook are already the two most widely used online apps, so the combination of the two is already much trodden ground.

11. **Social networking + webcam:** Share feeds of parties, concerts, and other events with your social network in real time.

12. **Social networking + solar:** Let friends broadcast and earn bragging rights for the amount of their personal energy consumption coming from renewable sources like solar.

13. **Search + webcam:** Enable webcam feeds to be searched for images.

14. **Search + solar:** Solar installations search the Web for forecasts of overcast weather where short-term prices for solar-generated power might be expected to rise.

15. **Webcam + solar:** (a) Solar-powered webcams can film outdoor/remote locations and (b) webcams optimized can be for security monitoring of remote solar panel arrays.

Fourth, research the needs and solutions, discuss the most promising ones with your prospective customers and others, and sort the needs in order from most to least promising. Which are real, unsatisfied needs, and which are just technologies in search of needs but with none readily in sight? Eliminate the combinations for which you cannot find a real customer need.

Suppose, based on your research and discussions, you conclude that two of the combinations are most promising:

• **NLP + social networking:** Automate chat for meeting people online, for users who aren't adept at typing or small talk, or for any user to save time by letting the automated "attendant" handle it

- **GPS + social networking:** Be alerted when friends of friends whom you haven't met are in the near vicinity

Consider repeating the exercise for combinations of three technologies. Starting with six different technologies yields twenty different combinations of technologies taken three at a time. Again: is each combination novel? Without being constrained by the customer needs you identified previously, what need might the combination be used to satisfy?

Let's say that, based on your brainstorming and discussions with prospective customers, you think one of the three-way combinations has potential:

- **GPS + social networking + webcam:** This is the same as #6 in the list of fifteen with the addition of webcam so friends of friends who haven't met can see and interact with each other online. A mobile application could let you know when you are within a certain range of one of your friends' friends, and the webcam could let you see and talk to each other and decide whether to meet.

In this example, the number of combinations of different technologies taken three at a time (20) is only slightly more than the number taken two at a time (15) because the number of technologies (6) is relatively small. In the world at large, where we have thousands of potential technologies to work with, the number of combinations taken three at a time is much larger than the number taken two at a time. For just a hundred technologies, the number of combinations taken two at a time is 4,950; the number taken three at a time is 161,700. However, the more technologies you try to add into the combination, the harder it is to find a real customer need that it satisfies. The more technologies in the combination, the smaller the percentage of them that will be readily useful. Nonetheless, as you become familiar with new technologies, the number of combinations at your disposal and your potential to find new combinations that satisfy needs grows very rapidly.

Build this new habit: Each time you become aware of a new technology, brainstorm what new customer need it might be used to satisfy in combination with one or more of the other technologies you know about.

Even after you have determined which needs suggested by these combinations are real and unsatisfied, you will be more successful addressing some of those needs than others. In chapter 13, "Matching Needs to Your Resources and Passions," we'll see how to further select the needs that best fit you.

ALL INNOVATION IS JUST LIKE YOUR INNOVATION

In his gem of a book, *The Nature of Technology* (Simon and Schuster, 2009), economist W. Brian Arthur makes the case that virtually *all* innovation is a combination of other technologies. The technologies on which the light bulb is based are themselves combinations of other technologies, which are based on still earlier technologies, and so on, all the way back to man's first innovation, probably a hand-held tool invented over two million years ago. Any two technologies are thus related to each other, either closely or distantly, connected by a genealogical tree like the one in figure 11.2. So technology evolution is highly analogous to biological evolution.[4]

I find it exciting and inspiring that the very approach we are using to differentiate your business—deliberately seeking novel combinations of technologies that you and your cofounder know something about—is, on a very small scale, the same process by which all innovation takes place. Not unlike looking up at the sky at night and knowing that everyone on earth sees the same stars.

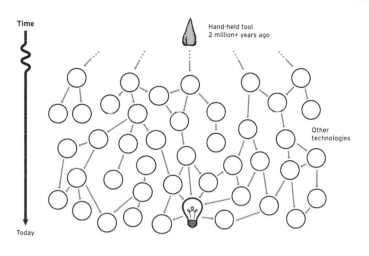

Time

Hand-held tool
2 million+ years ago

Other
technologies

Today

—— *Figure 11.2* ——

Technology evolution.

EXERCISES

1. As described earlier, make a table listing all pairs of technologies you know about firsthand and try to think of needs each combination might address. Cross out the ones for which you cannot think of useful applications. Keep going until you think of at least several new needs addressed by those combinations.

2. The Google Glass wearable computer can display Internet information through an optical head-mounted display and supports natural language voice commands for hands-free operation. Learn more about Google Glass on Wikipedia. Consider the combinations of Google Glass with the technologies you already know about or skills you already possess. What new customer needs might the combinations satisfy?

CORE LESSONS

- Combinations of new, fast-growing technologies harbor great entrepreneurial opportunities. You could be early or even first to apply a combination to satisfy a particular customer need.

- The number of technology combinations—and possibilities for innovation—increases very rapidly as you add each new technology to your list.

- Build this new habit: Each time you become aware of a new technology, brainstorm what new customer need(s) it might satisfy in combination with one or more of the other technologies you know about.

- This combining of technologies is, on a small scale, an example of how virtually all new innovation takes place.

12

1 + 1 = 3:
CHOOSING A COFOUNDER
AND TEAM MEMBERS

If you can laugh together, you can work together.
  —*Robert Orben*

By 2006, CustomerSat's software had become complex and unwieldy. Too many quick fixes by too-junior software developers for too many years had caused reliability problems, performance bottlenecks, and security holes. We had lost a previous head of engineering, in part, because these problems seemed insurmountable.

Into this maelstrom came Dickey Singh, our new head of technology and engineering. A member of the Sikh faith, Dickey's passions include keeping up with the latest software technology trends every day. At CustomerSat, Dickey went straight to work. He uniquely comprehended the complexity of our software in its entirety, pinpointing the problems and devising novel ways to address them. As a result, we avoided having to replace or rewrite much existing code, a huge advantage for a legacy code base, which you risk breaking if you modify. I sometimes wonder if we were able to hire an executive of Dickey's stature and quality because other US hiring managers did not know what to make of his turban. "Doesn't fit our culture," I can imagine them thinking. If so, it was their huge loss and our huge gain.

With his broad and deep knowledge of technology, Dickey attracts first-rate software engineers from around the world to work with him. He quickly took over software development, quality assurance, web operations, tech support, and IT. As a result, work became much easier for me; I was freed up from these areas to focus on marketing, sales, and customers. Two years later, CustomerSat was acquired in a transaction to which Dickey had added much value. There's no one I'd rather start a company with more than Dickey.[1]

Your chances of success more than double with the right cofounder:[2] $1 + 1 = 3$.

Full disclosure: I started both my companies without a cofounder. Doing so has some advantages: You can move very swiftly, you don't have to shave or be civil (at least until you get your first coworker or customer), and someone who cares less about your business than you do doesn't hold you back. But having the right cofounder has even more advantages. Here are three of them:

- It is hard to do, and impossible to be good at, everything yourself. The right cofounder brings not just manpower but also skills, other resources (STARS), and advantages complementary to yours. Your cofounder's advantages and yours can be combined in many more ways to satisfy customer needs than either of your sets of advantages can be separately. You and the right cofounder are much more powerful together than on your own.

- You will need to collaborate with team members as you grow. Having a cofounder lets you immediately start building skills in teamwork, achieving consensus, resolving conflicts, and creating a positive working environment. You can't develop these skills working independently, but with even a single cofounder, you can.

- The right cofounder challenges you, making you stronger, and boosts you up when you are down. And vice versa. Ideally you create a positive feedback loop with each other.

What makes you and a cofounder right for each other? Table 12.1 shows three main factors to consider and look for.

Table 12.1. What to look for in a cofounder.		
Factor	Includes	Relationship to you
Character	Honesty, passion, perseverance, positive attitude, intelligence, flexibility, kindness . . .	Independent of you and your mission
Fit with you and your STARS	Mutual trust, respect, and reinforcement Complementary resources and advantages	Relative to you
Fit with your mission	Shared passion and vision	Cocreated with you

Character, the first factor, is independent of you and your mission. It is the most important factor long term: The cofounder who embodies it will continue to add value no matter how your organization grows and evolves. The second, fit with you and your STARS, includes mutual trust and STARS that complement yours. The third, fit with your mission, has to be cocreated with you. You'll see that passion and perseverance arise in all three factors.

A measure of the overall fit between you and a prospective cofounder is the product of these three factors. All three are essential; if any one of them is absent, the overall score is zero.

As you think about these qualities in potential cofounders, remember: they are wondering about the same qualities in you. What is your character? Can they trust you? Are your STARS complementary to theirs? Can you and they cocreate a mission that they can become passionate about? How do they perceive your overall score as a cofounder? Candidly assess these factors from all sides.

Getting to know and trust someone takes time. Ideally, your cofounder is someone you have worked with before. You will already have experience with his or her values, character, ups and downs, and how they respond to deadlines and other pressures.

Start-up "speed-dating" events (popular in Silicon Valley) purport to help entrepreneurs find cofounders through a rapid-fire series of meetings with different people, each lasting three to five minutes. Such meetings can help build your network with the understanding that you will have to invest much more time getting to know each person; their skills, attitudes, compatibility with you; and so on. Don't expect such events to produce a cofounder for you right away.

Choosing your cofounder or cofounders may be the most important decision you make in your venture. They and your relationship with them will affect everyone who comes later in your venture. In the words of serial entrepreneur Naval Ravikant, cofounder and coauthor of the *VentureHacks* blog site, "If it doesn't feel right, keep looking. If you're compromising, keep looking."

CHARACTER

Character is a composite of qualities (honesty, perseverance, courage, etc.) and includes both attitudes and behaviors, which determine and reinforce each other (either positively or negatively).

Reputation is the shadow. Character is the tree.
  —Abraham Lincoln

Think of character as overall human quality. Larry Reed, president of the Foundation for Economic Education, lists nine qualities that he sees as most important to character: honesty, humility, responsibility, principle (having something you believe in), self-discipline, courage, self-reliance, optimism, and long-term focus.[3] Characterfirst.com lists forty-nine qualities, adding such attributes as attentiveness, compassion, creativity, flexibility, generosity, initiative, patience, and thriftiness.[4] You decide which of these qualities are most important to your venture and in your cofounder, and how much weight you place on each quality.

Whichever character qualities you emphasize, recognize the importance of both inward values (*attitudes*) and outward actions (*behaviors*). Valuing honesty (an attitude) doesn't count for much if the individual doesn't act honestly (behavior). Conversely, honest behavior without honesty as a value may be opportunistic and inconsistent. Only over time does observing behavior give us insight into a person's values and attitudes. On first meeting you can gauge some behavioral qualities of character such as attentiveness and punctuality, but it takes longer to assess others such as flexibility, honesty, and perseverance, and values and attitudes such as passion and loyalty.

In chapter 1 we discussed how your passion and perseverance create a feedback loop: Passion makes time fly, making it easier to persevere; the more tenaciously you persevere, the more passionate you become, and so on. So passion (an attitude) and perseverance (a behavior) mutually determine and reinforce the other. Positive feedback between actions on the one hand and attitudes and inner strengths on the other, help build those behaviors, attitudes, and strengths—and consequently character (see figure 12.1). For example, in addition to perseverance and passion, behaving

- enthusiastically . . . makes us feel enthusiastic,

- courageously . . . builds courage in us,

- honestly . . . reinforces our inclination to be honest,

- loyally . . . instills loyalty in us.

So I define character as *inward values (attitudes) and outward actions (behaviors) that mutually determine and reinforce each other.*[5] Just as positive reinforcement between passion and perseverance helps make the activity we are passionate about a *habit*, so does positive reinforcement between other attitudes and behaviors help make habits of those character qualities. A quick way to build a character quality is to start acting as if you already embody it.

Feedback loops also work in the opposite direction. If I consistently act timidly or pessimistically or tiredly, those behaviors will dampen my courage, optimism, and enthusiasm. A quick way to lose a character quality is to act as if you have lost it.

Again, as you think about these qualities in your cofounder, remember: he or she is wondering about the same qualities in you.

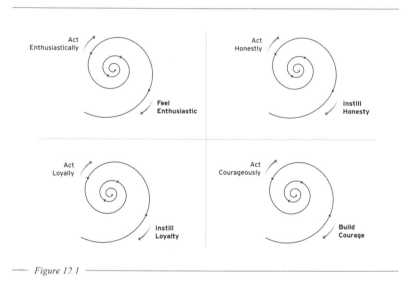

—— *Figure 12.1* ——

Actions and attitudes reinforce each other.

EXERCISES

1. Using whatever qualities you most value and metrics you think most appropriate, candidly self-assess your character. Some or all of the (inner) strengths you listed in chapter 6 may be among your character qualities, but so, probably, are qualities you would like to develop that are not on your list.

2. Identify several character qualities you would like to further strengthen and believe will be important in your new venture.

3. Choose one of those qualities and do something every day this week to further strengthen it.

EXTRA CREDIT

Take a risk. Invite one or more prospective cofounders with whom you already have solid relationships to read this chapter. Share with them the character qualities you would most like to further strengthen in yourself. Ask them if they would be willing to do the same self-assessment and share the qualities they would most like to further strengthen with you. Don't pressure them in any way. If they choose not to participate, they are probably not ready to be cofounders with you. But if they share their self-assessments. The fact that you have made yourselves vulnerable to the other, and in effect, trusted the other not to exploit that vulnerability, will have further strengthened your relationship and been a step toward becoming cofounders.

FIT WITH YOU

TRUST

Trust is the most essential aspect of the fit between you and your cofounder. Trusting your cofounder means that you and your cofounder are confident that each of you will

1. do (or perform or deliver) what you say you will do or have committed to, to the extent that circumstances are within your control or power to do so; and

2. act with your and your business's best interests in mind.[6]

The first one implies that you each have the skills and other means to fulfill the commitment and do not overcommit. If a situation cannot be controlled, you may not know what the other person is going to do, but you have confidence it will be the best the circumstances allow. Both numbers 1 and 2 imply an alignment between intentions and actions. The more uncertain the environment and the more independent judgment required by either cofounder, the more valuable is 2 than 1. Your consistently fulfilling your commitments and acting in your cofounder's and your business's interests is the best way to build trust and confidence in each other.

COMPLEMENTARY STARS

Two people with identical resources and advantages bring more manpower to your venture but no new ingredients. So your cofounder's STARS and yours should be *complementary*, which according to the dictionary means—"combining in such a way as to enhance or extend each other's resources and advantages." Dickey's skills, background, and relationship network and mine were highly complementary, for example: computer and software engineering for him, consultative sales and product management for me.

You want someone who is different from you.
You don't want to breed with your siblings.
—Reese Jones, serial technology entrepreneur

To see how complementary prospective cofounder's STARS are to yours, start with the self-assessment you did in chapter 6, in which you listed your STARS in a table with five rows (table 6.1). Invite your prospective cofounder to create a similar table of her STARS. Then combine your two tables, row by row, to see all the STARS you have to work with.

In chapter 13 and later, we match customer needs with your cofounders' resources and advantages and yours to choose the need that fits best overall. As you go through those chapters, you and your cofounder will see different ways of aligning your respective resources and advantages to best satisfy your targeted customer need. For example, if satisfying your customer need requires designing and developing both hardware and software, one of you might handle hardware, and the other, software; or (perhaps later) one of you might handle all technology, and the other, business issues.

Complementary advantages allow you and your cofounder to satisfy a larger need better than you would otherwise. If you try to handle the inventory and baking and packaging and cleaning and marketing and selling and deliveries and accounting for your healthy snacks business, you will be able to serve only a small set of customers, perhaps those in your immediate neighborhood. But if you have a cofounder who can handle some of these tasks—perhaps the inventory, baking, packaging, and cleaning, while you handle the sales, delivery, marketing, and accounting—you can serve and satisfy hungry consumers across a larger geographical area. As we have seen, advantages and the needs they satisfy are specific to and need to fit each other, like puzzle pieces. Similarly, your cofounder's advantages and yours also need to fit each other's (see figure 12.2). With complementary advantages you and your cofounder together can satisfy a larger or broader customer need than either of you can separately.

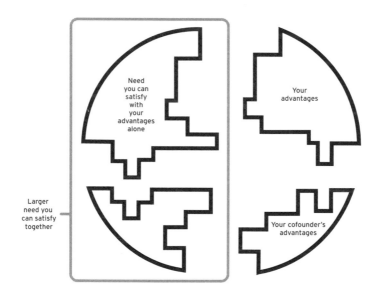

Figure 12.2

Complementary advantages.

Just as passion and perseverance create positive feedback loops in you, so can your cofounder's passion and perseverance and yours create positive and reinforcing feedback in each other. At CustomerSat, Dickey would develop and share with me an idea for a possible new software solution; I would have him explain it to me repeatedly until I understood it. When I could finally explain it in my own words that would often clarify and suggest refinements to the solution, which Dickey would then make. This back and forth would repeat. Over time, we would evolve completely different words to describe the solution that would most resonate with and engage our customers. Some of these solutions made it to market and helped us generate new business and grow. I find such mutually respectful collaborations deeply satisfying and rewarding. If you experience such rewarding collaborations with someone else, latch on to him or her.

Feedback loops can also cause negative reinforcement. If one of you thinks the other is not doing his or her fair share of the work, or is spending time on the wrong things, that can breed resentment. That, in turn, can strain the relationship and discourage the other person, causing further resentment, stress, and estrangement. This type of problem can only be corrected by some combination of changed behavior, good communication, or ending the relationship.

So the fit between you and your cofounder is a matter of trust, complementary STARS, and aligned priorities and goals. Again in the words of Naval Ravikant, "If one founder only cares about building a cool product; another, only about making money; and yet another, only about fame, it won't work. Pay close attention—true motivations are revealed, not declared."[7]

FIT WITH YOUR MISSION

If you and your cofounder can find or cocreate a mission to which both of you contribute something essential, both of you will bring advantages to it and increase your likelihood of success. Plus, both of you are more likely to be passionate about something you've created together.

In chapter 13 and later, we match customer needs to resources and advantages. Consider how you might adapt the customer need you satisfy so your cofounder's resources and advantages and yours are most complementary and best fit the need.

In addition to complementary resources and advantages, both of you should ideally contribute something important to your vision, like ingredients in a recipe. Assume that the customer need you satisfy and your business plan will be different, and likely more ambitious, after you and your cofounder team up. Your plan should be different and larger because your previous plan would not have incorporated all the advantages your cofounder brings to the mix.

REACHING AGREEMENT

After the two of you decide to become cofounders, discuss, agree on, and outline in writing such ownership issues as equity or profit/loss splits, rights of first refusal, and what happens if one of you leaves or dies. If significant assets are involved, use a lawyer to help you think through all the contingencies and draft an agreement from your outline. Doing so will ensure you have the same clear understanding of your arrangement and can avoid a lawsuit later.

Similarly, if things aren't going to work out between you and your cofounder, the sooner you recognize that fact, the better. If your involvement together has been brief and only one of you is interested in pursuing the venture, perhaps it could be as simple as shaking hands and parting ways. If you have pooled or jointly created any assets, such as tools, equipment, designs, or databases, return or divide them as equitably as you can and document what you have done to avoid any question later.

THE "COFOUNDER" TITLE LASTS FOREVER

Choosing a cofounder is like getting married. This person may be attractive right now; but will you still view them that way several years from now? Will you be grateful—or regret—that you are partners? Or worse, will you resent that person, his or her lack of dedication and/or negative attitude?

Most titles—VP, CEO, chairman, software developer, even husband or wife—last only for the duration, usually limited, that a person serves in that role. In contrast, unless the cofounder relationship is terminated very quickly after it is formed, once a cofounder, always a cofounder: The title is for life. Your cofounder's reputation will long be associated with your company. You may be tempted to choose a cofounder who has valuable skills or knowledge you need right now without regard to long-term fit. Be cautious of doing this.

If you can't find the right person, that needn't stop you from getting started. Figure 12.3 shows alternative ways to engage individuals who can help build your business. If someone has the right skills but you have questions about their long-term fit with you and your mission, consider hiring them as a contractor. Or if they are a promising team member, as we discuss later, and have strong character but lack the right skills, consider bringing them on as a trainee. Trainee could range from entry- to executive-level, for example, on-boarding a prospective VP of marketing as director of product management. If none of these approaches seem to apply or work, adjust your mission so you can satisfy it just by using your existing resources, or until you find the right person.

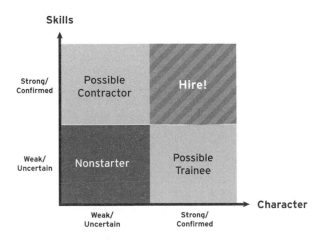

Figure 12.3

Hiring decisions depend on skills and character.

DIFFERENT IS BETTER THAN BETTER IN TEAM MEMBERS TOO

The same three factors that make for the right cofounder—character, fit with the team, and fit with the mission—apply to team members. Each team member that you bring on influences the environment for everyone else that follows. So don't take any hire lightly. In the words of Y Combinator founder Paul Graham, this is your one chance to create an all-star team.

> *The success or failure of a start-up*
> *depends on the first ten employees.*
> —Steve Jobs

THE VALUE OF COGNITIVE DIVERSITY

Diversity today usually suggests differences in ethnicity, gender, age, or sexual orientation. Such physical or identity diversity can have value in customer-facing employees where a customer may prefer to be served by someone who looks, speaks, or acts a certain way, perhaps in the same or opposite way that the customer does. Especially for intimate roles such as physician, nurse, chiropractor, or personal trainer, many people prefer that their service providers be the same gender as them. Gender is a factor for actors, actresses, and sex workers, of course. Beyond such special cases, however, studies show that physical or identity diversity has little impact on start-up team or business success, either positive or negative.[8]

In contrast, diversity in how people think about problems and make decisions—*cognitive diversity*—really does make a team stronger. Some people are abstract thinkers, others are concrete; some are high risk-reward oriented, others risk averse; some are relationship oriented, others are more transactional when interacting with others. University of Michigan's Scott Page, professor of complex systems, political science, and economics, finds that cognitive diversity trumps cognitive homogeneity: Collections of people with diverse problem-solving perspectives and heuristics outperform collections of people who rely on homogeneous perspectives and heuristics. He even maintains that cognitive diversity trumps ability.[9] Different is better than better with team members too.

Cognitively diverse people not only think differently but also sense their environments differently. Neuroscientist David Eagleman, author of *Incognito: The Secret Lives of the Brain* (Pantheon, 2011), tells us that different people pick up on different elements of their environments and thus live in different microrealities based on the subset of the world they're able to detect. Cognitively diverse teams thus both *collect* more complete data describing the world and can also *process* that data in more ways.

Most people prefer to work with people who think like them. If you keep hiring people who think like your existing team members, you may find after a while that everyone thinks the same way. You suddenly have a meta-issue to deal with beyond just hiring the best possible person for the job. It *is* more challenging to work with people who do not think like you. So there is an optimal diversity: It's somewhere in the middle of everyone thinking the same way and everyone thinking differently.[10]

BUILD A WHOLE-BRAINED TEAM

Many measurement instruments and models capture elements of cognitive styles and preference, including the Myers–Briggs Type Indicator (MBTI), Learning Orientation Questionnaire, DISC assessment, and Herrmann Brain Dominance Instrument (HBDI). *Whole brained* refers to a cognitively diverse team. A whole-brained team includes a mix of analytical, creative, safekeeping/security-oriented, and emotional individuals.

If you are up to five or six team members and all tend be analytical thinkers, you will likely benefit from your next hire being more oriented toward sensing, developing, and maintaining interpersonal relationships. If all your team members tend to think in broad, abstract concepts, consider making your next hire someone who is more detail oriented and specific. Of course, you'll only realize the benefits of diversifying your team in this way if the new team members share their perspectives and help make decisions.

DISTANCE ADVANCED IS AS IMPORTANT AS ABSOLUTE POSITION

Normally we think about someone's accomplishments in *absolute* terms. We ask if they have a high school and college degree; if so, from which school(s); and what they have accomplished since then. But comparing different individual's accomplishments this way can be misleading, because some people start out much further ahead than others.

In addition to evaluating an individual's accomplishments in absolute terms, consider how far they have come relative to where they started—that is, the *distance advanced*. Give someone extra credit for starting further behind than others, overcoming obstacles, catching up, or having accomplished the same amount in less time. In other words, how far has the person come on his or her own merit and in how much time? Distance advanced may better predict someone's trajectory and future potential, which is what you are ultimately interested in.

For example, assuming other factors being equal, if two people

- have a similar command of English, and English is the native language of one of them and the second (or third) language learned by the other, then the nonnative speaker has learned and achieved relatively more on a "command of English" dimension than the native English speaker;

- have comparable academic records, but one's parents were professors and the other's did not go to college, then the latter individual has advanced relatively further than the other on an academic dimension; and

- seem comparable overall but one could have been discriminated against because of handicap, gender, race, faith, sexual orientation, or otherwise, then the one who could have been discriminated against has likely come further than the other.

Have hiring managers who know little about the Sikh faith discriminated against Dickey Singh because of his turban and beard? He would emphatically deny it, demonstrating his utter unwillingness to be a victim, a character quality I much admire in him. But I'm not so sure. In any event, if others irrationally discriminate and you do not, they lose out and better people come to you.

Discount your assessment of distance advanced to the extent that reverse discrimination may be a factor. If someone has benefited from nepotism (they got a job with an organization because a relative works there), affirmative action (they have received preferential treatment based on race or physical or identity attribute), or legacy admission (they got into a college or university because a parent went there), that was not on their own merit. If other factors are equal, someone who has not benefited from such preferences has advanced further on their own merit than the person who has benefitted from preferential treatment.

Past performance—including behavior, attitudes, achievements, reputation, and your entire experience with an individual—is all we have to rely on in evaluating that person. Sensibly, investment documents remind us that past performance is no guarantee of future performance. The same is true of prospective team members.

GOOD QUESTION!

Q

Do cofounders need to be at about the same stage of life and career? Our ages are thirty and fifty.

A

Age difference may make your cofounder's skills and yours more complementary. One of you may be more seasoned as an executive; the other, more attuned to a younger generation's preferences. Thirty-five years separate the ages of Lauren Walters and Will Hauser, cofounders of Two Degrees Food; their complementary perspectives may well have contributed to Two Degrees Food's success.

Nonetheless, the two of you should discuss the issue as it applies to you directly. Is your venture more important—or challenging—for one of you than the other? Do you bring different degrees of financial and career success and today have different priorities and goals? If so, these could be concerns. Will the older of you be ready to retire well before the other? If so, discuss such long-term transitions explicitly.

EXERCISES

1. Make a list of twenty friends and colleagues whom you know well. For each one, as best you know, write down what they are most passionate about. The subjects and activities they are passionate about may be very different from yours.

2. Now sort them either individually (first, second, third, etc.) or into groups (high, medium, low) in two ways:

    - In order from most to least passionate. Don't confuse passionate with outspoken. The person most dedicated to and engaged with a particular subject or activity may talk about it only rarely.

    - In order from how closely to how distantly related the subject or activity they are passionate about is to what your new venture is about.

3. Now look for individuals who rank high on both. If you sorted them into groups, identify those who are both in the high passion group and the "closely related to your start-up" group. I did this exercise for forty of my Facebook friends chosen at random and was surprised to discover three potential collaborators of whom I hadn't previously thought, one of whom I would seriously consider as a potential cofounder for a new venture.

If you meet someone both passionate and perseverant about *any* activity, even one very different from yours, take note. That person probably knows a lot and is bound for success in their field. Keep in touch with them. You might someday want to collaborate with or invest in them.

CORE LESSONS

- Your chances of success more than double with the right cofounder or business partner. 1 + 1 = 3.

- Three factors to look for in a cofounder are character, fit with you, and fit with your mission. All three may take time to assess.

- Character is a composite of many qualities—courage, honesty, passion, perseverance, etc. How you weight them is up to you.

- Character includes both attitudes and behaviors that determine and reinforce each other, either positively or negatively.

- Trusting a cofounder or team member means having confidence that they will do what they say they will when circumstances are under their control and that the actions they choose will in any event be in the best interests of your company.

- Seek a cofounder whose resources and advantages (STARS) are complementary to yours.

- Cocreate your mission with your cofounder so your cofounder's advantages complement yours in fulfilling that mission.

- Build a whole-brained, cognitively diverse team as you grow.

13

MATCHING NEEDS TO YOUR RESOURCES AND PASSIONS (STEP 5)

You're only someone that I used to love.
—*Barbra Streisand*

Are you (a) satisfied, (b) dissatisfied, or (c) neither satisfied nor dissatisfied?

Satisfaction surveys. They have a quirky language and logic all their own.

After two decades in the business, I have seen both their value and abuse. Confident, high-trust organizations that are open to feedback and are willing to act on it benefit hugely from surveys. Properly designed, deployed, and analyzed, surveys can yield insights from the tiniest detail (change the size of the font) to the most strategic (merge or acquire).

But satisfaction surveys don't work when compensation or other performance incentives link either too tightly to scores or not at all. Finding the right middle ground is a true art. If a salesperson cares more about getting all 5s (where 5 is excellent or very satisfied) than the service she provides you, the linkage is too tight. No coworker has ever suggested to me that a high score be excluded from the feedback she received. But I have heard every excuse in the book to exclude a low score. "We surveyed the wrong person." "The customer is dissatisfied with our partner, not with us." "He's just angling for a discount on his renewal agreement." "Of course he's upset, he's going through a divorce." "She's on her period." Tying survey results to team rather than to individual incentives is one way to discourage people from gaming the system.

At the other extreme, usually in agencies insulated from competition, feedback surveys do not result in rewards, penalties, or changed behavior. They simply let the organizations feel or appear customer oriented. I call it "customer theatre." Says Harvard Kennedy School professor Lant Pritchett, "Organizations that fail adopt camouflage to enable them to survive further failure."[1] For monopolies like the US Postal Service, Transportation Security Administration, and Departments of Motor Vehicles, satisfaction surveys are often part of that camouflage and theatre.

In part because they invite such gamesmanship, surveys are being augmented by new technologies. Surveys are best for gathering attitudinal data such as satisfaction, willingness to recommend, and likelihood of repurchase. But such data is "noisy" because respondents misrepresent their true attitudes, either deliberately (more gamesmanship) or unwittingly; and narrow bandwidth, because of the limited number of questions you can reasonably ask in a survey, and because many people simply won't respond. Complementing surveys are the clearer, high-bandwidth signals of behavioral data. What people actually purchased again and again, what they searched for online, what series of screens they followed in a mobile app, or what paths they took to reach a physical destination cannot easily be misrepresented. Such behavioral data used to be expensive to gather, track, analyze, and extrapolate, but advances in databases, microsensors, GPS, and analytics have transformed the field, driving the explosion of big data. No questionnaires are needed to observe and experiment on customer behavior[2], which enables companies to gather insights on all customers, whether or not they deliberately respond. While surveys used to be the primary source of customer insights, increasingly they complement, nuance, and validate behavioral data today.

Having worked in the industry for twenty-five years, online surveys strongly fit my STARS. But I'm less passionate about standalone surveys today than twenty-five years ago when they were new: I feel the way Barbra Streisand does in the line that opened this chapter. Put me in the upper left quadrant (limited motivation) of the left resources-passion chart in figure 13.1. My passion has shifted to customer intelligence, a newer field that encompasses survey, behavioral, and contextual[3] data about customers, where I'm in the upper right quadrant (best likelihood of success) in the right resources-passion chart. This is where you want to be on your own resources-passion chart.

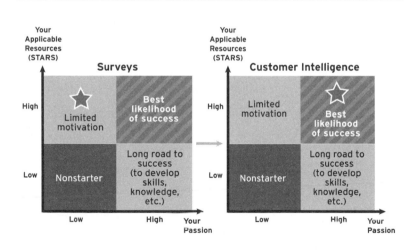

Figure 13.1

Resources-passion charts for two different solution categories:
surveys and customer intelligence.

Your venture should align with your resources *and* your passions. Resources provide rational alignment; passion provides emotional alignment.

WHICH CUSTOMER NEEDS AND SOLUTIONS FIT YOU BEST?

Say you and your cofounder, if applicable, have identified four customer needs and possible solutions:

Customer need	Possible solution
1. Graffiti-proof paint for cities in humid climates	New chemical formula that makes graffiti easily removable in humid climates
2. Underwater GPS for scuba divers	Wrist device that shows diver position and underwater path traversed
3. Automatic English-Spanish translation between patient and doctor	Smartphone-based real-time translation service
4. Automated chat for meeting people online	Smartphone app chats with potential dates you would like to meet

Now make a copy of your STARS chart for each customer need and solution like table 13.1 and 13.2 (we're only showing two, but you would make one for each customer need you have identified). On each chart, highlight the resources that you think significantly contribute to your ability to satisfy that need with that solution. Then in a separate row on each chart, indicate how passionate you are about that need and solution. If you and your cofounder differ in passion for a need and solution, indicate that as well.

Table 13.1. Customer need #1: Graffiti-proof paint for cities in humid climates.		
Possible solution: New chemical formula that makes graffiti easily removable in humid climates		
Letter	Category	Resource
S	Skills	-Chemistry (bachelor's degree) -3 years' work experience in medical services -Scuba certification -Conversational Spanish

Letter	Category	Resource
T	Technologies	-Social networking (Facebook, LinkedIn, Twitter) -Online search (e.g., Google) -Mobile phone cameras -Natural language processing (NLP) -Global Positioning System (GPS) tools
A	Assets and Accomplishments	**Assets** *Physical* -Laptop, printer, and high-speed Internet access -Hardware prototype *Financial* -Savings -Full-time job and income (medical services) *Knowledge* -Software design and prototype -Know my hometown well (born and raised here) **Accomplishments** -Earning a college degree -Completing a project on time and under budget
R	Relationships and Reputation	**Relationships** -Family who can provide help and encouragement -Mentors who can provide advice -Coworkers as potential cofounders, employees, customers -Alumni association **Reputation** -Friends I trust and who trust me -Recommendations -Strong credit score
S	Strengths (Inner)	-Leadership (led soccer team to regional championship) -Diligence/perseverance (got a raise and made honor role this quarter despite broken foot) -Compassion (helped neighbors after their house flooded) -Entrepreneurship (bought up friends' DVDs and sold them online for a profit) -Excellent health

Resource fit: Weak.

Passion level: So-so. Sounds like a hassle dealing with municipalities. Not excited about selling to (sometimes corrupt) Latin American municipal governments.

Overall fit: Weak.

Additional resources needed: Formula for graffiti-proof paint; business development and sales in Central America, Asia, Africa.

	Table 13.2. Customer need #4: Automated chat for meeting people online.	
Possible solution: Smartphone app chats with potential dates you would like to meet		
Letter	Category	Resource
S	Skills	-Chemistry (bachelor's degree) -3 years' work experience in medical services -Scuba certification -Conversational Spanish
T	Technologies	-Social networking (Facebook, LinkedIn, Twitter) -Online search (e.g., Google) -Mobile phone camera -NLP -GPS
A	Assets and accomplishments	**Assets** *Physical* -Laptop, printer, and high-speed Internet access -Hardware prototype *Financial* -Savings -Full-time job and income (medical services) *Knowledge* -Software design and prototype -Know my hometown well (born and raised here) **Accomplishments** -Earning a college degree -Completing a project on time and under budget
R	Relationships and reputation	**Relationships** -Family who can provide help and encouragement -Mentors who can provide advice -Coworkers as potential cofounders, employees, customers -Alumni association **Reputation** -Friends I trust and who trust me -Recommendations -Strong credit score

Letter	Category	Resource
S	Strengths (inner)	-Leadership (led soccer team to regional championship)
		-Diligence/perseverance (got a raise and made honor role this quarter despite broken foot)
		-Compassion (helped neighbors after their house flooded)
		-Entrepreneurship (bought up friends' DVDs and sold them online for a profit)
		-Excellent health

Resource fit: Fair. No skills in mobile app development; limited technical experience in automated interpretation of text and response.

Passion level: High This would be really cool. Would be fun to develop and use. Can see it becoming very popular.

Overall fit: Good.

Additional resources needed: Mobile app development; automated interpretation of text and response.

As we saw in chapter 6, among your STARS,

- your skills, technologies, knowledge assets, and professional relationships tend to vary *most* in value by customer need and solution;

- your physical assets vary *somewhat*;

- your financial assets, personal relationships, and (inner) strengths vary *least* (i.e., they are most generally applicable no matter which need and solution you address).

To assess which needs and solutions fit you best, your skills, technologies, knowledge assets, and professional relationships generally carry the most weight. But if one or more of your more generic resources seem particularly important for certain needs and solutions, then highlight those resources as well on your charts.

For example, say your STARS charts show that you are a "Microsoft Office Pro," an expert with Word documents, PowerPoint presentations, and Excel spreadsheets. But all four of your customer needs and solutions make use of these skills to about the same degree, so they won't help you choose one need and solution over another. Given that, you don't highlight "Microsoft Office Pro." Conversely, if one of your customer needs and solutions were corporate marketing services—writing brochures, preparing presentations, and forecasting sales—then you might well highlight "Microsoft Office Pro" for that need and solution.

Finally, considering both the fit with your STARS and your passion for each customer need and solution, rate the *overall* fit between you and each need and solution, and indicate that in a separate row on each chart. Don't be discouraged if your overall fits seem weak at this early stage—you will strengthen them.

Optionally, add one more row to each chart showing what additional resources you need to best satisfy that need. This row gives you a head start on the next step, Step 6, Develop or Acquire Resources to Strengthen the Fit between the customer need and possible solution, on the one hand, and your resources and passions, on the other.

Now, stand back and look at your charts.

WHAT ARE YOUR CHARTS TELLING YOU?

Of these four customer needs and solutions, you characterize the overall fit with your resources and passions as Weak for #1, Fair for #2, and Good for #3 and #4 (right-most column in table 13.3).

It's good to pare back the list, if possible, because we still have much work ahead that includes generating, eliminating, and refining more needs and solutions. The fewer needs and solutions you have to take through the remaining steps, the better you can define and evaluate each remaining need and solution.

You decide to eliminate #1, the weakest fit overall. Customer need #2 you rated only Fair, but you decide to see if you can acquire or develop resources to improve the fit (Step 6) before eliminating it. We will also be doing our best to improve the fits with the other remaining cases, #3 and #4.

Table 13.3. Overall fit with you.				
Customer need	Proposed solution	Your applicable resources	Passion	Overall fit with you
1. Graffiti-proof paint for cities in humid climates	New chemical formula that makes graffiti easily remov-able in humid climates	Chemistry degree (BS) — Weak	So-so	Weak
2. Underwater GPS for scuba divers	Wrist device that shows diver position and underwater path traversed	-Scuba certification -GPS — Weak	High	Fair
3. Automatic English-Spanish trans-lation between patient and doctor	Smartphone-based real-time translation service	-3 years' work experience in medical services -Conversational Spanish -NLP -Full-time job and income (medical services) — Good	Good	Good
4. Automated chat for meet-ing people online	Smartphone app chats with potential dates you would like to meet	-NLP -GPS -Social networking -Mobile camera — Fair	High	Good

In summary: in Step 5, we have assessed the fit between each customer need and possible solution on the one hand, with your resources and passions on the other. Next, we discuss how to stretch your resources by being frugal (chapter 14), and improve your fit with your remaining needs and solutions by developing or acquiring resources (step 6, chapter 15). Later, in steps 7 and 8, we again assess each fit after evaluating your competition.

GOOD QUESTION!

Q

Should it matter which and how many of my resources apply to a particular need? If I am really passionate about addressing a need, shouldn't I do so even if I have no resources applicable to it?

A

If your goal is to start a successful—growing, thriving, self-sustaining, profitable—business, your likelihood of achieving this will be greater if you can apply significant skills and other resources. Conversely, if you simply want to explore or develop a hobby for which you don't need a competitive advantage to be successful and for which you have little or no requirement or expectation to become self-sustaining or profitable, then freely consider any field for which you have few or no applicable resources other than your passions. Here, however, we will assume your goal is to build a business, whether for profit or not for profit, rather than to explore or develop a hobby.

Let's say that for the need about which you are most passionate you have *no* significant skills or resources. Far be it from me to advise you not to follow your passion. Rather, follow it and over time you will develop new skills, knowledge, and other resources for satisfying that need. You will need extra perseverance and time to compensate for your lack of resources. After a while, you will be able to add these new resources to your chart. But every unsatisfied customer need has a limited life, and someone else could well satisfy it before you do. So consider all these factors when choosing a customer need to address.

EXERCISE

Make charts of your resources like the STARS charts in this chapter (table 13.1 and 13.2) for several of the customer needs and solutions you are most passionate about. In each chart, highlight your resources applicable to one of those needs and solutions, and indicate how much passion you feel for that need and solution as well. Which customer need(s) and solution(s) have the best overall fit with your passions and STARS?

CORE LESSONS

- Your venture should align with your resources and your passions alike. Resources provide rational alignment; passion provides emotional alignment.

- Your skills, technologies, knowledge assets, and professional relationships tend to be the resources most specific to, and thus generally carry the most weight when choosing among, customer needs and solutions.

- If your goal is to start a successful business—one that will grow, thrive, and be self-sustaining and profitable—passion is necessary but not sufficient. Applicable resources are necessary as well.

14

THE FREEDOM OF FRUGALITY

Be frugal, and you can be generous.
   —*Lao Tzu*

Twenty-nine-year-old software entrepreneur Nick Winter owns only ninety-nine physical things. Two pairs of jeans. Four T-shirts. One laptop. One iPhone. One wedding ring. Here's the entire list of ninety-nine items:[1]

backpack	deodorant	letters
backpack	desk	monitor
birth certificate	desk	monitor
bobblehead doll	diploma	nail clippers
boosted board (electric	DVD drive	notebook (small)
longboard)	earplugs (bag of)	pants, convertible
boosted board charger	exercise ball	pants, dark gray
bowl	eye mask	pants, gray
boxers	first-aid and sewing kit	pants, light gray
boxers	flash drive	passport
boxers	fork	pen
boxers	headphones	pens (bundle of)
business cards (box)	helmet	phone
cable	hoodie	pillow
cable	iPad	polo shirt
cable	iPhone power cable and	polo shirt
cable	adaptor	power strip
cable, audio	jeans	razor
chair	jeans	razor base station
checkbook	keys	rubber plant
comforter	laptop	shirt
cup	laptop power cable	shirt

shirt	snake plant	sweater
shirt	socks, toe	t-shirt
shirt	socks, wool	t-shirt
shirt	speakers	t-shirt
shirt	speedo	t-shirt
shirt	spoon	tie
shoes, barefoot	spork	toothbrush
shoes, business	spork	towel
shoes, hiking	sport jacket	wallet
shoes, leather	suit	water bottle
shoes, Vibrams	suit	wedding ring
slow cooker	sun alarm (wake-up light)	

Why would you give or throw away hundreds of physical things you own to get down to ninety-nine items? It would be a way to simplify your life and be able to focus on what is really important to you, including your start-up. "All of us tend to accumulate stuff but ignore its costs: the physical space, mental space, and emotional space," says Nick. Eliminating stuff forces you to choose carefully what is useful and valuable to you and minimizes these extraneous costs.

Consider your clothes. If 90 percent of the time you wear only 10 percent of them, those other 90 percent of your clothes clutter up your closet and make it harder to find the 10 percent of your clothing you are usually looking for. Besides taking up space, they need hangers and periodic airing out even if you don't wear those items. Over time, they are likely going out of style, no longer fitting you as well, or both. You are losing money on them. In Nick's words, they "dilute" the other good stuff you own.

Nick's passion is hacking personal motivation—that is, fooling our brains into getting them to want to do what we want them to do. He cofounded *CodeCombat*, a multiplayer game that teaches people to code, and wrote the book *The Motivation Hacker*, which provides dozens of practical techniques for eliminating distractions. His owning only ninety-nine physical things is part of that regimen. Fellow minimalist Andy Brett similarly owns only ninety-nine things (andybrett .com/things).

Frugality has a bad name. It goes counter to the glamorous ads and images of affluence that constantly bombard us. It suggests dreary scrimping, hoarding, and denying the pleasures of life. But frugality is actually just the opposite. It is about eliminating the unimportant to focus on what we prize most highly in life. And it needn't be dreary. Despite Nick's limited wardrobe, I have never seen him poorly or inappropriately dressed. Just the opposite. The few clothes he owns are stylish and fit him perfectly.

Nick and Andy are on the (extreme) leading edge of the trend toward simpler and more focused living. Despite owning only ninety-nine possessions, they still enjoy the latest communications, education, entertainment, health services, and more, through free or mostly free online services such as Skype, YouTube, edX, and Coursera. Of course, these may still be distractions, but they take up no space, don't decline in value, and can be turned off or deleted in a keystroke. Nick and Andy enjoy many other products and services without owning them through online sharing—for example, Getaround (cars), Uber (taxi services), Airbnb (lodging), and Rentalic (everyday tools and equipment). With these new online and sharing alternatives, there are fewer reasons for us to buy and own stuff.

> *Own nothing. Have everything.*
> *—Napster*

I deeply resonate with this trend, although I haven't taken it to the extreme that Nick and Andy have. Like you, I have hundreds of physical possessions—clothes, books, furniture, tools, electronics, kitchen items, and more—that I have accumulated over my life, last year, and last week. Most of these I rarely use or have forgotten about. Six years ago, I gained new freedom by throwing out or giving away hundreds of items, most of little value, and downsizing from a three-story townhouse in Menlo Park to a compact condo in a San Francisco high-rise. I still had hundreds of possessions, but less clutter and fewer constraints, which let me enjoy experiences more, like travel and time with friends and family. I also became much more reluctant to buy anything that takes up space.

More recently, inspired by Nick's example, I went through my condo and further threw out or gave away over a hundred articles of clothing, books, and kitchen items. Suddenly a cramped, cluttered clothes closet, office, and cabinets became spacious. I now have ample storage and room to work.

Many noted technology entrepreneurs, executives, and investors have chosen the minimalist life. Tim Cook, CEO of Apple; Mark Zuckerberg, founder of Facebook; Drew Houston, cofounder of Dropbox; Tony Hsieh, CEO of Zappos; Aaron Patzer, founder of Mint.com; and David Cheriton of Stanford, are all worth hundreds of millions, if not billions, but for the most part live modestly and certainly far below their means.

Is Nick rich or poor? I don't know or care. He is rich in ideas and thought. I learn something important from him when we get together. Those things matter.

Ninety-nine physical possessions is not a magic number. The optimal number varies from person to person. But Nick and Andy prove how little we truly need.

This chapter is about the benefits of frugality: frugality with distracting physical objects, with low-value activities, and yes, with money.

SKIP STARBUCKS

Let's say you buy just two cups of Starbucks coffee each weekday, one in the morning and one in the afternoon. It's your midmorning or midafternoon pick-me-up. You buy medium-sized "Pike Place" coffees, nothing extravagant. In San Francisco, with a modest tip, those two cups of coffee come to about $5 a day. Multiplying that by five days a week and fifty weeks per year, you get $1,250 per year. Some of my friends routinely do this despite the fact that their offices have gourmet coffee machines that employees can use as much as they wish free of charge.

All that Starbucks spending adds up. $1,250 could buy a gourmet coffeemaker for your start-up and enough fresh ground Colombian coffee to serve several employees for many months. Kick your Starbucks habit for a year and you have already paid for a very nice perk for your first few employees.

AVOID BANKRUPTCY

Every company that went bankrupt first approached, then fell below, a threshold where management, creditors, or auditors believed it lacked the resources or credit to be an ongoing concern. If management had previously cut expenses, thus preserving cash, then they may not have had to declare bankruptcy at all. But without being so proactive, at some point the resources over which the company had discretion, before a court-appointed trustee assumed control, fell below that threshold.

For some of these bankruptcies, especially smaller ones, an extra $1,250 would have made all the difference. This amount of money could provide just enough breathing room—to pay a creditor or key employee until a cash payment was received, an important order came in, or a new product could be demonstrated that persuaded investors to invest—for the company to survive. Skipping a year of Starbucks could indeed be just enough to save your start-up from bankruptcy or closure.

Any number of consumer expenses other than Starbucks—eating out, alcohol, cigarettes, drugs, clothes, travel, theatre tickets, you name it—could easily tally to over a thousand dollars per year. Look for the easiest savings to make in your daily habits. If it is Starbucks, consider trying a low-cost alternative like making your coffee at home or the office. (I buy gourmet green jasmine tea from Mighty Leaf, my favorite brand, for about 40¢ per tea bag in bulk quantities.) When you need a midmorning or midafternoon pick-me-up, rather than go to Starbucks, take your mug and go for a walk with it. Perhaps invite a colleague to join you or make a courtesy business call during your walk. You'll enjoy exercise, fresh air, and save precious capital for your venture at the same time.

In an era of yawning federal deficits and artificially low interest rates, worrying about saving a thousand dollars here or there may seem old-fashioned. It is not. If you don't believe me, just wait until the next economic downturn, rapid rise in interest rates, or financial crisis. You will be thankful you were frugal when you didn't need to be.

LIVE WELL BELOW YOUR MEANS

A mansion in an upscale neighborhood. A resort vacation timeshare. Luxury foreign cars. Expensive suits and jewelry. Private schools for the kids. First-class travel. Signs of financial security, right?

Don't you believe it. According to Thomas J. Stanley and William D. Danko, authors of *The Millionaire Next Door* (Longstreet Press, 1996), most millionaires in the United States live well below their means, in middle-class neighborhoods, driving American-made cars, wearing off-the-rack suits. Living frugally is a key reason they are millionaires. Financial independence is more important to them than displaying high social status. About two-thirds are self-employed. Most of their businesses are "dull-normal," as the book describes them: welding contractors, mobile-home park owners, exterminators, diesel engine rebuilder/distributors, janitorial services contractors, recruiters, paving contractors, among many others. Most of their net worth and annual income derives from their businesses.

A crude measure of long-term financial security is your net worth (the total value of your home, savings, and other assets and investments, less mortgage and other debt) divided by your annual spending—food, clothing, shelter, household expenses, travel, entertainment, and so on—excluding spending on investments. This ratio tells you approximately how many years you could live, at your current lifestyle level without having to work, before you run out of money.[2] If Liam has a net worth of $250,000 and his annual spend is $100,000, he could live on his savings for approximately two and a half years. If Olivia has a net worth of $500,000 and an annual spend of $50,000, she could live on her savings for over ten years.[3] In this example, Olivia has over four times the financial security of Liam.

Living frugally improves both the numerator and denominator of this ratio by

- giving you more to save and invest, increasing your net worth (numerator goes up) and

- reducing your annual spending (denominator goes down).

Frugality increases your long-term financial security in not one, but two, ways!

When the number of additional years you can live at your desired lifestyle level without working exceeds your life expectancy, you have reached "escape velocity"—you never have to work again. Go online to determine your additional life expectancy, given your current age and gender.[4] If you are under seventy-five, it will be approximately eighty-five minus your age. At age forty-five, for example, you have an additional life expectancy of approximately 85 − 45 = 40 years. Again using our crude formula (please do a more exact calculation with the help of a financial advisor, if necessary), you can reach escape velocity at age forty-five in any of the following ways:

Net Worth	Annual Spending
$1 million	$25,000
$2 million	$50,000
$4 million	$100,000

These are just three of an infinite number of trade-offs. If you aspire not to work, one of these trade-offs will be optimal for you. You can do it!

REINFORCE FRUGALITY

We naturally want to impress the people around us. As a result, we tend to project what we think will impress them. Most people are impressed by extravagant visible possessions—fancy cars, houses, jewelry, and clothes. Acquiring and displaying these items often give us a sense of well-being, at least in the short term. But doing so will generally not help us reach our goals. It's just the opposite: They consume resources that we could otherwise invest in our businesses today or, through savings, tomorrow. Consequently, we need to seek out and surround ourselves with people who talk, think, and care less about visible possessions and more about the things that are truly important to us: dreams, goals, and our progress toward them.

Social scientists tell us we are most inclined to acquire and display extravagance when we are (a) feeling insecure, (b) trying to distance or differentiate ourselves from those around us, or (c) to win a date, life partner, or job. Ask yourself, when are you most tempted to acquire and display extravagance? Does that behavior further your goals or detract from them? Are you allowing those around you who don't share your values to control you?

I've been lucky to find a social group in San Francisco of people passionate about ideas, learning, innovation, entrepreneurship, and personal health and longevity. It's a mix of people of all ages, ethnicities, sexual orientations, and no doubt, net worths. Even though our community includes at least one billionaire, I don't hear people talking about this individual's money (or anyone else's). I treasure these qualities of my community.

Here's a test: Can you be honest with those in your social circle about your priorities? Perhaps say, "Rather than go to a theatre to see that movie, let's wait until it comes out on Netflix or YouTube and I'll host a party for all of us at my house to watch it." It's not a question of not being able to afford the movies; it's a question of spending money on what is most important or where you get the best return. If your circle of friends accept and support you on this, you've found a good group (see figure 14.1).

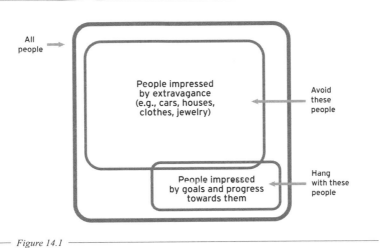

——— *Figure 14.1* ———————————

People to avoid and people to hang out with.

PERSONAL AND BUSINESS FRUGALITY

Here are specific suggestions to achieve freedom through frugality.

In Your Personal Life

• **Visualize what you want to free up time, space, and mindshare for**—your business; your spouse, significant other, or family; peace of mind; financial security; doing good in the world. Write these down; post them on your refrigerator or bathroom mirror; make them conspicuous to your conscious and unconscious mind.

• **Pay off credit cards.** This is the most expensive form of debt. Pay them off as soon as possible, if not immediately.

• **Pay bills online.** Every commercial bank now offers online banking; if you are not familiar with it, ask your bank about it. Automate fixed monthly payments like rent, mortgage, and home Internet access. You'll save time, postage, and late fees.

- **Invest in 401(k) accounts.** Employer-matched 401(k) plans are generally good investments. If these are available to you, take full advantage of them.

- **Be wary of impulse purchases.** Wait at least ten days before making an expensive purchase. During that time, research alternatives, compare prices, and consider whether the value of the item exceeds its costs—taking up space, requiring maintenance, losing resale value. If possible, rent the item for a limited time, either to try it out or for as long as you need it, before or instead of buying it.

- **Enjoy free entertainment.** YouTube offers thousands of times as many choices as your local movie theatre and the "tickets" are free. Movies in theatres necessarily appeal to the lowest common denominator; on YouTube you are likely to find videos that exactly match your interests.

- **Do it yourself (DIY).** Instead of going out with friends to pricey restaurants or clubs, invite them to a home-cooked meal or potluck. Rather than buy an expensive gift, make something edible, wearable, downloadable, readable, or functional. Visit a MakerFaire (makerfaire.com) for inspiration. You'll possibly gain a new skill and your gift will be much more personal.

- **Automate your investment account.** A new class of brokerage firms eliminates costly retail offices and still costlier account execs, and automates portfolio management to maximize returns after taxes and net of fees. Services are provided online or by phone only. Examples are Wealthfront and Betterment. Take a look.

In Your Business

- **Work out of your home as long as possible.** When you outgrow it, if customers rarely visit your offices, seek out the least expensive office space available. Refurbished warehouses are often low cost yet the most hip office work spaces in many cities today. Invite team members to help decorate and personalize work spaces. If you end up with more space than you need, consider subleasing it.

Decisive Technology's initial offices, 1020 Corporation Way, were then the least expensive in Palo Alto. CustomerSat's initial offices in Mountain View were nicer—we had our own restrooms. When CustomerSat outgrew those offices, we chose offices that had cubicles prenetworked and ready for us to move into—"plug and play," in Silicon Valley parlance—meaning that we saved on office configuration and setup.

Today, most software companies in San Francisco use open offices instead of cubicles or private offices. Plentiful conference rooms of varying sizes enable private conversations when needed.

- **Move paperwork online.** Replace printing, paper, and postage for agreements, invoices, and receipts—whether for customers, employees, suppliers, investors, resellers, or partners—with online documents and messages. Let your customers know in advance that you handle all such communications online; consider making that a requirement for doing business with you.

- **Seek multiple bids on every major purchase.** If you can quote a lower price from a competitor of one of your suppliers, that supplier will often match that price to win your business. Beyond saving money, you will discover new products and services that may better serve your needs.

- **Reward and recognize employees for suggesting ways to save money.** By the time you have several coworkers who are fully trained and productive, their aggregate knowledge of many aspects of your business will exceed yours. Their suggestions may range from installing motion sensors to turn lights on and off, to acquiring software to crowdsource customer support (enabling and incentivizing your customers to support each other).

- **Set an example yourself.** Don't enjoy travel, accommodations, or any other services in any class higher than your coworkers do. At CustomerSat, my cubicle was identical to everyone else's until we were acquired. I never had to deal with complaints about office size or location. On business trips in our earliest days, as many as four coworkers might share the same hotel room or suite, myself included. Providing visible perks exclusively to officers and executives in a start-up today is just wrong. At Decisive, I knew I had made a hiring mistake when a VP Sales insisted on flying business class to Europe rather than economy class like the rest of us. Team members will view themselves entitled to take the same liberties you do. So don't take liberties with company expenses.

- **Discuss frugality with potential coworkers before they come on board.** In Silicon Valley, companies like Google, Facebook, and Twitter routinely provide gourmet meals to their employees, and people from other well-established companies will be used to other perks as well. Will those candidates be comfortable and productive working in your closer, sparser environment? If not, better to recognize this before hiring, and not hire them, than to have to manage a problem later.

- **Anticipate resentment.** Employees with less equity will often be less frugal about your business than you—they have less to gain by saving the company money. They may even resent your frugality. Be sensitive to this, remembering what they may have given up to work for your company. Gently remind them that frugality increases the value of everyone's stock, including theirs.

- **Align your company perks with industry norms.** As your company's financial strength allows, do your best to align your company's perks with the norms of your industry. You compete for people with other companies in your industry; not aligning will eventually put your company at a hiring disadvantage.

EXERCISES

1. Could you improve your life by giving, throwing away, or selling some of your belongings? If so, which ones? Give, throw away, or sell those items.

2. When are you most likely to spend money that detracts from achieving your long-term goals? What can you do today to anticipate those moments and avoid spending that money?

3. Identify one of your regular consumer expenses whose primary benefit is your immediate gratification and eliminate that expense. Find a no-cost or low-cost alternative to fill the same need.

4. Given your age and annual spending today, calculate your "escape velocity" today—the net worth for which you would never have to work again.

5. Given your age and net worth today, calculate your maximum annual spending corresponding to your escape velocity today.

6. If you are not yet retired, choose a retirement age at which you stop working and your desired annual spending as of that age. What is your required net worth to make this possible?

7. Make a list of five people in your life most impressed by extravagance. How do they demonstrate it? How can you most effectively reduce any negative influence they may have, directly or indirectly, on your spending behavior? Make a similar list of five individuals who do, or you believe would be willing to, most encourage you to live frugally and make progress toward your goals. How do those individuals demonstrate that behavior and willingness? How can you most expand your interactions with them, strengthen their influence on you, or both?

CORE LESSONS

- Frugality may suggest dreary scrimping and hoarding, but it is actually just the opposite: It is about eliminating the unimportant to focus on what we prize most highly in life.

- With new online and sharing alternatives, there is less need to buy and own stuff.

- Many of the world's most successful entrepreneurs, executives, and investors deliberately choose to live simply, far below their means.

- Look for the easiest savings to make in your daily habits.

- Frugality increases your long-term financial security.

- When the next economic downturn, rapid rise in interest rates, or financial crisis comes, you will be thankful you were frugal when you didn't need to be.

- Seek out and surround yourself with people who talk, think, and care less about visible possessions and more about the things that are truly important to you: dreams, goals, and your progress toward them.

15

MIND THE GAPS (STEP 6): TEN WAYS TO DEVELOP AND ACQUIRE RESOURCES

In the plains the grass grows tall, since
there is no one to cut it. There is no one
to water it either.
   —*Vera Nazarian*[1]

Strengthening the fits between you, your possible customer needs, and solutions—an ever-constant process as you define, launch, and grow your business—requires developing and acquiring resources (STARS). Customer needs, technologies, and competitors are always changing, so gaps—whether hairline cracks or yawning canyons—are continuously opening between them. In chapter 2, we defined a need as a gap between a preferable and current state. Here we use the term *gap* to refer to a difference between requirements for satisfying a customer need and your resources. The left column of table 15.1 offers ten ways to close those gaps.[2] The first few ways you will likely use earlier; the last few ways, later. The right columns of the table indicate which of your STARS can be strengthened through these ways of minding gaps.

Table 15.1. STARS strengthened by minding the gaps.					
Ways to mind gaps	S	T	A	R	S
1. Attract cofounder(s)	✔	✔	✔	✔	✔
2. Hire team members	✔	✔	✔	✔	✔
3. Routinely stretch beyond your comfort zone			✔	✔	✔
4. Serve customers	✔		✔	✔	
5. Acquire tools, equipment, machinery, software, online services		✔	✔	✔	
6. Invest in training or information sources; hire consultants to learn	✔	✔	✔	✔	
7. Develop or refine a prototype or solution		✔	✔	✔	
8. Partner with another entrepreneur or organization		✔	✔		
9. Attract investors	✔	✔	✔	✔	✔
10. Merge with or be acquired by another organization	✔	✔	✔	✔	✔

STARS = Skills, Technologies, Assets and Accomplishments, Relationships and Reputation, Strengths (Inner).

As does any management team, my fellow execs at Decisive and CustomerSat and I developed and acquired resources continuously. Things we did well, in my view, included quickly assembling and developing expert teams in software development, sales and support, and consulting; hiring many top-notch professionals and managers; developing and executing compelling product strategies; attracting quality customers and investors; and readying the companies to be acquired at timely moments. My mistakes included assigning certain managers to the wrong roles; not adequately rewarding and retaining others; and not adequately investing in IT and finance systems to streamline service delivery. I could talk about these at length, but our focus here is on you and your start-up.

Table 15.2 shows specific examples of strengthening the fit between you and your customer need and/or solution by minding the gaps.

Table 15.2. Strengthening the fit between you and your customer need/solution.	
Ways to mind gaps	**Examples**
1. Attract cofounder(s)	–Add essential skills and knowledge complementary to yours
2. Hire team members	–Add design, programming, service delivery, sales, business development, and other skills & capacity
3. Routinely do something substantial that stretches you beyond your comfort zone and/or builds character	–Read a challenging book or take an advanced course in your field –Quit smoking –Lose unneeded pounds to reach a healthy weight –Take a ropes course –Take up a new sport or hobby –Run for or be appointed to public or private office relevant to your field (e.g., for an alumni, professional, or trade association) –Become conversational in a foreign language relevant to your business –Skydive or bungee jump
4. Serve customers	Build relationships with key customers: –From whom you can discover and master customer requirements –Who offer good long-term revenue and profit potential –Whose recommendation of you will favorably influence key customers to do business with you
5. Acquire tools, equipment, machinery, software, online services	–Uniquely differentiate your product or service –Deliver solutions more quickly or cheaply –Avoid the time and risk of trying to build new tools or software yourself
6. Invest in training or information sources; hire consultants to learn	–Gain solution, customer, or process expertise more quickly –Uniquely differentiate your product or service (e.g., enhance your solution with an online service that no one else is using to address the same customer need)

Ways to mind gaps	Examples
7. Develop or refine a prototype or solution	–Build a working prototype of your solution –Add features to your solution suggested during customer test –Differentiate your solution by uniquely incorporating a new technology
8. Partner with another entrepreneur or organization	Gain access to –Proprietary technology to better differentiate your solution –In-place manufacturing for rapid scale-up –Sales force or resellers for broader distribution or customer support –Established brand applied to your solution for credibility and awareness
9. Attract investors	Acquire –Capital for growing your team –Knowledge of your field and financing –Connections to prospective customers and partners
10. Merge with or be acquired by another organization	See 8 and 9

Figure 15.1 presents how you might use these techniques to strengthen the fit between you and each of the four customer needs and solutions discussed in chapter 13. For each customer need and solution, as indicated by the arrows in the figure, developing or acquiring the highlighted resources strengthens the overall fit between you, your customer need, and solution.

Customer Need	Proposed Solution	Your Applicable Resources	Additional Resources Developed or Acquired	Overall Fit with You
1. Graffiti-proof paint for cities in humid climates	New chemical formula that makes graffiti easily removable in humid climates	Chemistry degree (BS)		Weak
			· Formula for graffiti-proof paint · Business development and sales in Central America, Asia, and Africa	Good
2. Underwater GPS for scuba divers	Wrist device that shows diver position and underwater path traversed	· Scuba certification · GPS		Fair
			Ability to couple GPS receiver with a diver-based inertial guidance system	Good
3. Automatic English-Spanish translation between patient and doctor	Smartphone-based real time translation service	· Three years' work experience in medical services · Conversational Spanish · NLP · Full-time job and income (medical svs)		Good
			Detailed knowledge of existing real-time translation services for smart-phones	Very Good
4. Automated chat for meeting people online	Smartphone app chats with potential dates you would like to meet	· NLP · GPS · Social networking · Web cameras (webcams)		Good
			· Mobile app development · Automated interpretation of text and response	Very Good

—— *Figure 15.1* ——————————————————————————

Develop or acquire resources to strengthen overall fit with you.

YOU ARE ALWAYS MINDING GAPS

Strengthening the fit between you, your business, and your customer need continues indefinitely. This step—Develop or Acquire Resources to Strengthen Fit—arises again and again in our process. In the flowchart in figure 2.5, you'll see Step 6 recur in four different places, each with a slightly different focus, as shown in table 15.3.

Table 15.3. Step 6: Develop or acquire resources to strengthen fit.				
#	After step . . .	Step #6	Before step . . .	Focus
1	#5–Basic fit: Match needs and solutions with resources and passions	Develop or Acquire Resources to Strengthen Fit	#7–Determine advantages relative to competitors for each need and solution	**Broad.** Before considering competition, how strong is the general fit between you and the customer need?
2	#7–Advanced fit: Match needs and solutions with advantages and passions		#8–Choose your best opportunity	**Specific.** Focus on a specific need and solution to be different from competition.
3	#9–Launch your best need-solution-advantage-passion fit		#10–Scale up	**Fine-grain.** Get specific to a need, solution, and delivery model. These will reveal resources you need to scale up.
4	#10–Scale up		Repeat of various steps	**Continuously refine.** Track changes in needs, solutions, and competition over time.

EXERCISES

1. For the customer needs that best fit your resources and passions, make a summary table like table 13.3 "Overall Fit with You" on page 163.

2. For each of your customer needs, show additional resources you could acquire or develop to best improve each fit.

CORE LESSONS

- Acquiring or developing resources is one key way to improve the fit between you and your resources on one hand, and your customer need and possible solution on the other. (The other key way is refining or downsizing your customer need to better fit your existing resources, as you saw in chapter 5.)

- The early improvements you make in each fit are broad. The improvements gradually become more specific and fine-grained as you hone in on a specific customer need and solution.

- Strengthening the fit between your business and your customer need continues indefinitely, even after you launch and scale up your solution.

16

AVOIDING COMPETITORS (STEP 7)

The greatest victories are won without conflict.
—*Sun Tzu*

Are texting and voice calls competitors? Good question.

Texting and voice calls are fundamentally different. Among many other differences, one uses typing, the other, speaking.

For example, if Alexzander

- wants to convey a brief message to a friend across town,

- knows the friend is in class and can't answer a voice call,

- does not want the people around him to overhear him, or

- is under twenty-one (according to Pew Research,[1] 97 percent of cell phone owners ages eighteen to twenty-nine text), as is his friend, with whom he texts often,

there is only one choice, to Alexzander's mind: texting. Most young people I know who grew up with texting don't view voice and texting as competitors at all.

Similarly, if Brionna

- wants to chat at length with a friend across town;

- has arthritis that makes texting difficult;

- is relaxing at home, as is her friend, so talking on the phone is not an issue; or

- is over sixty-five (again according to Pew Research, only 35 percent of cell phone owners over age sixty-five text), as is her friend, with whom she has never texted,

there is only one choice, to Brionna's mind: a voice call. Most seniors I know do not consider texting and voice competitors at all.

So texting and voice calls are not competitors? But wait. Those are two extreme cases. Alexzander and Brionna each have customer needs particularly well suited for texting and voice calls, respectively. Change any of those needs even slightly and the choice becomes less clear. What if instead, Cruz

- wants to convey a message that requires a bit of explanation or discussion to a friend across town,

- has both texted and made voice calls to his friend,

- is age thirty to sixty-four, as is his friend.

For these customer needs, Cruz might go either way or both (text first then call, or call first and text a postscript). Survey even just a handful of your friends and you'll find that, for many of their messages, they have switched from voice to text in recent years. Indeed, texting is growing at 100 percent per year,[2] while the amount of time consumers spend making voice calls has fallen every year since 2007.[3]

So are texting and voice call competitors?

Yes, *when they satisfy the same customer needs.*

BECOME YOUR COMPETITOR'S CUSTOMER

To know a potential competitor, talk to its customers and ideally become a customer yourself. What customer needs does each competitor and its solutions satisfy, and how well? We asked similar questions in chapters 3 and 4 to discover unsatisfied customer needs; in this chapter and the next, we ask them to discover your competitive advantages and disadvantages.

Beyond your firsthand experiences with competitors' solutions and customers, you should do the following:

- Study competitors' websites, subscribe to their communications, and test their mobile apps, if they have them.

- If applicable, talk to their distributors or retailers.

- Visit sites such as Compete.com to see how much traffic their sites are experiencing and Yelp to see what customers and reviewers say about them.

If the competitor is another start-up and has a board of directors, how strong and relevant is the board's experience, and how interested in and committed to the company do the board members appear to be? If the company has raised money, how much and from whom? How do the company and its employees present itself, online, at their offices or stores, on the phone, and in person? How competent and experienced does their management team appear to be? How engaged is the founder or owner? What sort of buzz—what people are saying or posting—surrounds the business? Given the customer need and resources, how directly or indirectly do you anticipate you will compete?

> *Successful strategy derives from the differences*
> *between competitors with a consequent difference*
> *in their behavior. Your most dangerous competitors*
> *are those that are most like you.*
> —*Bruce Henderson, founder, Boston Consulting Group*

BE DIFFERENT; AVOID COMPETING DIRECTLY

As we saw in chapter 9 "Different Is Better than Better," you and your solution may be either

- **similar but better than your competitors'** (you have advantages along the same dimensions of customer need)—let's call these "improvements," or

- **different from your competitors'** (you have advantages along customer need dimensions that are different from those of other solutions but important to some customers)—let's call these "unique features."

Especially if your solution is similar but better and you compete directly in a well-established category like gourmet coffee, mobile payments, or health and fitness apps, the going will be tough, as Bruce Henderson notes in the previous quote. Competitors are more likely to see you as a threat, protect their turf, challenge or copy your improvements, and even attack you. In contrast, if your solutions are different, you avoid competing directly. Competitors may overlook or dismiss you, or even want to partner with you, which is good (just make sure they are not trying to steal knowledge or people from you).

Detroit auto manufacturers overlooked or dismissed Japanese auto imports. (Initially, Japanese auto quality was shoddy, a perception that Detroit retained too long after Japanese manufacturers improved quality.) Department stores overlooked or dismissed big-box retailers. Daily newspapers overlooked or dismissed online news. Further examples abound:

These solutions	Were or are being replaced by
Laptops	Smartphones and tablets
Calculators	Calculator apps
Road atlases	GPS and Google Maps
Digital cameras	Smartphones
Car keys	Keyless entry systems
Taxicabs	Uber and Lyft

These retail channels	Were or are being replaced by
Bookstores	Amazon
Blockbuster video stores	Netflix
Music retailers	Apple iTunes and iPod
Shoe retailers	Zappos

Whatever the reasons—oversight, dismissal, inertia, complacency, or structural difficulties of responding—they enabled new entrants like you to gain footholds in their markets.

In every case, new technologies gave the replacing solutions an advantage. Not only do you not want to overlook such "different" competitors; you want to *be* one of those very different, overlooked, or dismissed competitors. Seek either different dimensions of need along which competitors do not focus or a different customer set for which your advantages are strongest. The more different your solution and customer set, the less you have to worry about the overall strength of your competitors relative to you.

EXERCISES

1. Make a list of competitors for one or more of the customer needs you might satisfy.

2. Put them in order from most similar to your solution to least similar.

3. For each competitor, list two or three dimensions along which it competes and at least one different dimension along which you will compete.

CORE LESSONS

- Your competitors are companies or solutions that satisfy the same customer needs as you do.

- If you and others compete along the same customer need dimensions, competitors will more likely see you as a threat, protect their turf, and even attack you. In contrast, if your solutions are different, you avoid competing directly. Competitors may overlook, dismiss, or even want to partner with you.

- Be one of those different, overlooked, or dismissed competitors.

- Applying new technology is the best way to be overlooked or dismissed by established competitors, which is where you want to be.

- The more different your solution, the less you have to worry about how strong your competitors' resources are relative to yours.

17

WHERE DO YOUR STARS SHINE BRIGHTEST?
RECOGNIZING YOUR ADVANTAGES

Dear grass blade, ask not to be as tall as the tree,
But ask, "Am I the best grass blade that ever could be?"
  —Manpreet Kaur Singh

In chapter 9 "Different Is Better than Better," we saw how HP and Dell laptops were each better than the other, while the Apple Mac was different in valuable ways to some customers.[1] Apple was in a much stronger competitive position. Now, let's discover a systematic way of visualizing your advantages and disadvantages relative to competitors'.

In Scenario 1 (table 17.1), we compare HP and Dell laptops along three dimensions. In screen size, HP has an advantage (indicated by the "++" sign); in speed, HP is at a disadvantage (indicated by "– –"); and in storage, the two are about equal ("="). If we drew the chart the other way around, with Dell on the left, HP in the middle, and Dell's advantage or disadvantage over HP's on the right, Dell would have the disadvantage for screen size, an advantage for speed, and equal for storage. Either way, neither vendor has a clear advantage or disadvantage.

Table 17.1. Scenario 1: Advantages and disadvantages.			
Customer need/ product feature	HP	Dell	HP advantage or disadvantage?
Screen size	+++	+	++
Speed	+	+++	--
Storage	++	++	=

Note: Ratings are fictional, for illustration only.

The set of advantages and disadvantages in Scenario 1 is a tenuous competitive position even for established incumbents such as HP and Dell. It is certainly not a good place for a start-up.

Now, let's say a new entrant, Apple, competes with both HP and Dell (Scenario 2; table 17.2). When you have multiple competitors, there are many ways to gauge advantage or disadvantage; here, we'll simply compare the Apple Mac with the average of HP and Dell laptops. Again, to keep it simple, let's say that along these three dimensions, Apple's ratings are equal to the average of HP and Dell. Then Apple has neither advantage nor disadvantage along any dimension. At first glance, it appears that the three vendors are about evenly matched overall, with Apple falling midway between HP and Dell on the first and second feature, and equal to HP and Dell on the third.

Table 17.2. Scenario 2: Advantages and disadvantages.				
Customer need/ product feature	Apple	HP	Dell	Apple advantage or disadvantage?
Screen size	++	+++	+	=
Speed	++	+	+++	=
Storage	++	++	++	=
Video editing	+++	0	0	+++
Music production	+++	0	0	+++
Professional photography	+++	0	0	+++

But wait. The Apple Mac also has strong features along three *different* dimensions where the Windows laptops have none: video, music, and photos. Along these three dimensions, Apple has strong advantages, as indicated by the three "+++" symbols.

Not all laptop users value these additional dimensions, but for users who do, Apple is their clear first choice. This gives Apple a secure customer base from which to grow. If more and more laptop users value these dimensions, and Apple can retain its advantages in them, Apple's overall competitive position should strengthen further over time.

These advantages on different dimensions strengthen Apple's competitive position and give Apple a stronger position overall than HP and Dell have against each other. Different is better than better.

HP and Dell actually compete on many more than just three dimensions, and in fact, each has unique dimensions. But their unique dimensions are much less important to customers than their common dimensions. Here's how you can tell. Do most customers say that they could readily substitute Dell and HP laptops for each other? If so, those customers don't perceive the laptops as having important unique dimensions.

Similarly, the Apple Mac has more than three unique dimensions; the ones in table 17.2 are just three significant ones. But in Apple's case, most customers would say they could *not* substitute a Windows or any other laptop for a Mac, indicating the importance customers attribute to Apple's advantages.

YOUR ADVANTAGES VARY

Your advantages vary from need to need and customer set to customer set. Given your cofounder's knowledge and experience and yours, you may have an advantage for servicing diesel engines but none for hybrid vehicles, an advantage for Androids but none for iPhones, or an advantage for games but none for enterprise software. If you are based in Chicago and your chief competitor is based in Hong Kong, all other things being equal, you will have an advantage among Chicago-based customers and your competitor will have an advantage for addressing the same need among Hong Kong–based customers.[2] To broaden and strengthen your advantages, you will likely need to develop or acquire resources, as we saw in chapter 15.

Who decides what is better, different, both better and different, or not an advantage at all? Your customers, of course. If you are in doubt as to whether an advantage is unique or merely an improvement, consider it an improvement. Seek to further differentiate or strengthen it to make it truly unique.

HOW TEXTING OVERTOOK VOICE CALLS

The explosive growth of texting over the past fifteen years as a "different" competitor with unique advantages over voice calls provides a good model to emulate relative to your competitors. Before the year 2000, voice calling dwarfed text messaging; few people would have guessed that texting would overtake voice calls in less than a decade. Then, messaging used pagers or other devices separate from cell phones. The messages themselves were most often simple numeric strings: phone numbers to call someone back, or machine-generated alerts for technicians or traders. In 2000, AT&T introduced the first text messaging for cell phones.[3] Typing text messages on cell phones' numeric keypads was cumbersome (for example, pressing the number "2" three times for the letter "C"). Voice service providers saw messaging as incremental business, not competitive, since numeric messages often resulted in follow-up voice calls.

From 2000 to 2007, more and more cell phones supported messaging and alphanumeric keyboards that made texting easier. Voice services had long competed on sound quality, operator service, coverage, and price, but now they also had to compete with text messages. Messaging had advantages over voice along many dimensions:

- Quicker for short messages (avoid waiting for party to answer; dispense with small talk)

- Less obtrusive (phone doesn't ring)

- More discreet (those around you can't overhear what you are texting, and the texted party can't hear background noise that discloses your location as a bar or dance club)

- Better for messaging across time zones (doesn't demand an immediate response when recipient may be sleeping)

- No need for recipient to find pen or pencil to jot down phone numbers and street addresses

- Earlier conversations are automatically archived for future reference

- Can include hyperlinks in text messages

- Autocorrect grammar, ideal for foreign language learners

After 2006, user costs for texting started to fall rapidly, as cell phone service providers offered flat rate, unlimited texting contracts, and mobile apps enabled free texting. Texting use skyrocketed. In 2007, the number of text messages overtook the number of voice calls.[4]

Since 2007, texting has further expanded into still more dimensions: attaching images and videos, broadcasting to distribution lists, and supporting tweets with searchable hashtags. In this multidimensional space of customer needs, texting's region has continued to expand and separate from voice calls. Besides texting, online booking sites and apps have also cannibalized voice calls. For example, Google Maps, Booking.com, TripAdvisor, Expedia, Hotels.com, and Amazon enable users to get directions, make reservations, and place orders without picking up the phone. Voice calling is particularly vulnerable to texting because voice's position is defined only by the *absence* of customer needs on at least two of messaging's dimensions, unobtrusive and discreet. (Few people want their communications to be obtrusive or indiscreet.) Texting has not only defined the dimensions in which voice calls have to compete but also relegated voice calls to a shrinking region of that space.

Texting will continue to cannibalize voice calls for many years as younger generations who prefer texting replace older generations who prefer voice calls. From chapter 16, Alexzander (under twenty-one) is on the leading edge, and Brionna (over sixty-five), the trailing edge, of this trend. As these technology and demographic trends play out, texting will grow and compete less and less with voice calls. Either (1) texting and voice will continue to diverge, just as motor vehicles rarely compete with horses today, or (2) both texting and voice will be subsumed by other new technologies, just as Skype and FaceTime combine video, voice, and texting today.

FINANCIAL MODELING

It is easy to delude yourself about the strength of your advantages. Be sure to get feedback from prospective customers and others who don't pull their punches.

In the earlier examples, we looked at advantages and disadvantages *qualitatively*. This first level of competitive analysis can be done on a sheet of paper or even in your head. This is all you need for most decision making about which customer need you should address. But if a substantial investment rests on your decision, or you need to justify your decision to prospective investors, or you are considering two different alternatives that are so close you can't decide between them, then you may want to make your assessment *quantitatively*. Appendix C shows how to create financial models that you can use to test assumptions, ask "what if" questions, and project the financial impacts of decisions on your business.

EXERCISES

1. For several of the customer needs and solutions you are most passionate about, draw charts with one or more of your competitors like table 17.2. Along which dimensions do you have the strongest advantages?

2. Autonomous aerial vehicles ("drones") carrying video cameras are being used to map farmlands and spot crops that are inadequately irrigated or attacked by pests. With what conventional solutions do these new solutions compete? What are drones' advantages and disadvantages for this customer need?

3. Google Glass and Baidu Eye are wearable computers that use head-mounted cameras and recognize and understand your spoken commands. Google Glass's camera can take photos or videos on command. Glass also has a tiny head-mounted screen on which you can see a few lines of text, such as a patient's vital statistics or the first few results of a Google search. In contrast, Baidu Eye's camera has software that allows it to recognize objects. If you ask it about an object in front of you, such as an art piece in a museum, a pair of shoes in a display window, or an acquaintance whose name you can't remember, it searches for the information online and uses a synthetic voice to whisper it to you through an earphone. It has no head-mounted screen, but can use your smartphone to display information, if you wish. What customer needs are Google Glass and Baidu Eye each best suited to satisfy? What are the advantages and disadvantages of each solution?

CORE LESSONS

- Having advantages and solutions to satisfy customer needs different from needs that others satisfy lets you secure customers from which to grow your business.

- Seek to redefine customer needs so your competitors are defined by their inability to satisfy those needs (just as texting made communications private and unobtrusive even in public places, thus relegating voice calls to customers without those needs).

- It is easy to delude yourself about the strength of your advantages. Be sure to get others' assessments, especially from prospective customers who don't pull their punches, in addition to your own.

18

PARTNERING, RIGHTSIZING, AND UPSIZING

If I could solve all the problems myself, I would.
—Thomas Edison (when asked why he had
a team of twenty-one assistants)

In 2003, we CustomerSat execs had to decide whether to open a data center in Europe. Several major prospects, including Airbus in France and Deutsche Post in Germany, wanted us to host their data there; doing so would have given us a significant marketing advantage in Europe; and some of our execs strongly favored the idea. Our regional director and I visited several data centers in Europe as possible business partners. In those days data centers were not nearly as easily managed remotely as they are today. Even with a European data center partner, we would still have to extensively train the partner's staff, assign a full-time employee to the location, or both. The cost was significant; the decision was a tough call.

Along the way we recognized that the companies most insistent on storing data in Europe, public-private partnerships, were not representative of most companies there who cared little where data was stored geographically as long as it was secure. Finally, I asked Tien Tzuo, who was chief marketing officer at one of our important existing business partners, Salesforce, where they stored their European clients' data. Salesforce was the most successful company in software as a service

(SaaS), easily twenty times our size with major clients in the European Union, and a role model for CustomerSat. It turned out that, as a matter of public record, Salesforce hosted all their worldwide clients' data in North America.

We decided against the European data center.

This vignette illustrates three truths about business partners:

- They can help you reach customers you might not reach otherwise.

- Their benefits come with costs.

- They provide information flows that can help you make better decisions.

In this chapter, you will discover the wide range of benefits business partners can deliver, as well as their costs and risks; how partners can help you focus your resources where you add the most value; and how they can let you address a larger opportunity than you could otherwise.

A SMORGASBORD OF BUSINESS PARTNERS

Table 18.1 lists some of the many types of partners with the benefits, costs, and risks of each.[1]

Table 18.1. Partners, benefits, costs, and risks.				
Type of partner	Purpose	Examples	Benefits	Costs and risks
Technology	Acquire or license technology	-Technology firms -Inventors -Research universities	-Faster time to market -Opportunity for exclusive use of the technology for your application or industry	-License fees -Technology does not work as expected -Poor fit with target application -Provider cannot fulfill commitments

Type of partner	Purpose	Examples	Benefits	Costs and risks
Product research and development	Market research -Design and engineering -Software development	Generally industry specific, e.g.: -Consumer packaged goods (e.g., packaged foods, cosmetics, toiletries) -Consumer electronics -Enterprise software -Mobile apps -Office equipment	-Faster time to market -Leverage partner's technical expertise	-Engineering/ development fees -What you thought you specified is not what partner built -May need to retain partner indefinitely for changes, improvements, enhancements
Manufacturing	Low-cost, high-precision, or other production advantage	-Flextronics (Singapore) -Foxconn (Apple's Taiwanese manufacturing partner for iPad and iPhone in China)	-Low-cost, skilled labor -Faster ramp-up to volume production	-Production line setup -Communication of design specifications and changes -Differences of language and culture
Operations	Outsource "back office" functions: -Accounting -Order processing -Contact center -Data center -Human resources	Accounting and order processing: -Infosys -Genpact Contact center: -Convergys -TeleTech Data center: -Amazon -IBM -HP	-Focus on your essential advantage -Staffing flexibility -Reduce internal overhead -Economies of scale -Latest technology	-Training -Less commitment to your organization

Type of partner	Purpose	Examples	Benefits	Costs and risks
Marketing, media, advertising, public relations	-Win coverage by journalists, analysts, reviewers, bloggers, industry consultants -Promote your brand & solution to prospective customers	-Wide range of agencies freelancers -Generally industry specific	-Knowledge of media and readers reached -Knowledge of writers and their editorial interests -Skill at crystalizing/summarizing what is newsworthy -Creative talent	-Fees -Hard to measure performance
Distribution	Geographical coverage	Generally industry specific; for example, -Building materials and construction -Electrical -Electronics -Heating, ventilation, and air-conditioning -Janitorial and sanitation ("Jan/San") -Office supplies -Plastics	-Avoid shipping, billing, and returns from potentially thousands of customers -Avoid cost of warehousing and inventorying products -Gain access to new customers	-Training, discounts, incentives -Lose access to and knowledge of customer
Reseller	Sales, service, and support	Many—generally industry specific: -Manufacturers reps -Value-added resellers	-Established customer relationships -Industry and solution knowledge (e.g., Banking, Defense, IT)	-Training, discounts, incentives -Often sell what they know best or on which they earn the best commission (such as an established product) -Will typically lack your team's detailed knowledge of your solutions

Type of partner	Purpose	Examples	Benefits	Costs and risks
Retailing– physical stores	Brand, credibility	Established retail chains (e.g., Walmart, Nordstrom, Apple Stores)	Brand, credibility	-Training, discounts, incentives -Compete with many other products like yours -Retailer may drop you for reasons outside of your control
Retailing– online	Traffic, brand, credibility	-eBay -Amazon -Walmart.com -Staples.com	Traffic, brand, credibility	-Discounts and incentives -Often hard to be noticed

FOR WHICH STARS SHOULD YOU PARTNER?

Partners exist today to supply any or every resource—skill, technology, knowledge, customer relationship, etc.—that you can imagine. In deciding whether and which kinds of partners are right for you, ask to what extent a resource is or could be an advantage for the customer need you satisfy and how strong or complete the resource already is in your company, as in figure 18.1.

For partnering, resources fall into four categories:

- **Strategic (upper right quadrant):** If one of your resources is strong and a current or potential advantage, don't outsource it. Instead, build, maintain, and evolve that skill, technology, knowledge, or customer relationship yourself, to keep it in the Strategic quadrant (Arrow 1). *Examples*: Unique technology that enables your advantage; unique customer knowledge.

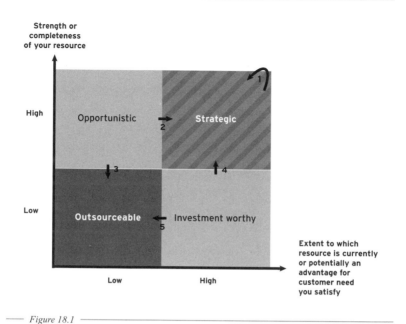

Figure 18.1

Four categories of resources: for which should you seek a partner?

- **Opportunistic (upper left quadrant):** If a resource is strong but not important for the customer need you currently satisfy, seek a way to benefit from it as long as doing so doesn't distract you from satisfying your primary customer need. Perhaps seek a related customer need for which the resource could be an advantage, find a partner to codevelop it, or lease it. *Examples*: Unique technology unrelated to your advantage; unneeded office or storage space in a prime location.

  If codeveloping and marketing the technology or space would be a significant distraction, consider simply licensing or leasing it as is or divesting it. If you do apply the resource to a customer need or codevelop it, the resource has the potential to become one of your advantages, in which case you will have reason to maintain, build, and evolve it. The resource would then move into the Strategic quadrant (Arrow 2). If you don't apply or develop the resource, its value will likely diminish as others with similar resources apply and develop theirs while yours stagnates. The resource moves down to the Outsourceable quadrant (Arrow 3). If you should later need that resource, a partner would have to provide it.

- **Investment-worthy (lower right quadrant):** If a resource has the potential to be an advantage but is not currently a strength, then develop, acquire, or license that resource. Perhaps start with a partner with the intent of learning from them to make the resource a Strategic advantage over time (Arrow 4). *Examples*: A technology closely adjacent to your advantage; your customer intelligence database, the value of which increases the longer you are in business.

  If you don't develop, acquire, or license the resource, it will lose its potential to become one of your advantages, and you will have no choice but to rely on a partner for it (Arrow 5). That may be okay if many potential partners could supply that resource; you will have plenty of leverage. But if only one partner is able to supply it, you could find yourself in a weak negotiating position. Worse, if that supplier views the customer need you satisfy as strategic for them, you may end up directly competing with them.

- **Outsourceable (lower left quadrant):** If a needed resource is not a current or potential advantage, and not strong or complete, let a partner provide it. Doing so lets you focus on what is most important to you and what you do best. The partners may provide skills, technology, or other resources. *Examples*: Facilities and temporary personnel during periods of peak demand (unless your business is providing these resources or services; e.g., human resources, production, retail sales, or accounting).

  The upper left and lower right quadrants are unstable: Resources tend not to stay in them for long. If you invest smartly in those potential advantages, they tend to shift to the upper right; if not, they tend to drift to the lower left. If you don't continuously invest in or apply an advantage or potential advantage, you will eventually lose it.

CHANNELS GOING DIRECT

Thanks to the Internet, to on-demand manufacturing,[2] and to advances in supply chain management,[3] global distribution is evolving from multitiered (your company to distributor to reseller to customer) to single tiered (your company to distributor or reseller to customer) to direct (your company to customer). Products ranging from books to computers to cars are increasingly being ordered online by customers, whether businesses or consumers, and shipped to them directly from manufacturer:

- **Books:** More and more books are being ordered online and directly delivered to consumers or downloaded to e-readers and tablets, rather than being shipped in hard copy from printer's or publisher's warehouses to retail book stores. As of 2014, e-book sales were an estimated 30 percent[4] of total book sales and growing rapidly.

- **Cars:** Tesla Motors, the innovative Palo Alto, California-based electric car manufacturer, markets its cars not through dealerships but through tiny showrooms in high–foot traffic malls. Consumers order the cars online; cars are manufactured to each consumer's specifications; and cars are delivered to consumers directly from Tesla's plant in Fremont, California. Eliminating dealers reduces inventory costs, eliminates price haggling, and improves the consumer experience.

- **Online sales:** Forrester estimates that by 2017, over 10 percent of US retail sales will use the Internet for online purchase, and over 60 percent for either online purchase or research.[5]

- **On-demand products via 3-D printers:** As with books, the specifications of physical products are increasingly being downloaded from central repositories. Three-dimensional (3-D) printer-equipped businesses, households, and retail outlets providing 3-D print services then realize those products. Early to adopt this trend are industrial and mechanical parts, whose exact shape and dimensions are more important than their physical appearance. Venture capitalist

Steve Jurvetson 3-D prints parts of his model rockets, for example. Soon we will also see 3-D printers creating many high-quality consumer products.

As you plan your distribution strategy, consider how you might exploit the trends of online ordering, direct delivery, and 3-D printing.

WHAT SIZE OPPORTUNITY IS OPTIMAL FOR YOU?

If you haven't done so already, in the next chapter you will compare your opportunities and choose the best one for you. In the exercises in chapter 5 "Think Big; Start Focused," you upsized, supersized, and "gigasized" each opportunity to help guide your long-term thinking about each one. You also downsized each opportunity to make certain your available resources and advantages could satisfy each one. Question: Which size of each opportunity should you compare with the others to choose the best one? Answer: Compare the *best* size for each customer need and solution for you, given your resources and advantages.

As you enlarge either the customer set you serve or the need you satisfy, you increase the size of your opportunity. At the same time, the strength of your advantage generally declines, and may even disappear, as you spread your limited resources more and more thinly.[6] So there is generally some range of opportunity—not too narrow and not too broad—that is optimal for you. What's the best way for you to find it?

MAKING TRADE-OFFS QUALITATIVELY

As a founder, you have to make more decisions every day than you can analyze with formal financial models and spreadsheets. To save time, let's see how you can think qualitatively about optimal size for each of your possible opportunities and only then build quantitative financial models, if necessary.

Take the customer need of "one-hour home or office delivery of prescription drugs" and your solution, a pharmacy on wheels with online orders transmitted directly to your nearest van that has a continuously updated and optimized driving route for rapid delivery. Say you are based in the San Francisco Bay Area and willing to start your delivery business in whichever city makes the most sense—San Francisco, Oakland, San Jose, Sacramento, or Santa Cruz. You research these five cities and conclude that you could make the most profitable deliveries quickly in the densely populated and generally affluent South of Market (SoMa) neighborhood of San Francisco. If your initial market test there were successful, you would upsize to all of San Francisco. If successful again, you would upsize to other cities in and around San Francisco, as shown in the bowling pin model in figure 18.2. Or you might upsize your customer need not geographically but instead by expanding the size or number of your vans and adding other popular, compact, high-value products to your "on wheels" inventories.

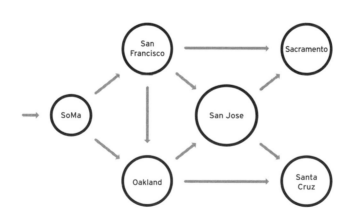

Figure 18.2

Upsizing customer need to other cities.

Let's say you decide to upsize geographically. As you do, your market and potential revenue grow. You don't know or need to know exactly how revenue will grow as you upsize geography. You do know that Oakland's population is less than San Francisco's and more spread out, while San Jose's is larger than San Francisco's and even more spread out than Oakland's.

As you upsize, you also incur additional costs. With a fixed set of resources, the resources you can devote to any city, and generally your advantage, decline. You don't know or need to know exactly how costs will increase as you upsize. You do know that, as you upsize, you have to buy or lease, equip, and maintain additional vans; buy more insurance; and hire additional drivers. Beyond that are costs associated with being more geographically dispersed. You may need to maintain one or more inventories of prescription drugs in each city to restock vans quickly; and you'll need to advertise your service across all the cities. You may also be more vulnerable to locally based competitors in those cities.

Will you enjoy any economies of scale by serving two or more cities? San Francisco and Oakland are only about ten miles apart on opposite sides of San Francisco Bay, but the bridge separating them is often clogged with traffic, and parts of Oakland experience high crime. Nonetheless, you can imagine that vans in your San Francisco fleet might also serve Oakland, either in an emergency or for an interim period until you scale up to separate fleets for each city. In contrast, San Jose, Sacramento, and Santa Cruz are over an hour's drive away and would surely require their own fleets from the outset. Knowing these factors, without doing any math, you guess that your optimal initial market size given your current resources is San Francisco (including South of Market) or San Francisco plus Oakland. (Instead of "guess," I could say "estimate" to sound more scientific.) For major decisions, you can build quantitative models to fine-tune your assumptions and further validate or invalidate your thinking (appendix C). Thinking through issues qualitatively first helps ground your models in reality.

PARTNERS EXTEND YOUR REACH

As you noted earlier, acquiring, outfitting, and maintaining vans, drivers, insurance, and inventory will take a lot of capital and limit your growth. Could partner(s) let you satisfy a larger customer need with your same resources?

Three popular GPS-enabled mobile apps—Uber, Lyft, and Waze—suggest ways to do this. Uber and Lyft partner with individuals who have excellent driving records and their own vehicles to be taxi drivers. The partners—the individuals—are independent contractors and their vehicles certified as attractive and comfortable. The Uber and Lyft mobile apps let customers hail the nearest available cab quickly. Waze's "partners" are its users, drivers who share real-time traffic and road information, saving each other time and fuel on daily commutes and road trips. After further research, you decide to similarly certify drivers and offer them a percentage of the revenue from pharmaceuticals they deliver with their own vehicles, thus saving your firm much capital. Since drivers may be carrying thousands of dollars worth of product, you decide you will need to bond them (i.e., require a form of insurance policy protecting you against theft). Furthermore, you decide to partner with existing pharmacies in each city to serve as inventory restocking points. Uber, Lyft, and Waze are all able to gather better information about customer demand and traffic patterns as a result of more and more drivers, allowing the three companies to offer better service to their customers. You believe you can do the same with pharmaceutical delivery.

Given all these factors, you guess (estimate) that your new optimal market expands from San Francisco or San Francisco-plus-Oakland to either San Francisco-plus-Oakland or San Francisco-plus-Oakland-plus-San Jose. Partnering has expanded your thinking and potential reach.

Thinking qualitatively first can be helpful for any decision and is all you need for many decisions. In effect, you are weighing in your mind as many factors that affect the decision as you can. Qualitative thinking can also let you quickly eliminate unattractive options from a long list. Once you have narrowed down the list, you can analyze the remaining options quantitatively, if necessary.

In chapter 20, we compare your different opportunities side by side to choose your best one. If "one-hour home or office delivery of prescription drugs" turns out to be one of your best opportunities, you can further evaluate it quantitatively. Alternatively, if "one-hour home or office delivery of prescription drugs" is not one of your best opportunities, there's no need to spend further time on it. You'll focus on other opportunities.

YOU AND YOUR PARTNERS FORM AN ECOSYSTEM

You, your partners, customers, suppliers, and competitors make up a dynamic ecosystem surrounding and including your company (see figure 18.3). These companies and individuals are constantly creating, satisfying, and eliminating needs and advantages. The companies and individuals react both to one another and to aggregate forces and outcomes—for example, costs, prices, technologies, and standards—that they cocreate. You saw how partners can deliver continuous streams of intelligence, whether it's Salesforce providing technology and marketing insights, or Waze, Uber, and Lyft drivers and passengers systematically providing traffic and weather data to each other. Your partners provide intelligence, and as moving parts in this dynamic ecosystem, contribute to your need for intelligence.[7] Be open to using them.

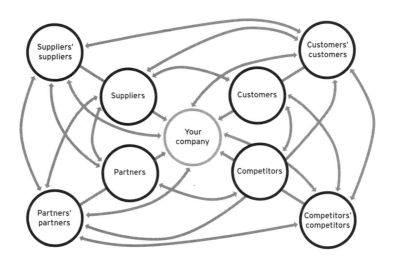

—— Figure 18.3 ————————————————————————

The ecosystem surrounding your company.

EXERCISES

1. Go with a group of friends into any nearby convenience store such as a 7-Eleven. Walk up and down the aisles. Taking no more than five minutes, without using calculators, and working individually, each of you estimate the market value of the inventory on the shelves. Afterward, compare your approaches and estimates. What can you learn from each other? If you can get an accurate figure from the store manager, compare your estimates with that figure as well. Reward the friend(s) whose estimates are closest either to the true figure or the median (half of the estimates above and half below) of all of your estimates, with a Red Bull or other beverage of her choice.

2. You believe that crowdsourced services to deliver anything and everything—from people (Uber and Lyft), to pharmaceuticals, to hard copy books and documents, to meals, to office supplies—will become widespread. What would be key features of a software solution that would enable any entrepreneur to start such a delivery service quickly and easily? What advantages and disadvantages would such a software business have over the crowdsourced delivery business of your choosing that you might start otherwise?

3. Your apartment window looks out on a busy freeway. Using a video camera and image recognition software, you can count the number of cars passing in each direction at any time of day, continuously. What customer needs might this information asset satisfy, and how might you turn it into an advantage and solution? If your friends in your city and elsewhere also have views of freeways and city streets from their apartment windows, how might you engage and partner with them?

CORE LESSONS

- Business partners can enable you to address a larger opportunity than would be possible with your resources alone.

- Business partners (a) can help you reach customers you might not reach otherwise, and (b) can provide information flows that can help you make better decisions or deliver greater value, but (c) require investment to develop and maintain.

- Build, maintain, and evolve resources that either are or have the potential to become advantages.

- Outsource resources and activities that do not give, or have the potential to give, you an advantage.

- Reason qualitatively about decisions before turning to quantitative analyses and spreadsheets. Doing so can save you time and help you avoid unrealistic financial models.

19

CREATING POSITIVE FEEDBACK LOOPS AMONG CUSTOMERS (NETWORK EFFECTS)

*A field was left to become pastureland. Castings
[earthworm feces] were thrown up month after month,
and these gradually increased in numbers as the pasture
improved . . . The average rate of accumulation . . . must
have been much slower at first, and afterwards
considerably quicker.*[1]

—Charles Darwin (describing positive feedback)

In chapter 1, we saw the power of positive feedback between passion and perseverance: Together they build and reinforce each other. Positive feedback loops were discussed again in chapter 12, "1 + 1 = 3," in the reinforcement of many attitudes and behaviors beyond passion and perseverance, including loyalty, courage, and enthusiasm, between you and your cofounder and among your team members.

Now we meet positive feedback loops again, this time among your customers. Consider Apple FaceTime, which allows iPhone, Mac, and iPad users to make video calls to each other over Wi-Fi or cellular connections. The more users in the FaceTime network, the more users the network attracts, because the attractiveness of the network

Thanks to Professor Marshall Van Alstyne of Boston University and the MIT Center for Digital Business for insightful discussions concerning this chapter.

and the amount you can use it are related to the number of people you can reach with it. Such positive feedback among customers is called a *network* effect.[2]

If a group of people attracts and is attracted to other members of the same group of people—such as video callers on FaceTime or classmates at a reunion—that is a *one-sided* network. If a group of users attracts and is attracted to a different group of users—such as consumers and merchants at a shopping mall or on eBay, job seekers and hiring employers on a recruitment site, men and women on a dating site, or users of a laptop or mobile device and application developers for that operating system or device—that is a *two-sided* network.[3] Where the users and sides come together (whether it's a cocktail lounge, website, or mobile app) is called a *platform*.

The geometric growth of the World Wide Web since its 1991 public launch epitomizes network effects: More users attract more content providers who attract more users.[4] "Winner take all" companies whose overwhelming market shares define and dominate product categories, such as Google, Facebook, Apple, and Microsoft, invariably reflect network effects.

HOW DO NETWORKS MAKE MONEY?

Networks may charge users based on

- the extent of their use of the platform (subscription fees, usage fees),

- the extent of features they have access to (feature fees), or

- purchases of goods on the platform (sales fees, virtual goods, and in-app purchases; i.e., purchases made within an application).

"Freemium" pricing, in which premium (i.e., paying) users subsidize other (free or discounted-fee) users, thus attracting more users and making the platform more attractive to premium and free users alike, is a means by which networks of all types can attract and retain users. We cover freemiums in chapter 21 "Five Pricing Principles." Networks may also generate revenue through advertisers.

Are the users on either or both sides of your platform "customers"? What if you are paid not by users but by advertisers who value the access to those users that your platform provides? Some people say that only those who pay you money are your customers. But since the success of your network business relies on the loyalty of your users whether or not they pay you directly, I recommend thinking of all your users and advertisers as your customers. If you lose any group, you have no business.

Any business, including yours, can create and enjoy network effects. In this chapter, you'll see how.

ONE-SIDED NETWORKS

Let's start with one-sided networks. In each example in table 19.1, more users attract more users for communicating, collaborating, transacting, or socializing. Each network creates a positive feedback loop among the users who attract and are attracted to other members of the same group.

Table 19.1. One-sided networks.			
Type	Examples	Users	Platform revenue sources
Physical/ offline	Social gatherings	Friends	Not applicable
	Sporting events	Fans	Attendee fees, advertising
	Karaoke bars	Karaoke singers	
	Industry conferences	Professionals	
	Workshops and symposia	Academicians	
	MakerFaire (exposition)	"Makers" and hobbyists	
	Burning Man (festival)	"Burners"	
	Davos and TED conferences	World leaders (by invitation or selection)	

Type	Examples	Users	Platform revenue sources
Virtual/ online	FaceTime, Skype	Video callers	Mobile data usage and feature fees
	WhatsApp	Voice callers, texters	
	Online multiplayer games (*World of Warcraft, Farmville*)	Game players	Subscription fees, virtual goods, or both
	Dating and social sites (Match.com, Scruff, Grindr)	Gay people	Subscription fees, advertising

In some one-sided networks, more users benefit from more users (positive feedback loop) even if they don't attract each other directly. For example, Google Search improves with more users: Their searches better inform others' searches.[5] Waze improves its effectiveness as a provider of traffic and road information as more drivers use its mobile app and report information.

ADVERTISERS

To reduce fees and obstacles for users to join the network, to further generate revenue, or to do both, platforms may also invite advertisers. An advertiser may be a party to the network—a member of one of its "sides"—for example, a surf club member who also makes and sells surfboards, a consulting geophysicist at an American Geophysical Union conference, an inventor at MakerFaire, or a buyer or seller on eBay. Or the advertiser may be a separate party to the network, for example, an insurance, transportation, or brokerage services provider at any of these venues or sites.

Table 19.2 gives examples of one-sided networks with advertisers.

In other one-sided networks, the same users play two distinct roles. On Facebook, LinkedIn, Twitter, and YouTube, content contributors and consumers attract each other (positive feedback loop). To the extent that users play these roles interchangeably, the networks are one-sided. To the extent that users playing those roles form distinct groups, they are two-sided (see table 19.3).

Table 19.2. One-sided networks with advertising.

Type	Example	Side 1	Advertisers and partners
Physical/ offline	Industry conferences with trade shows	Attendees	Sponsors
	Stadium sporting events	Fans	In-stadium billboards and advertisers
	Rock concerts	Fans	Sponsors
Virtual/ online	Google Search	Users	Google AdWords customers
	Waze (driver crowdsourced traffic info)	Drivers	Fast-food and other merchants targeting commuters

Table 19.3. Networks with the same users playing two distinct roles.

Type	Example	Roles	Platform Revenue Sources
Virtual/ online	Facebook	-Status updaters -Status readers	Advertising, payments for Facebook-based games
	LinkedIn	-Profile updaters -Profile readers	Advertising, premium subscriptions, talent solutions (premium accounts for recruiters)
	Twitter	-Tweeters -Followers	Advertising, data licensing
	You Tube	-Video publishers -Video viewers	Advertising (banner, search, video)
	Etsy, Pinterest	-Craft makers -Craft sellers	Sales fees, advertising
	Quora	-Question askers -Question answerers	None (at present)
	Wikipedia	-Article contributors -Article readers	Donations (nonprofit)

TWO-SIDED NETWORKS

In two-sided networks, users on the two sides are separate, well-defined groups who attract each other and create a positive feedback loop between the two sides. The examples in table 19.4 generally rely more on user fees than paid advertising for revenue. The side that is less price sensitive (Side 2 users in the table) often subsidizes users on the other side (Side 1). For example, many nightclubs attract more women through "ladies nights" (offering discounts on drinks and cover charges), thus attracting more men.[6]

Table 19.4. Two-sided networks.			
Type	Example	Side 1	Side 2
Physical/ offline	Farmers' markets, flea markets	Consumers	Merchants
	Nightclubs	Women	Men
	Managed care networks	Consumers	Physicians
Virtual/ online	Tinder (dating mobile app)	Women	Men
	eBay	Buyers	Sellers
	Mobile platforms (e.g., Apple iOS, Google Android)	Users	App developers
	Credit cards, PayPal	Consumers	Merchants
	Adobe portable document format (PDF)	Readers	Writers and publishers
	Video game platforms/consoles	Gamers	Game developers

Adobe Acrobat's portable document format (PDF) has writers who create documents and readers who view them. Readers are price sensitive and get the software free of charge. Writers, who want a large audience of readers, are charged for the software. In part due to this approach, half a billion users now read Adobe PDFs.[7]

In contrast to table 19.4, table 19.5 shows examples of two-sided networks that rely heavily on fees from advertisers or partners who are not already parties to the network.

Table 19.5. Two-sided networks with advertising.			
Examples	Side 1	Side 2	Advertisers and partners
Dating sites (OKCupid, Match.com)	Women	Men	Products and services for young adults
Online courses (e.g., Coursera)	Students	Professors/ courses	Products and services for young adults
Recruitment sites	Job seekers	Employers	
Review sites (TripAdvisor, Yelp)	Consumers	Reviewers	Hotels, restaurants, bars, and other merchants

ADVERTISING ALONE IS NOT ENOUGH

Some start-ups mistakenly expect to create network effects when they only have advertising and no users who mutually attract each other. Unless you have a significant technology advantage in targeting ads to make them sufficiently relevant and engaging to attract users—in which case you should probably productize and market the technology—don't rely on ads to attract users and create network effects. Think of a daily newspaper with no news and just advertising. #Boring.

If you don't have users who attract each other, focus on other possible advantages, such as content (CNN.com) or useful functionality (Google Maps). When your site starts to generate traffic, then you can expect to generate advertising revenue, not before. While you develop your content or functionality, work on building network effects at the same time. For example, CNN.com allows users to collaborate with reporters on "open stories" and share their own stories as well; Google, through Maps and other applications, allows users to share ratings and reviews of restaurants and other merchants.

CREATING NETWORK EFFECTS IN YOUR BUSINESS

Even if the business you contemplate is a "zero-sided network"—that is, your customers are wholly independent of each other, with seemingly no network effects at all—they still have something in common: They all do business with you. That is a seed from which to nurture and grow a network.

In this section, we look at five steps to evolve your business from zero-sided to a two-sided network. Virtually any business can benefit from the first four steps. Step 5 can demand major changes to your business, and so is not for every business.

1. BE A NETWORKER YOURSELF

Connect some of your customers individually. Would any two of your customers or prospects benefit from or enjoy knowing each other? If so, introduce them, as we saw in chapter 7 "Growing Your Mind from the Inside Out." Such thoughtful attention to customers' common interests, even if unrelated to your business, helps retain existing customers and attract new ones.

2. PROVIDE CONTENT YOUR CUSTOMERS VALUE

If you provide solutions for a hobby or sport, you can easily add a real-time feed to your website of the latest news and scores for major league professionals and teams. If you provide a solution for a business need, perhaps invite and host articles on the subject. CustomerSat had CustomerSat University: dozens of pages with practical tips and techniques for customer satisfaction professionals.

3. CREATE AN ONLINE COMMUNITY TO ENABLE YOUR CUSTOMERS TO COMMUNICATE DIRECTLY

If you provide solutions for a hobby or sport, would your customers like to pursue the hobby or play the sport together? If you provide solutions for businesses, would those businesses benefit from each other's knowledge and suggestions, perhaps surrounding your solution? If you babysit, would the parents you serve enjoy sharing tips on preschool?

Such an online community for your customers directly benefits your business as well. It can

- give you early feedback on your products and services to which you can respond quickly,

- improve your customer service and satisfaction as customers support each other, or

- provide a platform to introduce and promote new products or services to your customers.

In short, an online community enhances your customers' experience with you. But note: an online community amplifies your customers' satisfaction or dissatisfaction. If there is significant dissatisfaction among your customers, address that first.

4. ENABLE YOUR CUSTOMERS TO INTERACT BEYOND JUST ONLINE COMMUNICATION

For example, you could

- organize gatherings, matches, or games around the hobby or sport for which you provide solutions,

- enable the business professionals you serve to network with each other over coffee or drinks, or

- provide scheduling tools, perhaps for a monthly fee, to facilitate parents with young children to babysit for each other.

Some of these real-world events will also be opportunities to market and cross sell your solutions.

Finally, almost any network will benefit from appearing large and very active. To kick-start the 2010 launch of Quora, the online question-and-answer site we saw earlier, its founders posed and answered hundreds of questions themselves, making it look like the system already had hundreds of users, thus attracting more real users. Seems trivial? As of this writing, only four years later, Quora has raised $80 million in financing, at a value of hundreds of millions of dollars, despite having no revenue.[8]

5. GO TWO-SIDED

Again, virtually every start-up can benefit from the steps already covered. To go still further, consider turning your one-sided network into a two-sided network. There are two ways to do this. First, if the users in your one-sided network play two distinct roles, offer different marketing and services for those roles to differentiate them into distinct and mutually attracting sides. eBay, the online auction site, and Etsy, the handcrafts e-commerce site, started with one-sided networks of users who bought from and sold to *each other*. eBay started with collectors; Etsy, craftspeople. In each case, the users grew into distinct groups of buyers and sellers who attracted more of each other over time.

Alternatively, consider what other group(s) you could introduce to the network that would attract or be attracted to your existing customers. For example, if you provide services to any of the customers in the left-hand column in the next list, might the corresponding group in the right-hand column be interested in being part of your community?

Original Customers	Complementary Users
Game players	Game developers
Music composers	Lyricists
Dentists	Orthodontists
Architects	General contractors
Homebuyers	Real estate agents
Actors	Producers, directors, stage hands
Sports team players	Coaches
Software developers	Hardware developers

Yelp, an online service that enables consumers to search for local businesses and read reviews of them, built up the business/merchant and revenue-generating side of its network in a novel way. It started by providing users a searchable directory of local businesses that it gathered by "scraping" (automatically searching and copying) data from other sites. The directory service attracted consumers to Yelp's site. As Yelp built up consumer traffic, it persuaded merchants interested in that traffic to advertise on Yelp (for example, to buy the exclusive right to display an ad when consumers entered search terms and phrases such as "office furniture" in a particular zip code). This created a revenue stream for Yelp.[9]

Grafting an additional side of "complementary" users comes with risks: They may both turn off your original customers and distract you from serving your original customers. For example, too many real estate agents may repel homebuyers and dilute your focus from getting homebuyers the best deals.

If you did not originally conceive of your business as a network platform, turning it into one, especially a two-sided network, may mean changing your customer need, solution, competitors, and advantages. In short, it may mean changing your entire business. If you can envision a network business for which you believe you have significant advantages and that you believe has promise, add it to your list of opportunities. In chapter 20, you will choose your best opportunity from that list.

EXERCISE

How might your start-up most effectively create and benefit from network effects?

CORE LESSONS

- Network effects are positive feedback loops in which more users (customers) attract and are attracted to more users (customers). Networks may be one or two sided and may include advertisers.

- The side of a two-sided network that is more willing or able to pay, usually consisting of businesses or advertisers, may subsidize the side less willing or able to pay, usually consisting of individuals.

- Any business can create and build network effects among its customers. Techniques include making personal introductions; creating online communities; facilitating transactions, commerce, and relationships; and attracting complementary users and advertisers.

20

CHOOSE YOUR BEST OPPORTUNITY (STEP 8)

Excellence is the result of caring more than others
think is wise, risking more than others think is safe,
dreaming more than others think is practical,
and expecting more than others think is possible.
  —Ronnie Oldham

Let's say that you and your cofounder, if you have one, have now identified ten different customer needs and conceived of fourteen different solutions for them in areas about which you are either currently or becoming passionate. Your list, in table 20.1, demonstrates two good qualities:

- The breadth and depth of your interests and passions

- Your awareness of both businesses and consumers as possible customers (for five of the opportunities listed, your customer is a business)

Many first-time entrepreneurs limit their thinking about opportunities to consumer retail, such as clothing, home furnishings, and restaurants. But consumer retail is so visible to so many entrepreneurs that the opportunities tend to be highly competitive. Consumer retail spending is only part of the overall economy, which also includes business-to-business

(B2B) spending such as manufacturing automation, office supplies, and corporate information systems; and business-to-consumer (B2C) non-retail spending such as housing. You have found both B2B and B2C opportunities in areas you are passionate about. Good job!

Table 20.1. Target customers, their needs, and proposed solutions.		
Needs	Target Customers	Proposed Solutions
1. Remove graffiti quickly and easily	Cities with high humidity	Wall precoating formula and companion graffiti-removal compound (only works in humid climates)
2. Speed up 3-D printing; print textures on surfaces	3-D printer manufacturing or other 3-D software developers	Software for 3-D printers
3. Marketing for new suburb housing and urban high-rise devel.; see views from high-rise apartments and condos before buildings are erected	Suburban and urban real estate developers	Drone-attached, airborne video cams provide artful, time-lapsed housing devel. videos from ground-breaking to completion; and videos views from high-rise residential units
4. Alert athletes when they need to rehydrate (drink fluids)	Runners; other track and field athletes	Wristband detects electrolyte depletion in sweat; alerts wearer when to drink energy drink
5. Auto translate English and Spanish between patient and doctor	Hospital and medical center staff	Smartphone-based real-time translation service
6. Deliver print cartridges and/or repair office printers in one hour	Businesses in San Francisco and Oakland	Fleet of trained independent contractor drivers and their vehicles; driving routes continuously updated and optimized for rapid service and delivery
7. Show scuba divers direction and distance to dive boat or platform	Scuba divers, either commercial or recreational	Wrist device that shows diver position and underwater path traveled

8. Deliver prescription drugs in one hour	Busy professionals; immobile customers in San Francisco and Oakland	Fleet of independent contractor drivers and their vehicles; driving routes continuously updated and optimized for rapid delivery
9. Custom gift baskets	Gift basket givers who know exactly what they want to give	a. Purchaser can customize contents online
	Gift basket givers who are uncertain what to give	b. Recipient can customize contents online before shipping
		c. Site automatically customizes content via recipient's Facebook profile
10. Help people make friends online	Single or sociable smartphone users between ages 18-35	a. Get alerts when friends are nearby
	Single smartphone users between ages 18-35 who are busy or lack English and grammar skills	b. Online dating app with smart real-time messaging to greet people you are interested in, exchange pleasantries, optionally flirt, and alert you when you need to take over the conversation
	Single or sociable smartphone users between ages 18-35	c. Same as 10a or 10b with real-time video support (so you and other person can see each other as you talk with each other)

Note: The example customer needs and solutions listed here are representative only. They are fictional, untested, and may be neither commercially viable nor novel. Plus everyone else reading this book can see them. So please don't copy them. Come up with your own.

Ten is a lot of customer needs, and fourteen, a lot of solutions, to explore deeply and develop at the same time. If a few of these needs and solutions stand out far above the others for you, cross off all but those; or if a few of them engage you much less than others, at least cross those off your list.

As a first step, create a new table, similar to table 13.3 on page 163 but now more detailed. In chapter 13, for each customer need and solution, your table showed applicable resources, passion, and overall fit.

Your new table here goes further, showing possible partners, size of opportunity, advantages, passion, disadvantages, risks, and overall fit.[1]

Indicate the strengths of your advantages and disadvantages, as you see them, using whatever scale you wish, such as check marks, smiley faces, numbers (e.g., 0 to 10). Use the same scale for all needs and solutions.

Your scores depend as much on your passion and conviction for each solution and need as they do your tangible resources, advantages, and disadvantages. Others may challenge your assessments of your tangible resources or of your external risks; indeed, welcome them to do so. But no one can challenge your assessments of your passions except for you. Consequently, it is vital to be honest in your assessment. Don't give yourself a high score on passion for a particular need and solution just because you think you are supposed to. At the same time, remember that you can build passion through perseverance.

To focus and pare down your list of needs and solutions, we use four tools:

- Eliminate needs and solutions that least fit your advantages and passions.

- Combine (closely related) needs and solutions.

- Acquire or develop resources and advantages ("mind the gaps").

- Refine/resize needs and solutions.

The first two tools we apply in the next table. The third tool, acquire and develop resources, we first saw in chapter 15 "Mind the Gaps" (Step 6). We have applied it throughout our process and continue to apply it now. The fourth tool, refine/resize needs and solutions, we introduced in chapter 5 "Think Big; Start Focused" and saw again in chapter 18 "Partnering, Rightsizing, and Upsizing." Applying these tools, we come up with table 20.2.

Doing this exercise on your own, you would create a table that included every customer need and solution you were seriously considering so that you could see all the disadvantages, risks, and scores. Here however, in the interest of space, we've deleted six of the solutions from table 20.2 that you'd ultimately eliminate for the following reasons:

1. **Graffiti removal:** Chemical formula still requires development and testing; selling to municipal governments in Latin America and Southeast Asia has long sales cycles and many are corrupt.

2. **Faster 3-D printing:** Established 3-D printer manufacturers are already close to launching software using similar algorithms.

3. **High-rise apartment marketing via video cameras on drones:** Requires skilled supervision of drone during filming; labor-intensive post processing.

4. **Alerting athletes to rehydrate:** Potential competition from Fitbit and Fuelband.

5. **Auto translate English/Spanish between patients and doctors:** Similar solutions, though more expensive, are already available as options to hospital and clinic IT systems; would need extensive marketing to create awareness among doctors, nurses, and aids.

6. **Show scuba divers direction/distance to dive boat:** Technical risk—need to couple GPS receiver with a diver-based inertial guidance system; haven't been scuba diving for three years, would need to get back into the sport.

This leaves you with four customer needs and eight possible solutions in table 20.2.

For customer need 8, you eventually determine that it is more cost-effective to fulfill prescriptions centrally and only deliver using

Table 20.2. Selected customer needs and solutions with scores.

Customer Needs	Solutions	Possible Partners	Opportunity Size, Advantages, and Passion	Score	Disadvantages and Risks	Score	Overall Score
6. Repair office printers and deliver print cartridges in one hour	Fleet of trained independent contractor drivers and their vehicles; driving routes continuously updated and optimized for rapid service and delivery	-IT professionals with motor vehicles -Discount office equipment stores	-Often urgent when printer doesn't work in office -Can charge premium for one-hour, onsite service -Similar to 8 (delivery of Rx drugs)	+	-Printer repair is a basic IT skill -Several office equipment stores already make onsite service calls downtown	–	=
8. Deliver prescription drugs in one hour	Fleet of independent contractor drivers and their vehicles; driving routes continuously updated and optimized for rapid delivery	Possibly partner with existing pharmacies?	-Novel combo of existing tech: online payments and route optimization -No one is doing this!	++	-Existing pharmacy chains would have a major advantage -Significant capital investment -Inventory of drugs, some costly, on every vehicle; is there sufficient demand for one-hour delivery to justify extra inventory and labor cost?	–	+

		Partners	Pros		Cons		
9. Custom gift baskets, for people uncertain what to give	a. Purchaser can customize contents online	-Facebook (for access to app programming interface) -Outsource inventory, fulfillment, packaging and delivery?	Love gifts baskets and can assemble perfect one; can offer customers smart recs	+	Some gift basket sites doing this already	-	=
	b. Recipient can customize contents online		Could offer recommendations to recipient, too	+	Some sites already let recipients tailor gift baskets	-	=
	c. Auto customize content via recipient's Facebook profile		-Using Facebook for insights on gift recipient's likes and dislikes appears unique for gift baskets -Cofounder's expertise writing mobile Facebook apps	++	-Use of Facebook by apps as repository of personal information becoming more common -Would need to launch and scale quickly	-	+
10. Help people make friends online	a. Get alerts when friends of friends are near you	Facebook (for access to app programming interface)	Mainstream demand for this	=	Simple to design & build (low barriers to entry); more a feature than a product	-	-
	b. Online dating app with smart, real-time messaging to greet people you are interested in, exchange pleasantries, respond intelligently, and alert you when you need to take over the conversation		-People waste time chatting online. -Great for busy folks and those with limited English, spelling, or grammar.	+++	-User acceptance. The other party may get upset if/when they learn you are using a smart agent to chat with them. -Can agent be smart enough to appear human? What happens when two smart agents end up chatting with each other?	-	++
	c. Same as 10a and 10b with real-time video (so you & other person can see each other as you talk)		Enables you to see who you are talking to.	+	Simple to design and build (low barriers to entry); more a feature than a product	-	=

--Slight disadvantage; = Neither advantage nor disadvantage; +Slight advantage; ++Significant advantage; +++Strong advantage.

vehicles. In considering customer need 9, you note that 9a and 9b might be incorporated into 9c for a single site or application. With customer need 10, it seems that 10a and 10c could be combined into 10b, as features. Three of your needs and solutions—8, 9c, and 10b—get an overall score of one + mark or higher. After much back and forth, you and your cofounder decide that these three "finalists" genuinely reflect your top three choices, so we reduce the table to these three:

Solution	Overall Score	Description
8	+	One-hour home or office delivery of prescription drugs through "pharmacy on wheels."
9c	+	For givers who are uncertain what to give, gift baskets whose contents can be automatically customized based on recipient's Facebook profile.
10b	++	Online dating app with real-time messaging that politely greets people whose profiles you are interested in, exchanges pleasantries, responds intelligently, and alerts you when you need to take over the conversation.

+Slight advantage; ++Significant advantage.

YOU DECIDE

Drawing a table like table 20.2 can help you see pros and cons of each candidate and finalist clearly. If you somehow already know which one you want to go after, go for it. Again, don't raise your advantage ratings for that customer need and solution to make it look like you have the strongest advantages for that one. Instead, leave the advantages where they are and, if necessary, raise your passion rating to make that need and solution your top choice overall. If doing so doesn't reflect your true passion, something is wrong. It's fine to choose the customer need you are most passionate about, but if you have only a slight advantage overall, realize that you will have to work longer and harder to develop your resources and advantages.

Now it's time. Pick one and go for it!

GOOD QUESTION!

Q

My cofounder and I can't choose between two customer needs and solutions. Can we pursue both at the same time?

A

Only for as long as it takes you to choose between the two. The longer you postpone, the more time and resources you take away from the one you will actually pursue. If you both find yourselves gravitating to one of them, one of them pulling you toward it, you have your answer. Yes, it is possible, but rare, to start and successfully grow two very different businesses at the same time. My business school classmate and serial entrepreneur Jim Hornthal calls himself a "parallel entrepreneur" today, because he is working on four start-ups at the same time. But stick with "serial" for your first company or two. Like Jim, consider "parallel" only for your third, fourth, and higher start-ups. And even then, in Jim's words, only when you are able to engage crazy and dedicated talent to join you in each venture.

If you and your cofounder both have strongly different preferences, you may each decide to do your own thing and go separate ways. Before taking this step, think long and hard about the benefits of collaboration with your cofounder and how hard it is to find the right one as compared to tackling your chosen need and solution by yourself. But if both of you are not passionate about building the same company, it's not likely to work. This may be a hard decision.

EXERCISE

Make a table like table 20.2 showing Customer Needs, Solutions, Possible Partners, Size of Opportunity, etc. Cross out the needs and solutions to which you gave the lowest overall score. Combine others, if possible. Which need(s) and solution(s) stand out as your best opportunities?

CORE LESSONS

- For each possible customer need and solution, choose any method you like to score the size of opportunity, your advantages, passion, disadvantages, and risks. Net out the advantages and disadvantages to arrive at an overall score. See which needs and solutions have the highest overall scores.

- Others may reasonably challenge your assessments of size of opportunity, your tangible resources, advantages, and external risks. Only you can challenge your assessment of your passion. So be honest. At the same time, remember that perseverance can build passion.

- To focus and pare down your list, (1) eliminate low-ranking needs and solutions, (2) combine (closely related) needs and solutions, (3) acquire or develop resources and advantages ("mind the gaps"), and (4) refine/resize needs and solutions.

- Pick one and go for it!

21

FIVE PRICING PRINCIPLES

If you aren't paying for something,
you're not the customer,
you're the product being sold.
   —MetaFilter user blue_beetle

Would I pay $1,200 just to look up dead ancestors? No way. Not worth it.

But Ancestry.com was smarter than I am. They let me try out their site for free. After five days, I was hooked. They offered me a one-year subscription for only $300. When I signed up in 2011, I planned to use it for a year and cancel it. Wrong. After investing hours in research and building my family tree, I didn't want to lose my precious work or the genealogical updates that Ancestry.com periodically provides. Now after four years, I have paid Ancestry.com a total of you guessed it—$1,200. And despite the fact that a year may now go by without my even looking at Ancestry.com, I have no intention of canceling it.

In 1999, CustomerSat offered a thirty-day free trial of our online survey system. Think of this as an early version of SurveyMonkey. You could compose and deploy surveys and see their results, statistics, and charts free for thirty days. McGraw-Hill tried it out, conducted a survey, and received several hundred responses. After thirty days, we disabled access to their account. But McGraw-Hill wanted that data. They urgently cut and sent us a check for $18,000, which allowed them to access their account and create new surveys with up to a thousand responses for one year. It was the easiest $18,000 sale I've ever made.

These two stories highlight the power of enabling individuals and organizations to create something of value to them, and illustrate two principles of this chapter: use of subscriptions and freemiums. Entire books, scholarly journals, and graduate courses have been dedicated to pricing. This chapter touches on just five important principles. The first three contain a bit of simple math; after that, no math.

ESTIMATE AND BE ABLE TO ARTICULATE YOUR SOLUTION'S VALUE TO CUSTOMERS

To estimate the value of your solution to your customers, follow these four steps:[1]

1. Ask potential customers what product or service (or combination of product[s] and service[s]) they would purchase to satisfy the customer need that is most similar to the one you satisfy, if your solution were not available. Find out the price(s) of those product(s) and/or service(s).

2. Make a list of ways your customers perceive your solution to have advantages over competitors' alternative(s). Learn this list by heart and be able to articulate it at any time.

3. Make a similar list of ways your customers perceive your competitor's alternative solution to have advantages over your solution. Be honest. Get prospective customers to confirm.

4. Estimate the net value of your product's or service's advantages less the alternative's advantages, whether positive or negative, and add that net value to the price of your competitor's alternative. That is a good starting estimate for the value of your solution. You will revise this estimate as you get more real-world feedback from customers.

If possible, do this exercise for two or more different alternative solutions to arrive at an ever better estimate of the value of your solutions to your customers.

This exercise can help you pinpoint or confirm your target customer set. The customer set that values your solution most highly is often the best one for the launch of your minimum viable solution (see chapter 22) and to target first.

KNOW YOUR BREAKEVEN POINT

Breakeven is the point at which your company's revenues equal your costs—you neither make nor lose money. Having a sustainable business requires that your revenues exceed your costs, preferably sooner than later. Unless your business has another source of revenue such as a different customer set in a two-sided network (chapter 19), your breakeven point sets a lower boundary for what you can charge for your product or service.

Breakeven can be expressed as either the number of products or services (called "units") you must sell or amount of revenue you must generate in a time period, typically a month or quarter. In either case, breakeven is the revenue (net revenue, to be exact; also referred to as net sales) that equals your variable costs plus your fixed costs for that period. To determine your breakeven point, you need to know three things—net revenue per unit, variable costs per unit, and total fixed costs:

- **Net revenue**—from here on, we will generally use the term *net sales*—is revenue after discounts, whether to customers, your sales force in the form of commissions, or your sales channel (the last are called trade discounts), and excludes revenue from returned products for which customers' money was refunded, if any.[2]

  Suppose your list price is $100/unit. If you sell direct to customers who receive an average discount of 15 percent, and your sales force receives an average commission of 10 percent, your net sales per unit are ($100)(85%)(90%) = $76.50. If instead you sell through channels who get 30 percent discounts, out of which they may or may not offer discounts to their customers, your net sales per unit is $70. Any returns and refunds generally further reduce your average net sales per unit and raise your breakeven point.[3]

- **Variable costs** are directly attributable to products you sell or services you provide. They are incurred only if you produce (if you are a manufacturer), buy (if you are a retailer or reseller), or perform (if you are a service provider) and sell or resell the product or service. In short, the costs "vary" with units sold. Variable costs include materials, direct labor, shipping, and installation.

- **Fixed costs** include rent, utilities, R&D, advertising, insurance, overhead, and depreciation, which tend to be independent of the number of units produced or sold.

A few additional terms will come in handy:

- Your **contribution** per unit (or **gross profit** per unit) is net sales per unit minus variable costs per unit. Total contribution or gross profit—that is, total net sales minus total variables costs—is simply contribution per unit times the number of units sold.

- Your **gross margin** is contribution (or gross profit) divided by net sales.[4] If your variable costs were zero—this is rarely achieved but downloaded apps and software as a service (SaaS) can come very close—your gross margin would be 100 percent (very good). If your net sales equal variable costs, then your gross profit and gross margin are both zero (very bad).

- **Profit** = Net sales – Variables costs – Fixed costs. There are many definitions of profit. Here we use *operating* profit, which is calculated before deductions for interest and taxes, also referred to as EBIT (earnings before interest and taxes). If operating profit is calculated before deductions for depreciation and amortization as well, it is known as EBITDA (see appendix C).

Breakeven revenue is breakeven units multiplied by net sales per unit. Simple math shows:

- **Breakeven units** = Fixed costs/Contribution per unit[5]

- **Breakeven revenue** = Fixed costs/Gross margin.[6]

EXAMPLE

Your product: A stuffed toy bear that speaks to a child, understands its responses, and intelligently responds to many of those responses.

You and your cofounder designed, developed, and programmed the rugged board-level computer that is sewn into a bear made in China to your specifications. You have one employee who assembles, packages, and ships the bears; the three of you share a two-room office.

> **Distribution:** A regional toys retail chain
> **Proposed retail price per unit:** $100 (one bear = one unit)
> **Channel discount:** 30%
> **Estimated percent of bears that customers return:** 5%
> (typically within thirty days of purchase)

Therefore:
> **Average net sales per unit:**
> $100/unit × (100% – 30%) × (100% – 5%)
> = $100 × 70% × 95%
> = $66.50/unit

Variable costs: $26.50 per bear
Therefore

- **Contribution per unit:** $66.50 – $26.50 = $40
- **Gross margin:** $40/$66.50 = 60%

Your fixed costs: $10,000 per month

Therefore

- **Breakeven units:** ($10,000/month)/($40/unit) = 250 units/month
- **Breakeven revenue:**
  (250 units/month)($66.50/unit net sales) = $16,625/month net sales.[7]
  (250 units/month)($100/unit retail) = $25,000/month retail.[8]

Your breakeven units are sensitive to gross margin, your gross margin to contribution per unit, and your contribution per unit to sales price. In this example, if your retail price were increased by just 20 percent from $100 to $120 per unit, and variable and fixed costs were unchanged:

- Net sales per unit would increase by 20 percent from $66.50 to $79.80 per unit.

- Contribution per unit would increase by 33 percent from $40 to ($79.80 − $26.50) = $53.30 per unit.

- Gross margin would increase from 60 percent to ($53.30/$79.80) = 67%.

- Breakeven units would fall by 25 percent from 250 per month to 188 per month.

When net sales exceed fixed costs plus variable costs, operating profit is positive (figure 21.1). When net sales are less than fixed costs plus variable costs, you have a loss. If your net sales per unit are less than your variable costs per unit (meaning that the slope of the net sales line in figure 21.1 is less than the slope of your variable costs line), your contribution is always negative. Unless your business has another source of revenue, such as a different customer set in a two-sided network as you saw in chapter 19, you will never turn a profit no matter how many units you sell. In fact, the more units you sell, the greater your loss. Don't go there.

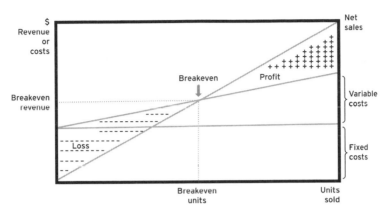

—— *Figure 21.1* ——————————————————————————————

Breakeven is the point at which net sales equal fixed costs + variable costs.

CREATE FORECASTS TO ESTIMATE THE PRICE THAT MAXIMIZES YOUR PROFIT; BUILD A FINANCIAL MODEL OF YOUR BUSINESS

Again, your profit is

Profit = Net sales – Total costs

= Net sales – (Variable costs + Fixed costs)

= (Net sales – Variable costs) – Fixed costs

= Total contribution – Fixed costs.

So for a given set of fixed costs, maximizing your profit means maximizing contribution. Total contribution depends on both sales price and number of units sold:

Total contribution = Contribution per unit × Units sold

= (Net sales per unit – Variable cost per unit)

× Units sold.

In your forecast, "Units sold" is your estimate of the number of units you would sell corresponding to the net sales per unit price.

To estimate the price that maximizes your contribution and profit, you estimate how many units you would sell at a range of sales prices. Suppose that you and your channel estimate you can sell the following number of bears (units) at each price in a typical month:[9]

Retail price per unit	Units sold per month (estimate)
$60	500
$80	400
$100	300
$120	200
$140	100

Let's now combine this forecast with the assumptions about your toy bear business in the example. In the next table, at a retail price of $100 per unit, at which you expect to sell 300 bears per month, your expected monthly profit reaches its maximum, namely $2,000 per month. At retail prices at $60 per unit or lower, you would expect to lose money, since your contribution per unit is so low. At retail prices of $140 per unit or higher, you would again expect to lose money, since your units sold per month are so low.

Retail price per unit	Units sold per month (est.)	Contribution per unit*	Total contribution per month	Profit per month**
$60	500	$13	$6,700	($3,300)
$80	400	$27	$10,680	$680
$100	**300**	**$40**	**$12,000**	**$2,000**
$120	200	$53	$10,660	$660
$140	100	$67	$6,660	($3,340)

*Contribution per unit = Retail price x 66.5% - $26.50; **Profit per month = Total contribution - $10,000 fixed costs.

If your forecast is correct—that's a big "if" that only real-world experience can confirm—then $100 per unit retail is indeed your sweet spot. To get a clearer picture of how profit varies by retail price, in figure 21.2 we graph the right-most column of this table. It shows that profit falls off quickly both above and below $100 per unit at this set of forecasts. This model would give you good reason, for example, to oppose any further discounts your sales channel might request, unless (1) those discounts applied only to bears sold in addition to the 300 per month currently forecast, and (2) you believed that such discounts would result in your channel selling more bears than otherwise.

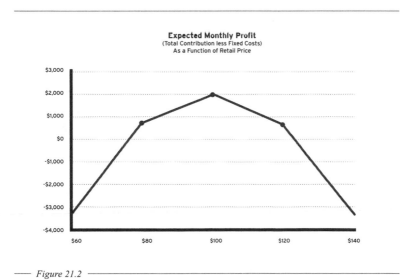

Expected Monthly Profit
(Total Contribution less Fixed Costs)
As a Function of Retail Price

Figure 21.2

Expected monthly profit as a function of retail price.

BUILD A FINANCIAL MODEL OF YOUR BUSINESS

A simple financial model of your business, such as you might build with Microsoft Excel, lets you try different assumptions and explore how best to allocate resources and maximize profit. For example, what if you increased advertising by $2,000 per month? Assuming other expenses did not change, fixed costs would increase from $10,000 per month to $12,000 per month. At a contribution of $40 per bear, you would have to sell an additional

($2,000 per month)/($40 per bear) = 50 bears per month

to cover the cost of the advertising. If, with the additional advertising, you and your channel forecast selling 80 more bears per month, your profit would increase by

(80 bears per month)($40 contribution per bear)
   – $2,000 per month advertising
   = $1,200/month.

But if the extra advertising didn't result in any additional sales, the extra $2,000 per month spent on advertising would wipe out the $2,000 profit per month from selling 300 bears per month. Your financial model lets you ask such "what if" questions to find the configuration of your business you think will be most successful. An example of a simple financial model is in appendix C.

If your model indicates that expected profit is zero or negative for the assumptions you think most reasonable, your business as you currently conceive of it may not be viable. One solution could be to work with a larger, national toy retail chain to increase sales. Another solution could be to focus on a smaller or different target customer set that most benefits from your solution and is thus less price sensitive, and raise prices. For example, would a family whose child has a hard time making friends, or lives some distance away from other children, be willing to pay more for an intelligent bear that provides companionship? With a smaller or different target customer set, perhaps you can avoid using channels and sell direct, thus eliminating channel discounts. Many businesses start out selling through their own websites with direct marketing, and expand into channels only after reaching or exceeding breakeven.

CREATE RECURRING REVENUE

Subscriptions, as you saw earlier with Ancestry.com and CustomerSat, have several advantages over single-order, one-time purchases of your solution:

- Subscriptions reduce the initial, upfront price for customers to try out your solution and thus help get more people using it.

- Customers are often willing to pay more in total than they would otherwise, in part for the convenience of having access to your solution at all times.

- You eliminate the cost of having to resell your solution to the customer periodically (subscriptions typically renew automatically every month, quarter, or year unless customers cancel them) and the associated accounting costs of invoicing and processing purchase orders, if applicable (subscriptions typically charge credit cards automatically).

- Recurring revenue streams are generally less volatile and more predictable than single-order revenue and thus reduce the riskiness of your company.

Many familiar products and services use subscriptions, of course:

Physical Products	Physical Services	Financial Services	Online/virtual Products and services
• Newspapers • Print magazines • "Book of the month" clubs • Consumables: fruits, gourmet teas and coffee, printer paper, ink cartridges, purified water, fresh vegetables, etc.	• Health club memberships • Stadium ticket subscriptions and concert series • Dance, sports, driving, and other skill-based lessons • Massage, yoga, and chiropractic treatments	• Credit cards • Insurance • Portfolio management • Installment plans	• Streaming video (e.g., Netflix) • Most business-to-business software as a service (SaaS) • Internet, cable TV, phone services • Music streaming (e.g., Spotify, Slacker)

Consider how you might define your solution as a subscription and your pricing to create a revenue stream to you:

- Any ongoing or recurring customer need could be satisfied by subscription: walking dogs, washing cars, or providing child care; shredding and recycling documents; servicing printers, lawn mowers, or drones; doing laundry, maintaining swimming pools, polishing silver, watering plants, taking out garbage, driving children to school, clearing sidewalks of snow, changing the wall art in office lobbies, cleaning pets' litter boxes, or replacing light bulbs in an office building, theatre, or stadium.

- Any physical product for which the amount consumed per period is predictable within some range could be delivered as a subscription. See "Consumables" in the previous table, for example.

GO FREEMIUM

Freemium[10] is merely a new name for a long-established and time-honored practice: offering a solution or the use of some of its features for free for either a specified period of time or indefinitely. Freemium pricing lets your users try your new solution without risk, gets them hooked on it, or both. Of those who try your solution, some users—the "premium" users—will opt to continue using it or upgrade to more features, thus generating revenue for you. The trick is to design the freemium to maximize revenue or the number of customers who convert from freemium to premium, without incurring too much in freemium costs.

The simplest forms of freemium, the free sample and free trial, have been around for millennia since humans started trading food and animal skins ("Taste this bear meat," or "try this woolly mammoth skin for a night"). They are most effective when your solution

- has benefits that are not obvious until users try it;

- enables users to design, build, or create something of lasting value to them (e.g., family tree in Ancestry.com; CustomerSat survey; a virtual farm in *Farmville*);

- is addictive (e.g., tasty snacks, games, cable TV); or

- is a platform in a one- or two-sided network—that is, your success depends on many users who either attract each other, convert from free to premium, or both. (See chapter 19).

Freemiums may be either of limited or unlimited duration. They may also be either subsets of premium features (users pay to upgrade to complete premium feature set or can make in-app purchases) or complete premium feature sets (i.e., even premium features are free).

The next list gives examples of when to use these four combinations. Free product or services may be of

Limited Duration + Complete Premium Feature Set

- Complete feature set required to fully experience product (e.g., test drive a Tesla for a weekend)

- Movie, TV, and music streaming services with free access for thirty days (e.g., Netflix, Spotify)

Limited Duration + Subset of Premium Feature Set

- Access to full feature set "gives away the store" (e.g., tech database or analytical tool for which one-time use provides answer)

- Access to full feature set incurs significant expense (e.g., gym membership trial excludes custom personal training program due to labor required)

Unlimited Duration + Complete Premium Feature Set

- One- or two-sided network where all revenue comes from advertisers or sponsors (e.g., Google, Facebook, Twitter, Instagram, YouTube, Waze)

Unlimited Duration + Subset of Premium Feature Set

- One- or two-sided network where free users attract more paid users (e.g., LinkedIn, Match.com, Skype, Viber)

- When users could choose to upgrade from free to premium functionality at any time in the future (e.g., *Norton Antivirus* software)

- When users might make in-app purchases at any time in the future (e.g., *Farmville, Angry Birds*)

- Free access to abstracts of technical articles only (not full articles); or free access to a limited number of articles per month

Our opening quote, "If you aren't paying for it . . . you're the product," applies to the Unlimited duration + Complete premium feature set combination, when most or all of the revenue comes from advertisers.

In deciding the duration and extent of a freemium, here are several factors to consider:

- The degree to which a free user may attract a paid user or advertisers

- The likelihood of a free user's conversion to a paid user (or make in-app purchases) as a function of time and extent of freemium feature set

- The cost of supporting a free user

- The extent of your advantage over competitors

In 2010, only about 6 percent of Skype's users purchased its video calling service premium features.[11] Much of the attraction of Skype to those premium users are the other 94 percent of Skype users with free accounts that they can easily reach on Skype.

Generally speaking, the greater your advantage over others satisfying similar customer needs, the less you have to give away. If your functionality is similar to others' solutions, you may need either to provide a freemium that is richer and more functional than a competitors', or to find a different business and revenue model. For example, if your competitors offer free subscriptions to businesses and earn revenue by selling data to advertisers or partners, consider a model in which you charge businesses directly and optimize your solution to their needs, not those of advertisers or partners. If your competitors offer fee-based subscriptions to individuals, consider offering free subscriptions to individuals paid for by advertising.

The freemium model may not apply if significant labor or other investment precludes free trials or samples, such as remodeling a kitchen, designing and implementing a corporate information system, or open-heart surgery. In such cases, your best marketing approach may be to describe the process or methodology you follow, explain why yours is the most qualified organization or team to carry out that process or methodology, and support your claims with customer testimonials. But apart from such cases, some version of freemium will likely be useful.

EXERCISES

1. For your company's solution

   a. Using value-based pricing, estimate your sales price and your net sales per unit. For your first year after first shipments to customers, estimate your average variable cost per unit and total fixed costs. Calculate your first-year breakeven point in both units and revenue.

   b. Forecast your unit sales for half a dozen or so prices ranging from half to double your estimated retail price. At what price do you maximize your gross profit and what is your operating profit at that price?

2. You are Charlie Price of Price and Son of Northampton, England (established 1890). You inherit your late father's shoe factory and business, which produces 25,000 pairs of classic but unexciting men's shoes per year. The shoes have a variable cost of £20 per pair. Retail shoe stores and chains in the United Kingdom sell them for an average retail price of £100 per pair and buy from you at a 40 percent trade discount. Your fixed costs of £1 million per year include depreciation but exclude interest expense.

   a. What is your annual profit before returns, interest, and taxes?

   b. On the premise that different is better than better, you consider changing your product from classic men's shoes to kinky boots, under the brand "Lola's." You estimate the total UK market for kinky boots to be about 5,000 pairs per year, but growing at 40 percent per year, thanks to the popular musical hit of the same name and your quality boots in this previously underserved market. The boots have a variable cost of £60 per pair including shipping. Your total fixed costs would increase by £50,000 the first year and £25,000 per year thereafter to promote and market your new boots.

      i. If you sell the boots directly for £500 per pair (no discounts), what share of the UK market do you need to achieve to breakeven in each of the first three years?

      ii. If you believe you can produce only 2,000 pairs of boots the first year, at what price do you need to sell them to breakeven?

     iii. How might you create an online community to build cus-
tomer loyalty and advocacy for Lola's Kinky Boots?

3. Your stuffed toy bears are intelligent enough to sense, speak, and respond to each other. How might you market and sell your bears on a subscription basis?

4. A few years ago I paid about US$17 and rose eighty-eight stories above ground to visit the Eureka Tower Skydeck, the highest observation deck in Melbourne, Australia, and the southern hemisphere. Once there, you discover "The Edge": for an additional US$10, you can enter a glass cube whose opaque floor suddenly became transparent and you felt as if you were floating eighty-eight stories above ground. For an additional US$13, you can get a framed photo of your horrified expression the moment the floor disappeared; and for an additional US$9, an extra copy of the photo. The total amount I ended up paying for all of these goods and services was just shy of US$50. How did I end up spending so much?

CORE LESSONS

- Estimate and be able to articulate your solution's value to customers.

- Know your breakeven point.

- Create forecasts to estimate the price that maximizes your profit.

- Create recurring revenue.

- Go freemium.

22

DESIGNING, CUSTOMER TESTING, AND LAUNCHING YOUR MINIMUM VIABLE SOLUTION (STEP 9)

[We] try to build the best services over the long term
by quickly releasing and learning from smaller iterations
rather than trying to get everything right all at once.
    —Mark Zuckerberg, CEO and cofounder, Facebook

All the brainstorming, research, analysis, and selection we have done so far lead to one place: getting your solution into the hands of real customers. You learn so much so rapidly at these stages—customer test and launch—that you want to get to them as quickly as possible.

Until real customers use your solution, you won't know for sure whether it is sufficient, and all its elements necessary, to satisfy a customer need. If your stuffed toy bear isn't soft and cute (solution not sufficient), it probably won't sell no matter how intelligently it talks and acts. If your enterprise mobile app has so many bells and whistles that business professionals can't figure it out (some features not necessary), or your competitors offer those customers a simpler solution before you do, your solution probably also won't sell or be adopted.

Your *Minimum Viable Solution*[1] (MVS) meets both conditions.

DESIGNING YOUR MVS

Think of your MVS as your solution's most important advantage packaged with the minimal set of features needed for its acceptance by customers and your channels (see figure 22.1 for a representative example). For your stuffed bear, your key advantage may be the intelligence; and the soft, cute, durable, and safe bear body and face, the minimum supporting feature set to ensure customer acceptance. Features such as the bear's wardrobe, accessories, and choice of color can be launched later, if customers want them. Your MVS gives you maximum flexibility to evolve your solution, apply your resources, and grow your business in whatever directions you discover are best, as a result of the information you gain from customers.

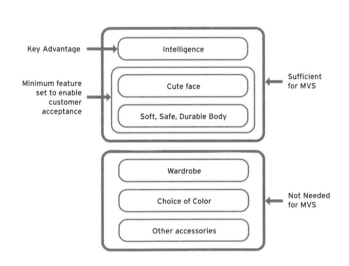

—— *Figure 22.1* ——

MVS design example.

Note: Necessary and sufficient features for a child's stuffed bear whose key advantage is intelligence. Your MVS comprises your key advantage and the minimal set of features needed to enable customer acceptance.

Apply the same minimalist thinking to your solution's key advantage, in this case, the bear's intelligence. The bear need not understand and respond to everything a child says or all the situations the child can get into; it just needs a meaningful set of important or common things that satisfy a definite customer need. For example, one intelligent bear MVS might recognize when a child is scared, hurt, or in danger; reassure and soothe the child; and send an alert to a parent or guardian. A different intelligent bear MVS might sense what the child finds amusing and make the child laugh. Still another might play the role of a cuddly teacher.

Apply this minimal thinking, testing, and design again and again to both advantages and enabling features, to whittle down your MVS. If the bear is a teacher, it needn't teach everything and comprehend every possible response. So we could narrow the bear's required intelligence even further. One MVS for a teaching bear might offer only foreign languages; another, geography; another, arithmetic. When you can't take anything else away without losing your advantage or disabling customer acceptance, you have reached your MVS.

My first company's initial product, Decisive Survey, was a full-blown Windows app when we launched it. Among other nonessential features, on its first release it automatically calculated skewness and kurtosis, two arcane statistics that customers rarely used. These were certainly not required at launch, because Decisive Survey's key advantage—parsing the text of completed email questionnaires to recognize respondents' answers to survey questions—did not rely on them.[2] By whittling down our MVS, we could have launched the app sooner with fewer resources, and going forward, maintained the software (i.e., fixed bugs and tested and validated new releases) more economically.

Your MVS may be a set of tools that enable your team members, certified consultants, or value-added resellers to provide unique services. Later, you may turn those tools into a solution that your ultimate customers can use directly. CustomerSat started with software tools that our consultants used to design, deploy, analyze, and report the results of online surveys for large corporations. After these tools were proven, we built a system incorporating their functionality that customers could use themselves. Beyond the knowledge we gained by serving customers with these tools, the services the tools enabled funded development of our self-service customer system. As a result, we were able to launch CustomerSat with much less capital than Decisive.

PROTOTYPING YOUR MVS

Prototype your MVS to gather the clearest feedback from prospective customers and partners:

- For **software**, mock up the series of screens the user would see. If the output is a customized graphic or report, perhaps create the report, manually if necessary, using the customer's actual data.

- For a **device**, prepare a model, blueprints, video tour, and/or form factor conveying size and shape.

- For a **consumable** such as food, drink, cosmetic, or toiletry, provide a real taste test or sample, and a mock up of packaging.

- For a **service** such as network installation, real estate or used car valuation, pool maintenance, auto repair, or housecleaning, provide the actual service to the client, perhaps at a discounted price, and solicit feedback.

If you are unsure which design is best, provide two or more prototypes of your MVS and let customers tell you which one or ones they like best and why.

Your prototypes will mature from mock-up to real solution over the course of prelaunch testing (discussed in the next section). When the test version of your solution reaches the stage that your team members can test the solution as if they were users, that's an *alpha* test. When your solution reaches the stage that the customers you select can get significant value from using it even if it is not finished, as well as give you useful feedback, that's a *beta* test.[3]

PRELAUNCH TESTING

Prelaunch testing resumes the real-world research and learning we started way back in chapters 3 and 4 when we interviewed prospective customers to understand their needs and brainstormed possible solutions. Prelaunch testing encompasses your MVS, pricing, sales channel, marketing, and overall solution delivery.

MINIMUM VIABLE SOLUTION

The more minimal your initial MVS or incremental the enhancements to an existing MVS, the clearer the customer feedback:

- If your MVS has multiple advantages over competitors and/or multiple improvements over previous versions, yet your target customers are not genuinely eager to adopt it, either that combination of "advantages and/or improvements" does not satisfy the customer need, or undue complexity is masking your advantages, or both.

- If your MVS has multiple advantages and/or improvements and does gain significant traction with customers, you know that combination of advantages and improvements is sufficient, although some of them may not be necessary.

- If your MVS has a single advantage or improvement and doesn't gain traction even after adding enabler and enabler, your advantage or improvement is not as compelling as you thought.

- If your MVS has a single advantage or improvement and gains traction, great—go for launch!

For example, if field sales, delivery, and logistics professionals clamor to buy the test version of your smartpen that uniquely reads handwritten numbers and the symbols +, −, ×, and ÷ and calculates and displays arithmetic results automatically, there's no need to hold off on launch until it can read alphabetic text or do more advanced math. You have your MVS. In contrast, if many smartpens already provide the same functions, your smartpen will likely not be viable without added functionality.

If you are a dentist, hairdresser, executive coach, optician, auto repair shop, masseur, or similar service provider: configure, test, and get comfortable with a web service or mobile app that enables your clients to self-schedule appointments, before making potentially more complex changes such as automated billing.

If you are a plumber, customer test and master new devices, like an electroacoustic microphone for finding leaks and the SeeSnake video camera to visually inspect and diagnose clogs from inside pipes, on separate service calls.

If you are a web or mobile app developer, consider incorporating A/B test tools into your app. A/B test tools randomly offer some of your users feature A (a new feature) and others feature B (either an existing feature or a different new feature) at the same time. The tools monitor and compare users' responses and show, for example, whether A or B led to more click-throughs or purchases. A/B test tools incorporate real-world experiments directly into your app.

Two nonadvantages do not add up to an advantage. In the mid-1980s, Xerox had two expensive, lackluster office products: a proprietary workstation for document management and publishing, and a bulky, tabletop laser printer. Xerox tried bundling the two together as a single offering. It went nowhere. Combining lackluster products generally makes them more, not less, disadvantaged.[4]

PRICING

If you plan to charge for your solution after it is launched, charging during prelaunch test will more faithfully reflect real-world conditions. The fee you charge should likely reflect a discount from your planned initial price, including the following factors:

- The risks your customers take and benefits they enjoy in using your MVS

- The benefits you gain from their feedback and recommendations

- The number of customers willing to test your MVS

The further along you are in prelaunch customer testing, the smaller the discount you should be able to negotiate from your planned initial price.

SALES CHANNEL

In chapter 12 "1 + 1 = 3" we saw the importance of you *and* your cofounder contributing to the vision and mission of your company. Doing so leverages the STARS of both cofounders and engages both of you in fulfilling that mission. Similarly, it is important for your sales channel—whether distributor, direct sales force, telemarketing team, resellers, or other—to contribute to your sales and launch plans. Doing so leverages the STARS of your sales channel and engages them in fulfilling your mission.

If you think your channel has little to contribute to your launch plans, either you may be undervaluing them (not seeing the true value of partnership with a group of people whose livelihood will depend, in part, on the success of your solution), or they genuinely aren't adding value. In the latter case, consider bypassing them and going straight to the parties, either downstream resellers or customers, to whom they sell. If you don't think you can bypass them, they may be adding more value than you realize.

MARKETING

Two key marketing questions are *What is your marketing message?* and *By which media will your message best reach your customers?*

Marketing Message

If you have followed the steps of *Unleash Your Inner Company* up to and through this chapter, you already know most of what you need for your marketing message: your target customer, the need(s) you satisfy, and your advantages over others satisfying the same need. What is left is choosing the means—words, images, sounds, and media—to convey your message. You have probably discussed your solution with team members and prospective customers so much that you have already discovered many of the best means to use.

One technique to develop the words for your marketing message is to first state the customer need you satisfy and your advantage and benefits exactly, in as many words as necessary, even if it is cumbersome. This gives you a target to aim for. Then make that statement concise, pithy, and memorable. For example, at CustomerSat, we started with a long, cumbersome statement like,

> We gather, analyze, and generate customized reports on customer feedback, for business professionals throughout the enterprise, to drive and coordinate responsive action that increases customer satisfaction, loyalty, and advocacy, thus increasing revenues and reducing costs of sales, marketing, operations, service and support, thereby increasing overall profit and corporate value.

After much iteration, we reduced this to the slogan that accompanied our logo:

> *Profit* from Customer Feedback

which captured both the key feature and benefit of our solution in just four words.

Media

First, whether business-to-consumer (B2C) or business-to-business (B2B), every business can benefit from a website, LinkedIn page, Facebook page, and Twitter account.

These serve as your business's public face.[5] They are free to set up but demanding to maintain: You have to keep them updated. Through them you can share success stories, customer testimonials, solution benefits and features, and how to contact you. Every business can also benefit from prospect and customer email lists for outbound communications linking your prospects and customers to your online resources.

If your business provides products or services that your customers order or use again and again, such as office supplies, online games, information services, construction materials, fast food, or hairdressing, consider offering a downloadable mobile app as well. A mobile app makes your company readily visible and accessible from the customer's mobile device; lets you promote new products and services to your customers directly; and can automate many of the steps of your solution delivery, including configuration, ordering, payment, and status updates.

Next, find the industry or community analysts, bloggers, and columnists who influence your target customers most directly. Read what each influencer has written and learn what issues are of greatest interest to him or her. When you feel your MVS is mature enough to make a positive impression, schedule a meeting. In the meeting, listen to the influencer's feedback and, if possible, incorporate one or more of his or her suggestions. Few actions convey more respect and build more goodwill with influencers than this. If they are willing, schedule follow-up meetings sometime later to show them how you incorporated their feedback into your solution. But don't add features for which you don't believe there is demand, or which don't fit your vision of the solution, just to please an influencer.

If your solution intersects two or more markets, seek out the influencers in each one. CustomerSat spanned market research, analytics, business intelligence, and customer feedback and reached out to the influencers in each of these markets. To prospective customers, it is particularly impressive and memorable to encounter your firm in two different markets, and it makes your firm appear larger and stronger.

If you are contemplating advertising on billboards or national TV for your launch, your initial target customer set is not adequately defined.

These media charge you for casting a wide net over consumers of all ages, living situations, and interests. Of all those consumers, ask yourself, "Which segments can most benefit from my solution?" Then find media that reach those segments specifically.

SOLUTION DELIVERY

Design, test, and refine the entire flow of your solution delivery including whichever of the following apply to you: ordering, scheduling, payment, manufacturing, shipping, installation, training, and service and support. After launch, customers will expect these business processes to be in place. Typical questions to answer here: How are manufacturing and shipping alerted of orders? Will a salesperson follow up after installation? When is training scheduled? Who do customers call for support?

Over the long term, plan to enable your customers to handle every task surrounding your solution—configuring, ordering, scheduling, shipping, paying for your solution, and/or getting service and support—online. Using tools and services readily available today, many of them free of charge, see how many of these tasks you can handle online from the outset.

> *If you aren't embarrassed by the first version*
> *of your product, you waited too long to launch.*
> —*Reid Hoffman, Cofounder, LinkedIn*

LAUNCHING YOUR MVS

Your learning continues from prelaunch through launch and beyond. Launch is different from prelaunch in that

- you publicly announce your solution,

- your solution delivery processes are in place, and

- your solution typically starts to generate revenue for your company.

"Launch" also means you will now get feedback based on real customer experience rather than on prospective customer opinions and perceptions alone.

Your initial customers will likely require special attention to ensure that they are satisfied, so carefully choose customers you believe will benefit most and from whom you will most benefit. Ideally, they should be up and running smoothly by the time you launch. Your choice of these customers should balance immediate benefits to you with long-term benefits.

Immediate Benefits

- **Learning**: Which customers will give you the most valuable feedback? Generally, these will be customers who can most benefit from your solution.

- **Require limited support**: Given your limited resources, choose customers who can either become self-sufficient or are low maintenance, and who have a high likelihood of success.

Long-Term Benefits

- **References**: The customers are ideally well known or highly regarded names and would be willing to serve as references or positively review or blog about your solution if their experiences are positive.

- **Revenue**: Customers purchase and/or subscribe to your solution if their experiences are positive.

Beyond the industry and community influencers we saw earlier, every single customer can help build your business. Your customers can do this online, by posting about you on Facebook, tweeting about you on Twitter, or favorably reviewing you on Yelp or TripAdvisor. They can also do so through old-fashioned word of mouth: telling their colleagues or friends what a positive experience they had with your product or service.

Your launch may be planned prospectively or recognized retrospectively. When your first important customer has been made happy by your product or service; when you receive your first purchase order; when many potential customers have heard and want to know more about your solution—you realize you have launched. It is the beginning of the positive feedback loop between you and your customers: you satisfy their needs; they give you feedback, pay, and recommend you; which builds your knowledge and advantages, enabling you to satisfy more needs— onward and upward.

GOOD QUESTION!

Q

My MVS incorporates my essential advantage but is just a circuit board connected to battery supply and output device. Prospective customers are turned off by its appearance. How can I get an accurate read in customer tests?

A

While some visionary customers may be able to see the potential of your MVS beyond its geeky packaging or lack of design, for most it will be a distraction. So provide enough of the real packaging or design so customers are not missing your advantage and benefits. Of course, for fashion, art, and many other categories, design may be your most important advantage and must be part of your MVS from the outset.

EXERCISES

When launched in 2005, Google Maps had a single technical advantage (and many disadvantages) relative to the entrenched market leader, AOL MapQuest. That advantage was users' ability to pan around a map, enabled by the then new technology, AJAX (short for asynchronous JavaScript + XML). Google linked Maps to its search home page, generating huge volumes of traffic for their map product. Shortly thereafter, Google added satellite images, and in 2007, Street View to Maps. By 2009, Google Maps had overtaken MapQuest as the number-one provider of maps and directions in the United States.[6]

1. Suppose that instead of Google, it was your start-up that had the AJAX-based Maps product that had to compete with AOL MapQuest. Your start-up lacks Google's enormous resources, popularity, and user base. How might your target customer and launch strategy differ from Google's to ensure market acceptance and success of the Maps product against your entrenched competitor AOL?

2. Now suppose you are AOL MapQuest today. How might you best compete with two market leaders, Google Maps and Apple Maps?

CORE LESSONS

- When you can't take anything else away without losing your advantage or disabling customer acceptance, you have reached your minimum viable solution (MVS).

- Design and build your MVS to enable prospective customers and sales and marketing partners to give you meaningful feedback on your solution.

- Prelaunch testing includes the MVS itself, sales channel(s), marketing, and solution ordering, delivery, and support, if applicable.

23

DON'T WASTE TIME RAISING MONEY

Poverty has no causes. Only prosperity has causes.
  —*Jane Jacobs*

Apart from "friends and family" seed funding, we haven't talked about raising money until now, almost the end of the book. Why have we waited so long?

- In chapter 6 "The Future Is in Your STARS," you saw that, in addition to your savings, your financial assets include your good credit history and trustworthiness, likely requirements for friends and family to consider lending you money or investing in your business.

- In chapter 14 "The Freedom of Frugality," we covered many techniques for living frugally and running your business frugally, enabling you to stretch your available funds.

- In chapter 6 and chapter 22 "Designing, Customer Testing, and Launching Your Minimum Viable Solution," we discussed how you can provide consulting and other services to generate funds for your business.

So why haven't we talked about raising capital from external sources—those other than friends and family—until now?

Because 98 percent (my unscientific estimate) of start-ups that try to do so—offer stock (sell equity) or seek bank loans (issue debt)—waste time doing so when it doesn't make sense or before they are ready. Were this not the case, banks and venture investors would receive only 2 percent as many proposals and business plans as they do, and virtually every plan or proposal would be a candidate for serious consideration by an investor or bank. As it is, most plans and proposals neither deserve nor receive serious consideration. If you follow the steps in *Unleash Your Inner Company*, you will avoid this pitfall.

Seeking capital (which includes both equity and debt) when it doesn't make sense or before you are ready, wastes everyone's time: yours, investors', and/or bankers'. Yes, do get outsiders' perspectives on your business, and welcome them from venture investors and bankers. But best to have gathered many of those perspectives already from friendly sources such as fellow entrepreneurs and executives in your network—and to have culled, refined, and integrated the perspectives into your plans or rejected them—before you meet with bankers or investors. When you do, they should not be the expert on your customer need, solution, competition, advantages, and finances; *you* should.

Seeking capital when it does make sense, at the right times, puts you in a strong negotiating position, helps your financing(s) come together quickly, and minimizes distractions from building your company. Let's say that you have fully leveraged the three bulleted techniques at the beginning of this chapter—"friends and family" seed funding, extended frugality, and generating revenue through services—but still need capital to grow your business as you would like.

WHAT ARE YOUR FINANCING OPTIONS?

Tables 23.1, 23.2, and 23.3 summarize eight popular forms of financing: two forms of crowdfunding, two forms of debt, three forms of equity, and the convertible note, which combines debt and equity.

CROWDFUNDING

Crowdfunding, a new and rapidly growing source of funding, enables you to raise funds from large numbers of individuals who each contribute a small amount. Most popular are reward- and donation-based crowdfunding sites such as Kickstarter and Indiegogo. These sites are ideal if you are developing a new product or conducting an initiative that has broad consumer appeal. The amount contributed, typically less than $100 per individual, might be the price of your cool new product with an attractive early buyer discount. Your supporters receive neither stock (equity) nor promissory notes (debt). Instead, you promise that they will receive your cool new product that their funds help develop, a perk, or some other acknowledgment of their support.

The newest form of crowdfunding, investment crowdfunding, lets you raise equity or issue debt. Crowdfunder, CircleUp, and AngelList are examples of investment crowdfunding sites. Individuals' investments may be as small as $1,000. At this writing, in the United States, equity crowdfunding still requires that investors be accredited.[1]

Table 23.1. Crowdfunding.			
Forms of financing	Typical uses	Specific requirements	Risks for lender or investor
Reward- or donation-based crowdfunding (typically $10K-$100K total)	-Reward-based: new product development -Donation-based: charitable or social project	-A cool product that people want to be early to own -An appealing mission that people want to support	-Product does not materialize -Funds are misspent
Investment crowdfunding (up to approx. $1 million total)—either debt or equity	-If debt, same typical uses as in table 23.2 -If equity, same typical uses as in table 23.3	-If debt, same requirements as in table 23.2 -If equity, same requirements as in table 23.3	-If debt, same risks as in table 23.2 -If equity, same risks as in table 23.3

Note: The time horizons of crowdfunded equity and debt are similar to those shown for equity and debt in tables 23.2 and 23.3.

If your firm has no customers, no cash flow, nor large and compelling upside potential, you are not in a position to raise equity or debt. But if your product has broad consumer appeal, you can consider reward-based crowdsourcing. A successful reward-based crowdfunding campaign (typically lasting sixty to ninety days) can lead to a successful investment crowdfunding campaign and even attract venture capital. Crowdfunding (see table 23.1) could be your start-up's first external financing.

DEBT VERSUS EQUITY

With both debt and equity, your investors expect a return, of course. With debt, they expect to receive their loan back with interest (usually in one to five years); with equity, they expect to be able to sell their stock at some point for more than they paid for it (generally in three to seven years).

The similarities end there. You are a candidate for a bank loan or line of credit only if you already have customers and cash flow (see table 23.2); you are a candidate for raising equity only if your firm has large and compelling upside potential. For loans, the bank or other financial services firm (say, American Express) who lends you the money has very limited say in running your business and no ownership in your business. Interest expense is tax deductible. When the loan is fully paid back (with interest and fees, if any), the relationship typically ends unless renewed by both parties.

In contrast, you don't have to pay back equity investments, and you don't have to use precious cash flow to cover interest expense (see table 23.3). If you go out of business and your stock becomes worthless, your investors get nothing. But your investors are co-owners of your business until you sell it or buy them out. They will likely have a major say in your business operations and decision making, so choosing equity investors can be as significant a decision as choosing cofounder(s).

Table 23.2. Debt.

Forms of financing	Typical uses	Specific requirements	Risks for lender or investor
Line of credit (< 1 year)	Short-term cash needs: -Working capital until accounts due are received -Inventory and payroll during peak periods (e.g., holiday season)	Strong cash flow; typically monthly, quarterly, or annual cyclicality in revenues	Positive peak of revenue cycle does not appear as expected (e.g., receivables are uncollectable)
Business loan (1-5 years)	-Equipment upgrade -Capacity expansion	Predictable revenue; investment will enable you to pay back loan	Investment does not pay off and borrower cannot repay loan (may lead to repossessing equipment)

Table 23.3. Equity.

Forms of financing	Typical uses	Specific requirements	Risks for lender or investor
Angel investment (typically up to $1 million)	Bringing innovation from design to market that: -Uniquely satisfies a widely held customer need -Could substantially reduce costs	Your opportunity fits with the passions, investment focus, or portfolio of the angel investor or venture capital firm	-Start-up does not perform as expected or hoped for -Down round (share price declines on subsequent round) or liquidation of business
Venture capital (typically $1 million & above)			
Corporate investment (typically $.5 million & above)		You have technology or other asset of value to the corporate investor	
Convertible Note (typically up to $1 million)	-Interest-bearing loan which is converted to equity, typically within 1-2 years -Allows postponing of equity round until start-up has achieved milestone(s)	Your opportunity fits with the passions, investment focus, or portfolio of the angel investor or venture capital firm	-Start-up does not perform as expected or hoped for -Down round (share price declines on subsequent round) or liquidation of business

If your business already has a revenue stream, demonstrated that it can generate cash, and has a large and compelling upside potential, both debt and equity can help fund your growth. Debt burdens your company with interest expense and potentially grave penalties in the event of default; selling equity dilutes the founders. If you are confident that your risk of default is small (be cautious), the optimum capital structure may be a mix of both.

ANGELS, VENTURE CAPITAL, AND CORPORATE CAPITAL

Angel investors are typically individuals, often former entrepreneurs, who have sold their companies and who now invest their own funds as equity in other entrepreneurs' start-ups. Angels bridge the gap between friends and family seed funding and venture capital.

In contrast to angels, venture capital (VC) firms primarily invest other people's money, typically from high net worth individuals, pension funds, foundations, university endowments, and insurance firms. As a result, they are able to make larger investments than angel investors. If a group of VC firms invests in an equity round (i.e., financing or deal) in your company, one of the VC firms will serve as lead investor. This firm sets the terms of the deal and typically takes a seat on the board of your company.

Corporate investors are generally as interested in gaining access to technology or market knowledge as in financial return on their investment, and so may be less sensitive to the price or terms of their investment than a venture capitalist would be. But they may try to limit your firm from doing business with their competitors or seek a right of first refusal if you are acquired. Be careful about agreeing to such terms that limit your company's options. Despite these concerns, corporate investment does not get as much consideration from entrepreneurs as it deserves, in my view. CustomerSat gained credibility, expertise in customer satisfaction measurement, and access to key accounts by having J.D. Power & Associates and NICE Systems as corporate investors.

CONVERTIBLE NOTES

A convertible note is debt that automatically converts into equity on the closing of a round of equity financing, typically within twelve to twenty-four months. A convertible note postpones the valuation of the company and its shares until the company has reached a milestone such as product launch, when the company should enjoy a higher valuation. Earlier investors in the convertible note are rewarded for their early support of the company through a "cap" that limits the price at which their loan converts into stock. Since convertible notes are debt, they can be issued more quickly and simply than stock, which typically has more complex terms, costs more in legal fees to set up, and takes longer to negotiate with investors.

DO YOU WANT OUTSIDE INVESTORS?

At the risk of belaboring the point, here are some reasons you may not want to sell stock:

- You believe you can adequately address your market opportunity and sustain and grow your business through cash generated by operations, business loans, or lines of credit.

- You don't want to have to sell or lose control of your company, as you will likely have to do to provide a return to your investors.

- You don't want to be accountable to outside investors or a board of directors.

If your market opportunity and vision do not require additional capital and you invite and accept outside investment nonetheless, in my experience you will probably end up with less equity in and possibly loss of control of substantially the same company you would have had without raising the money, the money you raise squandered, and/or disgruntled investors. Don't go there.

Beware: If new competitors unexpectedly win some of your best customers and you have few or no cash reserves, you may have few options.

In contrast, if your innovative solution uniquely satisfies a large opportunity that demands additional capital, your current or prospective customers are enthusiastic, and you are okay with being accountable to a board of directors and probably losing control of your company at some point, then raising equity (selling stock) is very likely the best option for you.

HOW DO YOU FIND INVESTORS?

Start cultivating them today, well in advance of your fund-raising. Go to AngelList and see which investors share common passions with you. Watch their videos on YouTube or read their blogs. For example, if both you and the investors have worked in publishing, or business analytics, or IT security, or foreign exchange, they will likely recognize and appreciate the customer need you have identified and further be able to add value.

Think of something not generally well known that you know well by virtue of your passion and perseverance in the field of common interest between you and the investor. Share that knowledge with her and invite her to talk about your mutual interest and expertise. When you talk by phone or meet, if you are confident in your knowledge, invite her to call on you if you could help with due diligence on an investment in the area about which both you and she are passionate. Keep in touch with investors until it is time for you to raise funds.

RAISE MONEY WHEN YOU REDUCE RISK OR RAISE UPSIDE POTENTIAL

What are the ideal times to raise equity? It is certainly not when you are out of money. Then you have minimal credibility and even less negotiating leverage. Nor is it when you can see that you are going to run out of money. The best times are *when you significantly reduce the risk or raise the upside potential in your company for your investors*. Investors may not believe that an investment in your start-up will enjoy a good return at the valuation that is acceptable to you. Demonstrably reducing investor risk, raising upside potential, or both increases the common ground between you and investors and makes your reaching agreement more likely.

Each time your start-up advances through one of five milestones (from idea to prototype to customers/users to revenue to positive cash flow), you significantly reduce investor risk:

- Positive cash flow eliminates the risk that you can generate revenue.

- Revenue eliminates the risk that you can get customers.

- Customers eliminate the risk that your prototype works (and satisfies a real customer need).

- A working prototype eliminates the risk that your idea can be reduced to practice.

Recall the "bowling pins" (customer needs that your business can satisfy) that we saw in chapter 5. The more persuasively you can demonstrate that your business uniquely satisfies a customer need, and can use that stronghold to satisfy another, and yet another, customer need—and thus knock down a whole series of bowling pins—the more you raise the upside potential of your company for investors.

So how does this translate into a fund-raising strategy?

BUILD INVESTORS' CONFIDENCE IN YOU

Seek funding before, and ideally close on funding shortly after, you reach a significant milestone that reduces risk, increases your upside potential, or both. Ideally, the seeking and the closing are at most a few months apart. During that time, your prospective investors get to see you in action.

For example, in your initial meeting with investors, you will lay out your customer need, your and your cofounders' applicable STARS, your solution, your competitors, and your advantages over them. In addition, you may assert that you will achieve a certain milestone—say, 100,000 downloads, 10,000 daily users, $100,000 in quarterly revenues, or a signed reseller or licensing agreement with a major partner in your industry—within, say, 90–120 days. Then, in a subsequent meeting before that deadline, you demonstrate that you have achieved the milestone to which you committed. This starts building your prospective investors' confidence in you. The more significant your achieved milestone, the greater the investors' confidence. Clearly, when you claim that you will reach a milestone, you want to be very confident that you will do so. Like a sword, this approach cuts both ways: If your performance falls very short of the milestone, it is better not to have asserted that you would achieve it in the first place.

This approach has two benefits:

- It has you raising money at the time when you have reduced risk, raised upside for prospective investors, or both.

- It starts building, in a small way, your relationship and track record with prospective investors even before they become investors.

If you are in the rare position where investors already know and have confidence in you, you may need to be concerned just about the first benefit and not the second. But even so, don't take your previous track record for granted, and realize that your firm's performance and yours during the fund-raising period will become part—the most recent and memorable part—of your overall track record.

HOW MUCH SHOULD YOU RAISE AND WHEN?

Let's say that, using the three bulleted techniques at the beginning of this chapter, you can generate enough funds, or have enough on hand, to achieve one or more milestones before raising equity. At which milestone should you raise capital, and how much, if any?

The timing and pace of your fund-raising depends on the size of your opportunity and the speed at which it is growing. To fully address a large, rapidly growing opportunity means growing your company more rapidly and thus raising or generating more money sooner. In contrast, if your opportunity is smaller or growing less rapidly, less capital will be required to address it.

Think of the next significant milestone for your business beyond the one you have most recently achieved. It may be either advancing your company to the next stage—prototype, customers, revenue, or positive cash flow—or knocking down the next "bowling pin" (customer need) in a series as you expand. How much you raise and when depends on three factors, each of which contain a different type of uncertainty:

1. **Time and money required to reach the next milestone:** This depends on your own organization. Despite the uncertainty, it should be the easiest of the three factors to assess.

2. **Increase in the value of your company by reaching that milestone:** This requires gathering comparative intelligence (amounts by which comparable companies have increased their valuations, either in financings, acquisitions, or initial public offerings).

3. **Amount by which your competition advances in the meantime:** This requires assessing your competitors specifically.

The more different you are from your competitors, the less you have to worry about #3; the less relevant comparable companies will be for #2, and the harder it will be to estimate your company's value; and the more you can simply focus on #1 in deciding how much to raise and when.

PUT YOURSELF IN INVESTORS' SHOES

When you buy shares in an established company, say, Apple or Google, you don't expect that your small investment will significantly increase the company's likelihood of success. Rather, you believe the company is already likely to be successful whether you invest or not, and you want to participate in that success. Assume that prospective investors have the same expectation when investing in your company.

Beyond the soundness of your plans, strength of your management team, and size of your opportunity, factors affecting whether investors will perceive you and your company as already likely to be successful include the following:

- How much you accomplished before starting your company

- How much you have accomplished since starting your company (e.g., assembling your team, prototyping your solution, engaging your first customers)

- How much your company progresses during fund-raising

- Others who have committed to investing in and supporting the company

- Your passion, self-confidence, perseverance, and vision

Not all investors have the "already likely to be successful" expectation—some fully expect to contribute significantly to your venture's success, and virtually all will try to persuade you that they will do so—but you will have more success fund-raising if you set this very high bar for what you and your company achieve before you approach investors, and how you present your company's future to them.

EXERCISES

1. Which form(s) of financing are likely to be best for your company in the next six months? In the next twelve months?

2. If raising equity is right for your business, how could you most significantly reduce risk, increase the upside potential of your company for investors, or both?

CORE LESSONS

- Seeking capital that make sense and at the right times puts you in a strong negotiating position, helps deals come together quickly, and minimizes distractions from building your company.

- Start with "friends and family" seed funding, extended frugality, and generating revenue through services.

- Consider the pros and cons of all forms of financing, including crowdfunding, debt, equity, and convertible notes.

- Start cultivating investors today, well in advance of your fund-raising.

- If raising equity is right for your business, time your funding to follow significant reductions in risk and/or increases in the upside potential of your company for investors.

- Assume that investors will invest in your company only if they believe it is already going to be successful.

24

SCALING YOUR BUSINESS (STEP 10)

A journey of a thousand miles begins with a single step.
—Lao Tzu

All of the world's largest, most successful companies were once start-ups. Apple and Google first operated out of garages. McDonald's started as a single restaurant; Walmart, as a single variety store; Starbucks, a single coffee shop. Facebook started in a dorm room. Every one of these enterprises started with a single customer.

To grow your business you need cash, either generated from operations or raised as capital (equity or debt). The more cash your operations generate, the less capital you need to raise. *Scalability* means the ability of your business to generate increasing cash—cash flow from operations—for each additional dollar of capital invested (figure 24.1 left chart).[1] Alternatively, scalability can be defined as increasing profit for each additional dollar of revenue (figure 24.1 right chart).[2] Either way, scalability broadly measures how many more customers you can serve or how much more revenue you can generate with minimal increases in costs.

In the figure 24.1 charts, the dark gray companies are more scalable, and more attractive investments, than the light gray companies.

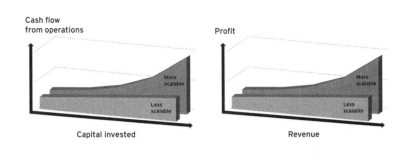

——— Figure 24.1 ———

Two definitions of scalability.

The more scalable (dark gray) companies are likely more highly automated and less labor intensive than the less scalable (light gray) companies—machines and computers can more readily handle large increases in workloads than people can. The more scalable companies are also probably more information intensive, whether in the form of intellectual property—trade secrets, patents, trademarks, copyrights, or software—or in detailed knowledge of customers, suppliers, processes, markets, geographies, or technologies. All of these give advantages to the company or can add value to the products and services that incorporate them without adding variable costs of materials or labor.

Software and software as a service (SaaS) companies, especially those with self-service customers and network effects such as Google and Facebook, are among the most scalable. For SaaS companies like these that both sell and deliver their services online, handling a tenfold increase in the volume of users may be as simple as adding a few servers.

Any business can be made more scalable. Even if you don't aspire to create a Global 2000 multinational—even if you are content to remain a sole proprietorship indefinitely—increasing your profitability, cash flow, and scalability

- helps you grow your business more rapidly and efficiently, with less capital;

- gives you more options for responding to competitors who might try to encroach on your business, or to other changes in market conditions; or

- increases your value to potential investors or acquirers.

> *All great things have small beginnings.*
> *—Peter Senge*

TWO WAYS TO BECOME MORE SCALABLE

You can improve your scalability by

- **Improving your operational performance (execution).** This means managing your existing business processes more effectively, efficiently, and economically.

- **Adopting a more scalable business model.** This means satisfying the same or similar customer needs but not being constrained by the business processes you currently use.

To compare the two approaches, here are four examples of each:

Improve operational performance	Adopt a more scalable model
Streamline processing of purchase orders and generating invoices.	Eliminate purchase orders and invoices; take credit and debit cards.
Enable telesales reps to take more phone orders per day.	Let customers place their own orders online.
Enable tech support staff to handle more inquiries and cases per hour.	Incentivize, recognize, and certify customers to support each other.
Provide online city maps and fleet GPS data to a (human) expediter to better coordinate delivery vehicles.	Share pickup and drop-off information with all vehicles and let the fleet self-organize.

Improving operational performance and adopting a more scalable model are *better* and *different* ways of running your business, respectively. Some may discount operational performance as secondary to business model, but both are essential for optimizing overall scalability, as is shown in figure 24.2.

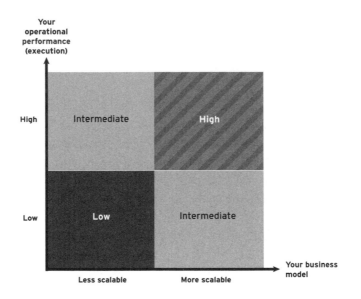

Figure 24.2

The actual level of scalability achieved depends on the operational performance and business model.

IMPROVING OPERATIONAL PERFORMANCE

Virtually every operational improvement enhances your growth potential. Metrics enable you to measure and manage operational performance. Here are some examples.

Operational Metrics

- **Average days outstanding of receivables:** Average number of days until customers pay your invoices

- **Returns:** Percent of units shipped that are returned

- **Inventory turnover ratio:** Net sales per average inventory at cost

- **Gross margin:** Gross profit (net sales minus variable costs) divided by net sales

- **Sales productivity:** Sales per account exec per year

- **Operating profit margin:** Operating profit (net sales minus variable costs minus fixed costs) divided by net sales

- **Working capital ratio:** Current assets (cash plus assets that can be sold for cash within twelve months) divided by current liabilities (debts which come due within the year)

- **Customer acquisition cost:** Average amount you spend to acquire each customer (sales, marketing, and advertising expense divided by number of customers acquired per period)

- **Customer satisfaction:** By touchpoint (e.g., website, customer service, account exec, installation, tech support) and by segment (e.g., demographics, technographics, and psychographics);[3] Overall satisfaction; Willingness to recommend; Net promoter score (NPS)

- **Burn rate:** Average cash consumed per month

- **Runway:** Cash reserves divided by average cash consumed per month

If on average you generate or consume $X in cash per month, did you generate or consume more or less this month? Find out what caused the changes so you can better manage them. If your accountant or tax advisor also serves other businesses, or you are a member of a local roundtable group of CEOs and founders, they may enable you to benchmark your performance—that is, compare it with that of other companies like yours. Table 24.1 suggests ways to improve your operational performance for several metrics.

Table 24.1. Ways to improve your metrics.	
Selected metrics	Possible ways to improve
Sales productivity	Instead of selling annual renewals, create evergreen subscriptions that renew automatically unless cancelled by customer.
Accounts receivable	–Offer customers discounts or rebates for immediate or timely payment. –Accept credit and debit cards.*
Inventories	Reduce inventory through on-demand manufacturing and tighter supply chain management.
Accounts payable	Approve expenses above specified thresholds depending on seniority of team member.
Profit margins	–Outsource nonstrategic functions to low-cost specialists. –Discontinue offerings with the lowest margins. –Raise prices.

*Despite their fees, accepting credit and debit cards can save you time and money (and make purchases easier for your customers) by minimizing cash handling, thus making you less vulnerable to theft and pilfering; eliminating the need for a credit department; and by reconciling payments, letting you focus on other aspects of managing and growing your business.

You saw in chapter 21 "Five Pricing Principles" that there is an optimal price range for your solution: Too low means not enough margin; too high means not enough demand. At either extreme, you limit or reduce net profit, cash flow, and scalability. Similarly, for a given business model, there is an optimal range of efficiency and economy. If your company is not lean enough, you never get very profitable; if you're too lean, you risk degrading the quality of your solution or losing valuable members of your workforce. As we saw in chapter 5 "Think Big; Start Focused" growing your venture is less like driving on a freeway and more like finding your way through a thick, steep, dark, rocky jungle with only a compass. Trial and error and experience help you sense the landscape and constantly move toward the ever-shifting optimal range.

Once you have reached what you believe are the optimal metrics ranges for managing your current operations, your best opportunities for further improvement are to identify and adopt a more scalable business model and processes, if possible.

ADOPTING A MORE SCALABLE MODEL

Capital Investments to Reduce Variable Costs

Capital investments—longer-term investments in areas such as physical plant, machinery, automation, and IT to improve productivity or increase capacity—are key to reducing your variable costs and increasing your gross margins and scalability. If you can then sell enough units to cover your higher fixed costs, you've made your business more scalable. Examples of such capital investments include the following:

- Automation to eliminate or enhance the productivity of manual labor

- IT systems that share customer and status information with team members and/or product or service information with customers, to streamline business processes and empower customers to serve themselves

- Software development to increase the intelligence of your solution—whether a home appliance, smartphone, drone, or stuffed bear—to deliver greater customer value at minimal additional variable cost

Around 2000, CustomerSat added a dozen popular statistics for each rating question in a client survey to our online reporting. One of our research consultants, Jose Ver, remarked that it saved him two days a month calculating the values manually, freeing him to provide more higher-value analysis and consulting for our clients. That is an example of automation eliminating and enhancing manual labor.

Example. In table 24.2 (upper left), your net sales (revenue after discounts) are $10 per unit. Before investing in automation or market expansion, you sell 10,000 units per quarter at a variable cost of $8/unit, with fixed costs of $10,000 per quarter, for a net profit after taxes of $8,000 per quarter.

Table 24.2. Income statements before and after investments in automation and market expansion.

		Before			Investment in automation (+$50,000 in fixed costs of operations) After	
	Before	Sell 10,000 units (at $10/unit)	$100,000		Sell 10,000 units (at $10/unit)	$100,000
		Less variable costs ($8/unit)	($80,000)		Less variable costs ($4/unit)	($40,000)
		Gross profit	$20,000		Gross profit	$60,000
		Less fixed costs	($10,000)	→	Less fixed costs	($60,000)
		Operating profit	$10,000		Operating profit	$0
		Less taxes	($2,000)		Less taxes	($0)
		Net profit	**$8,000**		Net profit	**$0**
		↓			↓	
Market expansion (+$10,000 in fixed costs of marketing)	**After**	Sell 20,000 units (at $10/unit)	$200,000		Sell 20,000 units (at $10/unit)	$200,000
		Less variable costs ($8/unit)	($160,000)		Less variable costs ($4/unit)	($80,000)
		Gross profit	$40,000		Gross profit	$120,000
		Less fixed costs	($20,000)	→	Less fixed costs	($70,000)
		Operating profit	$20,000		Operating profit	$50,000
		Less taxes	($4,000)		Less taxes	($10,000)
		Net profit	**$16,000**		Net profit	**$40,000**

Now suppose you can invest an additional $50,000 per quarter in automation—perhaps the operating, depreciation, and interest expenses for new equipment—and thereby reduce variable costs to $4/unit (upper right in table). If you still sell only 10,000 units per quarter, your net quarterly profit drops to zero, demonstrating the risk that capital investments pose for any entrepreneur.

But now let's say that if you invest an additional $10,000 per quarter in marketing (more fixed costs and risk), you can double your sales to 20,000 units (lower left in table). Without automation, your net profit after tax doubles from $8,000 to $16,000. Your after-tax profit margin— net profit after tax divided by net sales—is unchanged at 8 percent. In contrast, with automation and the same marketing investment, your net profit after tax and after-tax profit margin increase to $40,000 and 20 percent, respectively—two-and-a-half times as much as without automation (lower right in table), and five times the after-tax net profit you originally started with. You have made your business more scalable.

Your market needs to be large enough to make investments in scalability worthwhile, of course. If you serve a market of just ten thousand individuals worldwide, providing, say, a therapy for people with a rare disease, increasing production capacity to serve many more than that number of individuals won't help you.

Reengineer Your Business for Scalability

In their 1993 international best seller, *Reengineering the Corporation: A Manifesto for Business Revolution* (HarperCollins Business), Michael Hammer and Jim Champy advised managers to

1. analyze businesses not as sets of departments but as sets of cross-departmental business processes,

2. focus not on fixing old processes but on reengineering them, and

3. use information technology (IT) as a key enabler of reengineering.

One case study discussed in their book was the IBM Credit Corporation, which took a week to process applications for financing. The time was taken up by four groups of specialists, each supported by its own IT system, shuttling the applications back and forth. IBM Credit analyzed its processes and reengineered them by replacing these siloed specialists with generalists, each of whom handled applications from start to finish. Individuals in this newly defined role were supported by IT systems that combined all the information each of the four specialists previously had only separately. As a result, IBM Credit was able to reduce turnaround time from a week to four hours. Beyond improving customer satisfaction, these changes reduced the time required to bring new IBM Credit customers on board and the number of days until customers' first payments, improving cash flow. The change also enabled IBM Credit to handle many more customers with the same staff, improving scalability.

Reengineering the Corporation was written before commercial use of the Internet became widespread, and the book did not specifically focus on scalability. Nonetheless, its ideas and methods are as relevant today, and applicable to scalability, as they were over two decades ago. Technology is advancing ever faster, so periodically reexamining your business processes and the extent to which they leverage the latest IT is more important today than ever. Any business process that has remained unchanged for five years or longer probably uses outdated technology.

Table 24.3 offers examples of how three businesses could be reengineered for greater scalability given technologies available today or in the near future—the Internet, numerically controlled machine tools, and autonomous vehicles.

Customer Need	Business models		
	Less scalable ─────────────────────────────► More scalable		
Dating	Your professional matchmakers interview clients either by phone or in person to profile them; propose matches	Clients complete online profiles to indicate likes/dislikes; system matches clients with complementary profiles	Your solution accesses clients' Facebook and LinkedIn pages to profile them automatically and recommends matches with complementary profiles
Custom furniture	Skilled artisans handcraft furniture to clients' specifications	Clients design furniture online to fit their style and available space; pieces are created automatically using numerically controlled machine tools	Clients upload dimensions or floor plans of rooms and photos of furniture they would like to match; your solution drafts designs of pieces to fit clients' space and style; client reviews and fine-tunes designs; final pieces created using automated machine tools
Delivery services	Fleet of delivery vehicles and drivers	Partner with and certify drivers as contractors to drive their own vehicles	Autonomous vehicles (ground or air) pick up and make deliveries

Table 24.3. Scaling your business with technology.

Franchising

If your business is currently profitable; has a brand or trademark that has won customer loyalty and advocacy; and uses standardized, replicable, and teachable processes, then your business is a candidate for scaling through franchising. As franchisor (one who grants a franchise), you effectively license your successful business model and brand to other entrepreneurs. The franchisee, not you, makes the capital and other investments in buildings, staff, and operations, and absorbs the associated risk; you receive fees and royalties typically based on the franchisee's revenues. As a result, you can expand your business (usually geographically) with much less capital. Franchising has allowed McDonald's and Starbucks to grow rapidly around the world. Besides hamburgers and coffee shops, other categories that have scaled rapidly through franchising are listed next.

Popular Franchise Categories	Fast food
Accounting services	Fitness centers
Advertising and marketing	Hair salons
Automotive repair	Home improvement
Bakeries	Hotels
Business brokers	House cleaning
Car rental agencies	Ice cream parlors
Carpet cleaning	Internet cafes
Coffee shops	K–12 education
Commercial cleaners	Pet supplies
Commercial realtors	Printing
Convenience stores	Security services
Cosmetics	Senior care
Courier services	Tax preparation

In chapter 5 "Think Big; Start Focused," you saw how Shireen Yates of 6SensorLabs reengineered her business model for scalability at a very early stage. Shireen realized that creating a worldwide chain of bakeries to serve the millions of people with celiac disease would be costly, even with franchising. Instead, she and her cofounder developed a compact, portable device enabling anyone to test food for gluten. Selling a unique, lightweight device whose cost of goods (variable cost) is far less than its value to its target customers and that can economically be shipped anywhere in the world is a very scalable business.

Perhaps one day, 6SensorLabs will license its technology and design to other medical device manufacturers, and beyond that, charge customers a small fee to download the specs for the device and 3-D print it locally. Doing so will make 6SensorLabs even more scalable, akin to a SaaS company. Like choosing between hardcopy and e-books today, the choice of ordering product as atoms (hardware) or bits (software) will increasingly be up to the customer.

EXERCISES

1. Whether your current team consists of just you or many members, what tasks that either you or your team currently perform could you:

   - Delegate to another individual?

   - Automate?

   - Have customers perform on a self-service basis?

   - Outsource to another company?

2. Diagram your business processes as a series of steps, some in a series, some in parallel. Make a list of all possible paths from initial customer contact to solution delivery. Prioritize the paths from highest to lowest value to your business. Which paths and steps can you eliminate, automate, delegate, or outsource?

3. What is a business or industry that has not been widely franchised? What obstacles have kept it from doing so? How might applying new technologies sidestep those obstacles?

CORE LESSONS

- *Scalability* is the ability of your company to (1) generate increasing cash flow from operations for each additional dollar of capital invested, or (2) increase profit for each additional dollar of revenue.

- More scalable businesses are typically more highly automated, less labor intensive, and more information intensive, than their less scalable counterparts.

- You can improve your scalability either by improving operational performance (execution) or by adopting a more scalable business model.

- Capital investments are key to reducing your variable costs and increasing your gross margins and scalability.

- Use IT to reengineer business processes for greater scalability.

- Franchising can let you expand your business geographically with much less capital.

25

REGULATIONS:
THE HIDDEN ROADBLOCKS
TO YOUR SUCCESS

The end [purpose] of law is not to abolish
or restrain, but to preserve and enlarge freedom.
  —*John Locke*

Regulations are often inspired by noble ideals. Many, like driving on one side of the road, are beneficial; others are at least benign. Unfortunately, the regulations in this list and hundreds of thousands of others stifle entrepreneurship, innovation, or both:

- Texas requires every computer repair technician to get a private investigator's license.[1]

- Florida makes it illegal to buy or sell beer in 64-ounce reusable containers.

- Philadelphia requires anyone who receives any income reported on Internal Revenue Service (IRS) Form 1099 to purchase a "business privilege" license ($300).

- Nevada requires a license to teach how to apply makeup.

- Many cities prohibit online ride sharing (e.g., Uber and Lyft).

- New York City attempted (unsuccessfully) to ban the sale of many soft drinks in containers larger than 16 ounces.

Some regulation of economies and societies is necessary, healthy, and inescapable, as we see in the following pages. In contrast, the regulations above exist either to generate revenue for governments or their agencies through licenses, penalties, or exemptions; to impose our ideas of healthy living on others; or to protect politically important businesses or lobbying groups from competition. For example, the prohibition against 64-ounce containers protects major brewers against small craft breweries, and laws against ride-sharing services protect conventional cab companies.

What is the impact of regulations on entrepreneurship in general, and on your start-up in particular? What, if anything, can or should you do?

CASE STUDY 1: WORKER STATUS LAW

In 1992, when I started Decisive, you could freely hire a programmer or other contractor for as many hours or days per week as you could afford and as the individual was available. As your business grew, you could gradually increase the hours the contractor worked until you could afford to make him or her an employee. It made starting a cash-strapped business possible for a novice, first-time entrepreneur.

Today? It's much harder.

Today, complex and subjective rules govern whether any worker, even one working just a few hours a week, is considered a contractor or an employee. If deemed an employee, you must withhold income taxes, withhold and pay Social Security and Medicare taxes, pay unemployment taxes, and comply with countless other laws, rules and regulations. Each has its own myriad supporting documents and forms—for example, the six-page Form SS-8 and its instructions, "Determination of Worker Status for Purposes of Federal Employment Taxes and Income Tax Withholding."[2]

Satisfying the IRS that your worker is a contractor often requires a tax specialist or attorney, or having another firm hire the contractor as an employee and contract that person to you—a significant management burden and expense in either case. Worker status law reflects a focus on maximizing collectable taxes; none on business practicality or compliance costs.[3] For any entrepreneur, it is a costly hassle. For a first-time, cash-strapped entrepreneur, perhaps with limited skills or English proficiency? Probably overwhelming; possibly insurmountable. The solution is not more costly handholding or IRS customer service. Those do not scale and just cost taxpayers more. The right solution, as the IRS would be first to agree, is simpler regulation.

Unfortunately, the worker status example is just a drop in the ocean. Among many other US regulations that burden entrepreneurs are the Occupational Safety and Health Act (OSHA), environmental protection laws, equal opportunity, the Americans with Disabilities Act (ADA), tax liens,[4] minimum wages, and the "Affordable" Care Act (ACA)[5] to name a few. Added to these are myriad industry-specific, state, and local regulations. Regulations are rarely eliminated; they accumulate and grow. The 2012 Code of Federal Regulations' 174,545 pages increased by over 21 percent in a decade, according to the Congressional Research Service.[6] The Internal Revenue Service itself cites a 2008 report indicating that the number of pages in the tax code had more than tripled since 1975.[7]

REGULATIONS OPPOSE THE TREND

In most respects, starting a company has become easier in the past two decades, thanks to technology:

- Many more products and services exist today than twenty years ago, creating many more customer needs that entrepreneurs can satisfy, more niches that start-ups can occupy, and more opportunities for unique specialization and differentiation.

- Technical, communication, and other skills can be learned free through online courses.

- Software platforms have become more functional and smarter, enabling start-ups to do more with fewer developers.

- Many general-purpose, small-business services (e.g., accounting, customer scheduling, and online marketing) can now be automated online at low cost or free of charge, off-loading these tasks from entrepreneurs and allowing them to focus instead on what they do best.

- Geographically separated teams can more easily collaborate.

- Customers for niche solutions, suppliers for unique components, and collaborators who share your passions are all easier to find through online search tools.

- Entrepreneurs generally need less funding to get started, and can more easily identify and qualify funding sources.

Only regulations have made starting and growing a business harder. The regulations that most burden entrepreneurs vary widely by industry, type of business, and start-up. Here are some candidates for the United States:

Industry or Business Type	Most Onerous Regulations: Candidates
Software development	Limit on number of allowed H-1B visas
Medical devices	Food and drug
Construction	Occupational health and safety
Aerial vehicles	Federal aviation
Self-driving vehicles	Transportation
Real estate	Zoning; environmental protection
Delivery services	Transportation; municipal laws
Employ many teenagers	Minimum wage laws

In less regulated industries such as software and games, the biggest risks and uncertainties your business faces are the ones we cover in chapters 1–24: changing customer needs, demand, technologies, and competition. But in more regulated industries like financial services and health care, and increasingly in all industries, you not only have to become knowledgeable of current regulations but also make guesses about their probable momentum and direction. The biggest risks and uncertainties you face are likely to be the regulations themselves.

REGULATIONS DETER ENTREPRENEURSHIP AND EMPLOYMENT

Regulations deter entrepreneurship in at least three ways. Here are examples of each:

- **Getting started:** About one-third of US workers now require licenses to pursue their chosen occupations.[8] For example, over half of US states require a license to braid hair, a simple and safe practice dating back thousands of years. In some cases, braiders—many of them young black women who can ill afford the expense—must take irrelevant courses in cosmetology costing thousands of dollars.[9]

- **Innovation:** Start-up research and development budgets go not into innovation but increasingly to compliance with regulations that are often outdated. Until recently, restaurants and commercial kitchen ventilation suppliers had to comply with 1950s regulations that long predated demand ventilation and solid-state controls.[10]

- **Expansion:** Zoning and building codes raise costs of offices, warehouses, and factories. The Americans with Disabilities Act can require facilities to accommodate the disabled even if the requirements make no sense (e.g., wheelchair-compliant restrooms in the upper floors of buildings that don't have or require elevators). Many conditions of the Affordable Care Act (ACA) kick in when a company reaches fifty or one hundred employees.

Define any metric that you wish of potential entrepreneurs that combines ratings of such qualities as skill, passion, perseverance, self-confidence, ambition, and resources. Your metric will distribute the entrepreneurs along a curve, perhaps like the bell-shaped series of bars in figure 25.1. No matter how you define your metric, many potential entrepreneurs, especially at the low end of your rating scale, are being blocked by regulations. The numbers blocked each decade grow as regulations grow. The very men and women in society who find it hardest to provide for themselves and their families and live in self-sufficient dignity are blocked.

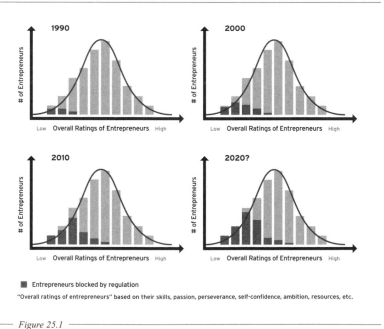

■ Entrepreneurs blocked by regulation

"Overall ratings of entrepreneurs" based on their skills, passion, perseverance, self-confidence, ambition, resources, etc.

Figure 25.1

As regulations grow, so does the number of blocked entrepreneurs.

According to a 2012 study of the US Census Bureau Longitudinal Business Database,[11] the number of new businesses created for every 10,000 working-age Americans has declined from approximately twenty-seven in the 1980s to twenty-five in the 1990s to twenty-two in the 2000s. Using data from the Bureau of Labor Statistics, the study also showed that the percentage of working-age Americans who are self-employed dropped by 13.6 percent from 1994 to 2011. As a percentage of all businesses, new firms dropped from 16 percent in 1977 to less than 8 percent in 2010.

These downward trends also affect employment. Start-ups provide jobs for both their founders and their employees, and an important few start-ups grow into sizable businesses. According to the US Small Business Administration (SBA), businesses with fewer than 500 employees create 64 percent of net new private-sector jobs.[12] The SBA also noted that key to job creation is not company size but youth—how recently the business was founded.[13] Older firms, whether large or small, tend to have stable headcounts; most of their growth comes from acquiring younger companies. It is the young firms that create jobs. But those firms are a rough and tumble lot: over half of start-ups go out of business within five years. Net job growth comes from the survivors. When fewer start-ups are being created, fewer survive, and job growth suffers. Given these trends, it's not surprising that the United States has stubborn unemployment.

REGULATIONS STIFLE INNOVATION AND REDUCE QUALITY OF LIFE

Here are two examples from the US Food and Drug Administration (FDA) alone.

Pharmaceuticals

The US Food and Drug Administration (FDA) has many incentives to withhold drugs and little incentive to approve them other than to mitigate the inevitable public outcry. A single death from an allowed drug subjects the FDA to criticism and embarrassment. But as long as a particular drug's use is not allowed, victims can't see how their lives are degraded in quality or unnecessarily cut short without access to it. Many of those thousands with life-threatening illnesses whose life the drug could save would, given the choice, very willingly take the drug even with its known risks. In 1990, Louis Lasagna, chairman of a presidential advisory panel on drug approval, estimated that thousands of lives were lost each year due to FDA delays in approval and marketing of drugs for cancer and AIDS. Indeed, it was public outcry that finally forced the FDA to approve those life-saving drugs.[14]

Medical Devices

Most US start-ups developing medical devices that require FDA Pre-market Approval (PMA) now sell their products first in Europe where CE mark[15] compliance is easier and faster to achieve.[16] As a result, Europeans enjoy earlier access to US medical technology than Americans, and the European medical device industry gains a home-field advantage. American consumers and industry all suffer.[17]

CASE STUDY 2: RENFE, SPAIN'S STATE-OWNED RAILWAY VERSUS ALSA AUTOBUS

In 2014, my friend Wojtek and I traveled from San Roque to Granada, a four-hour journey, on Renfe, Spain's state-owned railway. Our train had no services other than two vending machines and no Wi-Fi, so we spent the time looking out the window and dozing. It was like stepping back in time. Renfe was created with the nationalization of Spain's railroads in 1941. It seemed like little had changed since then.

Two days later, after visiting the magnificent Alhambra, we needed to travel again from Granada to Madrid. We were about to pay eighty euros per seat to reserve two seats on Renfe, when we heard about Alsa Autobus. This privately owned bus service took the same length of time, four and a half hours, as Renfe. But every passenger enjoyed a personal entertainment screen with choices of movies, music, and news. Wi-Fi allowed us to send and receive email and text messages. We could even follow our route with an interactive map, great for visitors like us. The best part: Alsa was only forty-two euros per seat from Granada to

Madrid, half as much as the same route on the Renfe nationalized railroad. Needless to say, we chose Alsa Autobus. In addition to everything else, *twice* during the four-and-a-half-hour trip, the hostess came by with free snacks, coffee, tea, and juice. Much nicer than the two vending machines on Renfe.

But the differences didn't stop there. The Renfe website appeared at first to give you a choice of Spanish, English, French, or Catalan. But after you selected your desired departure and destination and left the home page, the entire online reservation process reverted to Spanish. So you didn't really have a choice of languages at all. I call that marketing theatre. I asked our hotel receptionist for help, who told us about Alsa, which offers a choice of seven languages for the entire reservation process. For my part, I can't wait for my next journey on Alsa Autobus and hope I don't have to take Renfe again.

As an extreme form of regulation—a government-run monopoly— Renfe is insulated from market forces. It doesn't have to compete to survive. In contrast, a privately owned business like Alsa has to compete with other service providers to affordably deliver quality customer service and satisfaction. It must also provide shareholders a reasonable return on their investments, or it will be sold, restructured, or go out of business. In addition, state-owned Renfe is losing money, despite its monopoly, and is very much in debt. Citizens of Spain, the EU, or both will ultimately pay for its losses through higher taxes, debasement of the euro's value, or a combination of the two. In contrast to the cheaper Alsa Autobus who is paying taxes, state-owned Renfe is consuming tax revenues.

Railroads were advanced technology in the nineteenth century. Not so in the twenty-first. In very few years, compact, lightweight, self-driving electric taxis (see Case Study 3) will pick us up on demand at our points of origin and deliver us directly to our destinations.[18] No stations, schedules, unclean restrooms, or surly Amtrak employees.[19] Similarly, self-driving trucks will safely and quickly pick up, load, deliver, and unload cargo with no humans required. If these vehicles need parking, they will simply seek and find it wherever available. Many such transport providers will share the existing highway infrastructure. The required investment will be orders of magnitude less than that for railroads, enabling lots of suppliers (perhaps even you and me) to compete to provide the best service at the lowest prices. Renfe and Amtrak empower their respective governments: They centralize planning, control, and spending. But when compared to self-driving vehicles, railroads, with their inflexible schedules and itineraries, are unintelligent, capital consuming, and deficit generating. No conventional railroad, high-speed or otherwise, should be built in North America or Europe at public expense again.

THE BETTER LIFE POSSIBLE WITH LESS REGULATION IS MOSTLY INVISIBLE

Regulations are insidious: Only under special circumstances such as natural experiments can we see how negatively they affect the quality of our lives. Examples of natural experiments are arbitrary divisions of common regions and people as in the former East and West Germany, or North and South Korea. Starting with substantially the same resources as their repressed counterparts but with much greater freedom, West Germany and South Korea flourished while their counterparts stagnated or regressed. No one would choose to live as people did in the former East Germany or in North Korea today.

Occasionally we can glimpse other examples as well, such as between Renfe and Alsa Autobus, or between the US Postal Service (like Renfe, sustaining a huge deficit despite its government-protected monopoly) on one hand and FedEx or UPS on the other. But most of the time, we can't see how much state and federal regulation negatively affects our quality of life, because there is no choice, no visible alternative, no experimental control. As Bastiat said, how much better we could be living *is unseen*.[20] So please, whenever anyone suggests that a product, service, or industry—education, health care, transportation, communications, banking, you name it—should be further regulated or worse, nationalized, very deliberately think of East versus West Germany, North versus South Korea, Renfe versus Alsa Autobus, or the US Postal Service.

ORGANIC VERSUS IMPOSED REGULATION

Federal and state statutes and regulations rest on top of other regulatory layers already pervasive and deeply ingrained in societies and economies: social customs, markets, private agreements, and, where applicable, common law. I call these under layers *organic* regulation:

- Customs arise bottom-up from myriad social interactions.

- Markets emerge from buyers and sellers seeking, finding, and exchanging (i.e., self-organizing for mutual benefit) with one another.

- Common laws coevolve with society over decades and centuries.[21]

In contrast, I refer to federal and state statutes, regulatory agency requirements, and executive orders as *imposed* regulations to highlight their distinction from organic. They reflect a top-down civil law tradition and the objectives of governments, which may differ from those of the people the government is nominally serving. Table 25.1 offers a comparison of these two forms of regulation.

Common law originated in the United Kingdom in medieval times but has roots dating back to the Magna Carta (1215), which limited the rights of the Crown. In the common law tradition, independent judges and courts of law look for and select precedents for resolving disputes and enforcing contracts. If no precedent applies, judges are authorized to make law—define resolutions that best suit circumstances—and thereby establish precedents.

Table 25.1. Organic and Imposed Regulation: Traditions and Features (Legal, Social, and Economic)			
		Organic	Imposed
Traditions		Common law	Civil law
		Distributed (judges and juries)	Centralized (legislatures)
		Dispute-resolving*	Policy-implementing*
		-Not codified** -Evolutionary	-Codified** -Designed
Features		**Organic**	**Imposed**
Legal	Source of Law	Judges and juries looking to precedent	-Legislators (statutes) -Regulatory agencies -Executive orders
	Focus of Law	-Torts*** -"Persons, property, and promises (i.e., agreements)"	Comprehensive (anticipating and covering all cases)
Social		-Custom-based -Emergent	-Directive-based -Prescribed
Economic		-Supply and demand -Word of mouth -Positive (what is)	-Wage and price controls -Government subsidies -Normative (how authorities believe things should be)

*This characterization of common versus civil law is attributable to Mirjan Damaska, *The Faces of Justice and State Authority* (Yale University Press, 1986).
**Civil law is codified, (i.e., legislators and legal scholars continuously draft, update, and interpret compilations of the law). Common law is generally uncodified and captured through series of precedents based on real-world cases.
***Tort laws cover negligence (e.g., accidents), willful misconduct (e.g., assault, fraud, and theft), and strict liability (harming someone through a defective product).

If higher courts concur, a resolution can become the law of the land. Over the last two centuries, the United Kingdom, United States, Canada (except Quebec), Australia, New Zealand, South Africa, and Hong Kong have inherited English common law traditions.

In contrast, most of continental Europe, including France, Spain, and

Germany, has followed civil law traditions. Dating back to Roman times, emperors and legislatures provided rules for judges to follow. In the early nineteenth century, Napoleon initiated a comprehensive codification of civil law in France that brought clarity and consistency to the law and nullified much prior law. Codification helped Napoleon consolidate power. Judges became administrators who did not make law but merely applied it to the facts of cases. The influence of the Napoleonic Code led to civil law being adopted throughout much of Europe and later the world, particularly through the colonies of continental European powers.

I characterize civil law as a layer "on top of" common law, because common law closely fits the complex systems nature of societies and economies in ways that civil law does not. In complex systems, order and patterns emerge from the bottom up, not by top-down design. In societies and economies, for example, social interactions give rise to customs, and buyers and sellers give rise to wages and prices.[22] Both societies and economies are dynamic, never at equilibrium. They evolve, usually unpredictably: Imperceptible changes and developments today can have major impacts tomorrow.

The open-ended, uncodified nature of common law fits these dynamics well. Common law allows for variation (by thousands of judges) and selection (by other judges and higher courts),[23] and thus evolves, as do societies and economies. Common law is bound to reality through real-world cases. Distributing influence among thousands of judges not only enables laws to reflect and track evolving customs and technology; it makes it harder to corrupt the system as a whole. Noted author Nassim Nicholas Taleb calls common law "antifragile."[24] In the words of US Supreme Court Justice Oliver Wendell Holmes Jr., "The life of the [common] law has not been logic; it has been experience."[25]

In contrast, legislators and legal scholars codifying civil laws may be distant in space and time from people to whom and customs to which the law is applied. If top-down policy competes with or trumps fair and equitable outcomes, judges and their litigants have little power to resist. Imposed regulations extend to economics, of course, and include controls that limit buyers' and sellers' ability to self-organize for mutual benefit. For example, minimum wage laws can preclude managers from affording and hiring employees who would eagerly accept lower wages, an outcome that is disadvantageous to managers and employees alike. The variation and selection that enable common law to evolve with economies and societies are mostly absent in civil law. Finally, having one central decision-making body provides a single point of vulnerability to corruption.

Not surprisingly, given these factors, multiple studies have correlated technological innovation and economic growth with use of common law.[26] In *A Concise History of the Common Law*,[27] Theodore Plucknett credits common law with facilitating the Industrial Revolution. Innovations in early nineteenth-century England, such as contract and bankruptcy law and shares of jointly owned enterprises, enabled the large capital investments that machinery and steam power required. In "The Economic Consequences of Legal Origins," La Porta, Lopez-de-Silanes, and Shleifer note,

> Compared to French civil law, common law is associated with
>
> - better investor protection, which in turn is associated with improved financial development, better access to finance, and higher ownership dispersion;
>
> - lighter government ownership and regulation, which are in turn associated with less corruption, better functioning labor markets, and smaller unofficial economies; and
>
> - less formalized and more independent judicial systems, which are in turn associated with more secure property rights and better contract enforcement.[28]

Sadly, in the last two centuries, all "common law" countries, including the United Kingdom and United States, have made increasing use of statutory (i.e., civil) law. For France to adopt anything resembling

British common law would be as likely as the French suddenly preferring British to French cuisine. Judge-made precedent governs a declining proportion of litigation worldwide.[29] Beyond all their other limitations, civil law and imposed regulations have one more downside: unintended consequences.

UNINTENDED CONSEQUENCES OF IMPOSED REGULATIONS

Unintended consequences arise when regulations attempt to restrict or force interactions that are different from what people would voluntarily choose or agree to. Following are some examples:

- If minimum wages are set too high, employers reduce their use of labor, accelerate their use of automation and robots, or outsource jobs to companies overseas. We see minimum wage laws, for example, creating high teenage unemployment throughout much of North America and Europe.

- If the US Affordable Care Act imposes costs on businesses for employees working thirty or more hours per week, owners will convert formerly full-time employees to part time (bad for businesses and employees alike).

- If taxes on alcohol or cigarettes are too high, black markets in these goods arise.

- If the FAA unduly restricts testing and export of unmanned aerial vehicles (UAVs), US manufacturers will move to Canada, Australia, or other countries with markets less hamstrung by regulations, or lose global market share to non-US competitors.

Imposing more elaborate and complex regulations to plug loopholes does not eliminate unintended consequences. Just the opposite. Game theory tells us that any set of rules can be gamed, and adding rules simply creates more opportunities for gaming. The more complex and subjective the regulations, the more benefit gained by the few who are adequately funded (to afford the best legal teams, the most protracted legal wrangling, or bribery); suitably connected; and sufficiently influential to either seek and win favorable interpretations or exemptions, or discover further loopholes and determine how best to leverage and exploit them.

Attempting to block loopholes creates ever more labyrinthine laws that further advantage the funded, connected, and influential. That is not the answer. The only sustainable solution: fewer, simpler, and less obtrusive laws.

CASE STUDY 3: SELF-DRIVING CARS, UNMANNED AERIAL VEHICLES, DANGEROUS ANIMALS, PEEPING TOMS

Imposed regulations rely on penalties and prohibitions that discourage or disallow experimentation and innovation. In contrast, organic regulation relies on liability and responsibility, thus allowing experimentation and encouraging innovation while at the same time providing protections from harm to others.

THE IMPOSED APPROACH

Self-driving cars and commercial unmanned aerial vehicles (UAVs or "drones") are today illegal in the United States except under very restricted circumstances. Self-driving cars are disallowed in all but four states and the District of Columbia as of this writing and even those states require a human "driver" present. This is despite the cars' far superior driving records to humans': Self-driving cars don't get tired, distracted, intoxicated, or fall asleep.

Federal Aviation Administration (FAA) regulations for UAVs are even more restrictive. At this writing, they can fly only:

- well away from airports,

- up to 400 feet in altitude,

- within visual sight of their operators,

- during daylight hours, and

- for noncommercial purposes.

In effect, this limits allowed UAVs to hobbyists.[30] Limiting UAVs to within sight of their operators and during daylight hours discourages innovators from developing UAV capabilities such as

- recognizing airborne objects like birds, kites, and other drones;

- extrapolating the positions of those objects and moving quickly to avoid them; and

- if the objects are other drones, communicating with them to avoid collision.

Prohibitions limiting drone operations to within visual sight of operators, during daylight hours, and for noncommercial purposes together preclude real-world customer testing of business models for services such as aerial delivery of pharmaceuticals, spare parts, and electrical components.

These imposed regulations are reducing quality of life for hundreds of thousands of people—especially the handicapped; those in remote, inaccessible locations; those whose mobility is restricted due to natural disasters such as earthquakes; and extreme sports enthusiasts—not to mention businesses and hobbies like filmmaking, farming, and construction.

A drone manufacturer cannot even legally buy isolated private land in the United States to test drones, for example, to keep proprietary designs confidential. Drone manufacturers are allowed to conduct tests only at one of the FAA's public testing sites. Given these imposed regulations, it is hardly surprising that the top worldwide manufacturer of nonmilitary drones today is not US based but Chinese: Shenzhen-based

DJI Technology Company. DJI's drones are used for—you guessed it—filmmaking, farming, construction, extreme sports, and even finding earthquake survivors.

THE ORGANIC APPROACH

In contrast, organic regulation of self-driving cars and UAVs might look to precedents such as the liability and responsibility of the owners of dangerous animals[31] and to "Peeping Tom" laws. Common laws have long held owners responsible for controlling or restraining dangerous animals to protect other people. Owners of self-driving cars and UAVs that destroyed others' property or hurt or killed another person would be similarly responsible. Peeping Tom laws make it a crime to secretly peep into a room occupied by another person, or to secretly photograph or video that person or room. Such laws could apply to drones as well. To address negligence, willful misconduct, or strict liability (harming someone through a defective product) in the use of self-driving cars and UAVs, common law would likely provide for

- fines or imprisonment of the owners of irresponsible, invasive, or malicious self-driving cars or UAVs;

- owners being able to hold irresponsible manufacturers responsible; and

- the use of interceptor UAVs to defend life, property, and privacy from invasive or malicious UAVs.

Watch how rapidly common law alone—while protecting life, property, and privacy—fosters industry-wide advances in the intelligence, safety, and usefulness of self-driving cars and UAVs.

In a recent report on self-driving cars, the Rand Corporation noted, "Aggressive policymaker intervention is premature and would probably do more harm than good."[32]

Innovation requires freedom, and with freedom comes responsibility. We need to let entrepreneurs be free to innovate and take risks, but to hold them responsible if and when they harm life and property. Progress without risk taking is impossible.

> *[Common law] is a vast, continuous, and spontaneous*
> *collaboration between judges and the judged to discover*
> *the people's will in a series of real-world court cases—*
> *a collaboration like that among all the participants in a*
> *free market . . . The law is not legislated and enacted,*
> *but discovered.*
> *—Bruno Leoni*

VISUALIZING REGULATIONS

Let's see graphically the effects of imposed regulations. Say that five years ago, in some aspect of life, perhaps your health or the airspace above and around your home, what you are allowed to do by law was bounded by a new regulation, as in figure 25.2.

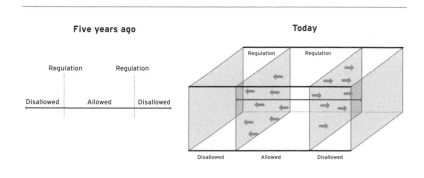

Figure 25.2

The regulatory environment—five years ago and today

321

Now fast-forward five years to the present. Regulations stay fixed while advances in knowledge, technology, and cooperation enable more dimensions of human needs to be satisfied that the regulations also preclude. During that time, perhaps, innovation has enabled intelligent UAVs, or Uber and Lyft crowdsourced taxi services, or neurogaming helmets with sensors that detect your emotional state and incorporate it into game play. What had previously been a single dimension of possibilities excluded by regulation is now many dimensions of human needs disallowed by those same regulations.

But these figures oversimplify the situation. The actual situation is far worse. The regulations are not clear, flat boundaries between what is allowed and disallowed but irregular and complex surfaces.

The longer, more complex, and subjective the regulation, the more irregular, complex, and blurry the surfaces. These surfaces take more time and money to explore and comprehend, and as we have seen, impart more advantage to the well funded and well connected.

There are hundreds of thousands of start-ups in mobile apps but relatively few in pharmaceuticals, aviation, construction, consumer banking, and medical devices. Why? Because mobile apps are less regulated. Regulations raise barriers to entry, strengthen the agencies that administer them, further entrench the positions of existing players, and increase the capital required of new market entrants. Deliberately or otherwise, entrepreneurs avoid more regulated industries in favor of less regulated industries.

Over 100,000 mobile apps compete today in the health and fitness segment (figure 25.3).[33] Few of these crowded apps will survive. If even a fraction of these entrepreneurs could be freed to address myriad opportunities in pharmaceuticals, aviation, construction, consumer banking, or medical devices, those fields would see much more rapid advances and humanity would be far ahead of where it is today.

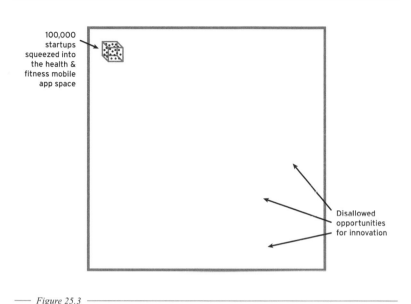

100,000
startups
squeezed into
the health &
fitness mobile
app space

Disallowed
opportunities
for innovation

—— *Figure 25.3* ——————————————————————

Regulations crowd companies.

THE UNITED STATES IS LOSING GROUND

The World Bank annually reports its Ease of Doing Business Index for approximately 189 countries and regions around the globe. The index measures how easy or hard it is for a local entrepreneur to open and run a small to medium-sized business when complying with relevant regulations. It measures and tracks changes in regulations affecting eleven areas in the life cycle of a business (see table 25.2). A favorable ease of doing business overall ranking (i.e., a low rank, starting with 1) means the regulatory environment is conducive to starting and operating a business in that country or region.

Table 25.2. World Bank Ease of Doing Business Index.

Index component	Criteria
1. Starting a business	Procedures, time, cost, minimum capital required to open business
2. Dealing with construction permits	Procedures, time, and cost to obtain construction permits, inspections, and utility connections
3. Getting electricity	Applications and contracts with electricity utilities, all necessary inspections and clearances from the utility and other agencies until the external and final connection works
4. Registering property	Procedures, time, and cost to transfer commercial real estate
5. Getting credit	Strength of legal rights index, depth of credit information index
6. Protecting minority investors	Strength of investor protection index: extent of disclosure index, extent of director liability index, and ease of shareholder suits index
7. Paying taxes	Number of tax payments, time to prepare and file tax returns and to pay taxes, total taxes as a share of profit before all taxes borne
8. Trading across borders	Documents, time, and cost to export and import
9. Enforcing contracts	Procedures, time, and cost to resolve a commercial dispute
10. Resolving insolvency	The time, cost, and outcome of insolvency proceedings involving domestic entities
11. Employing workers	Rigidity of employment index, redundancy costs

Sadly, the United States has declined on these metrics over the last decade in overall ranking from 3 to 7 (figure 25.4). In 2015, the United States has been surpassed in the World Bank's Ease of Doing Business ranking by Singapore, New Zealand, Hong Kong, Denmark, South Korea, and Norway.[34]

A great and worthy goal for the United States to regain its freedom and leadership in innovation and global competitiveness—a goal that I believe is both aggressive and achievable—would be to return to the #3 or #4 rank by the year 2020. And then to #1 by 2025.

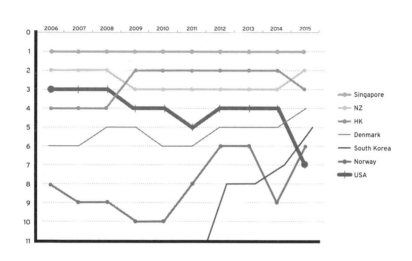

—— *Figure 25.4* ——

US ease of doing business is deteriorating rapidly.

Note: World Bank 2015 Rankings.

RECOMMENDATIONS

For the vast majority of the thousands of regulations you face, your best strategy will simply be to swallow your indignity and comply with them. Most will not be worth the time, cost, or hassle of challenging them. Beyond that, here are some specific suggestions.

Delegate or Outsource

As noted earlier in the chapter, you can hire experts or service providers to deal with much regulation, for example, contract with third-party firms to hire and pay contractors, payroll firms to handle payroll and deductions, accounting firms to handle taxes and filings, attorneys to handle articles of incorporation and stock purchase agreements, or you can rent or lease space in established office buildings to avoid dealing with building and zoning permits.

Seek Workarounds

If regulations disallow you from erecting a stationary structure, for example, can you add wheels and turn the structure into an allowed vehicle? Conversely, if a vehicle is disallowed, can you remove the wheels and turn it into an allowed stationary structure?

Seemingly bizarre practices may be workarounds to unseen regulations. For example, Ford Motor Company installs unneeded seats and windows to turn vans it manufactures in Turkey into passenger vehicles, only to rip them out and recycle them when the vehicles are imported to the United States. Doing so costs Ford hundreds of dollars per vehicle in materials and labor, but saves the company thousands of dollars per vehicle in taxes. US import tariffs leftover from a 1963 trade spat with Europe are 25 percent for delivery vans. The tariffs are a comparatively low 2.5 percent for passenger vehicles.[35]

If regulations are arcane, trivial, vague, blatantly unfair, or far out of date, no one may care or notice if you proceed in spite of them. But doing so can be risky; you could have to cease and desist from the practice, which might mean having to write off an investment; pay penalties; or go to court, pay fines, and get a criminal record. If you are uncertain, spending money on legal counsel today could save you much more in costs and hassle later on.

Choose Your Best Jurisdiction

If you know that your start-up will push up against regulatory boundaries such as with drones, self-driving cars, or biotech, assess the regulatory environment in the jurisdiction—county, state, or country—where you are considering founding your company. If the environment seems particularly burdensome and you are able to move, consider other jurisdictions. If you are in North America, consider Utah, North Dakota, or

Canada. If you are in Paris, consider London.[36] If you are anywhere in Europe, consider Ireland. If you are in Asia, consider Hong Kong. If you are in the Southern Hemisphere, consider New Zealand.

Consult with Entrepreneur Advocacy Groups

For example, the Institute for Justice (www.ij.org) helps defend entrepreneurs from regulations that block them from earning a living. Avail yourself of their resources and support them.

Leverage Social Media to Fight and Overturn the Regulation

As a Mother's Day present, nine-year-old Spencer Collins of Leawood, Kansas built a "Little Free Library" (littlefreelibrary.org)—a birdhouse-like bookcase on a post in his family's front yard through which neighbors could lend and borrow books for free. The Leawood City Council determined that the little library violated an ordinance disallowing detached structures such as sheds and above-ground pools in the residential community. As a result, Spencer's father created a Facebook page for the library that generated over 30,000 responses and a national outcry. At a city council meeting, Spencer told the council, "I want you to allow little free libraries because I love to read. Lots of people in the neighborhood used the library, and the books were always changing. I think it's good for Leawood."[37] The town council excepted little libraries from the ordinance. If a nine-year-old can marshal forces and successfully overturn a regulation, so can you.

Become an Advocate

Advocate policies and legislation that make the modern regulatory state more resilient, humane, and friendly to start-ups. Appendix E proposes seven ways to do so.

> *It is seldom that liberty of any kind is lost all at once.*
> *—David Hume*

26

THE ETHICS OF ENTREPRENEURSHIP:
MAKING THE WORLD MORE POSITIVE-SUM AND ABUNDANT

Capitalism takes more people out of poverty than aid.
  —Bono

"Ethical" usually means a person is honest, respectful, law-abiding, compassionate, and caring. Using this definition, which I like and aspire to, I see entrepreneurs as no more or less ethical as people in other fields. But I do believe that entrepreneurs are nonetheless a uniquely ethical bunch for an entirely different reason. Entrepreneurs create new positive-sum opportunities where only zero-sum, negative-sum, or no opportunities existed before. And that makes everyone better off.

WHAT ARE ZERO-, NEGATIVE-, AND POSITIVE-SUM?

Zero-sum means that any gains by one party in a transaction or interaction are equal to the losses by the other party or parties. One sports team wins, the other loses; one gambler wins the pot, the others lose.[1] The size of the "pie" is fixed: The only way to get more is for someone else to get less. In contrast, positive-sum means that all parties are better off. Value is created; the pie grows. Negative-sum means that the parties are worse off. Value is destroyed; the pie shrinks.

Wars are generally negative-sum, given the costs of lives, injuries, weapons, damage, and dislocations to both sides. Positive-sum exchanges are less conspicuous. For example

- any voluntary exchange such as a trade, purchase, or sale in which both sides perform as committed. If the exchange were not positive-sum, the parties would have no incentive to make the exchange,

- fruitful collaboration such as between you and your cofounder (chapter 12 "1 + 1 = 3"),

- any warm, loving, supportive relationship between two people, or

- contests in which one individual or team wins and others lose are zero-sum as far as rankings are concerned: If one advances in the ranks, others must fall behind. Only one can be ranked first, so that position is a scarce resource. But more broadly, if the losing players don't mind losing, enjoyed playing, and feel they became stronger, that is positive-sum: All players are better off.

Zero-sum matchups like the Super Bowl and World Series attract millions of viewers, and negative-sum conflicts like wars make international news. Positive-sum interactions, though greater in number—people are naturally incentivized to seek and engage in them—rarely make headlines. Conflict, not cooperation, rivets our attention. Two requirements for positive-sum exchanges are (1) communication between the parties to agree on what is exchanged, and (2) trust—that is, confidence that the other party will do what it says. Lose commitment and trust, and positive-sum exchanges either don't occur or become zero- or negative-sum.

ADAM SMITH RULES

The amount of mutual gain from any positive-sum interaction or transaction may be tiny. But add up billions of such exchanges every day among the billions of people on earth over the centuries, and you hugely advance the well-being of humanity.[2] Two hundred and fifty years ago, Adam Smith, a trenchant observer of humankind, recognized five requirements to sustain these advances:[3]

- **Free trade:** To ensure that transactions can take place

- **Light regulation:** Again to ensure that transactions can take place

- **Light taxes:** So taxes don't eliminate incentives for positive-sum interactions

- **Protection of private property:** To incentivize people to preserve and invest in what they own to enhance its value to them or to trade with others

- **Sound currency:** So the parties know what they are offering and receiving[4]

I call these the "Adam Smith Rules."[5] Smith (figure 26.1) didn't speak of positive feedback loops—he used the phrase "invisible hand" instead—but they arise again here among the parties of positive-sum interactions who seek or welcome such interactions, and engage in ever more of them with more and more people.

Figure 26.1

"Big Adam" Smith (1723–1790). He da man!

ENTREPRENEURSHIP AND POSITIVE-SUM EXCHANGES

Successful entrepreneurship, as with all voluntary interactions, is a series of positive-sum exchanges. No one has to buy your start-up's product or service. Just the opposite: Others have every reason to buy from someone already in business with an established reputation. To make that first sale, you have to work hard to provide value and satisfy the customer need. To make the second sale, you have to make certain the first customer is satisfied (word gets out). If you stop satisfying customers, they will go elsewhere.

The positive-sum exchanges are not just with your customers. It costs many times more to attract and train new team members than it does to retain existing ones. You have to continuously create win-wins to keep good team members. Otherwise, they will go elsewhere too.

But it doesn't stop there. Suppliers, investors, and potential partners don't have to deal with you, either. To succeed as an entrepreneur, you have to create positive-sum interactions with all your stakeholders.

Most people engage in positive-sum interactions every day. That's good. But entrepreneurs go further: They create *new* solutions that satisfy new customer needs. That makes the world more positive-sum in new ways and expands options and opportunities for everyone. To see how, let's go back a couple of million years to early caveman. Or maybe just fifty years to the popular 1960s animated sitcom, *The Flintstones*.

CAVEMAN ECONOMIES

Imagine an economy with just three individuals—Wilma, Barney, and Dino—and just one "product," meat. The line in the upper left of figure 26.2 represents this one-dimensional economy that satisfies a single human need, hunger. It is cold, the individuals lack tools, and hunting small rodents is their only option for survival. Since there are no other products, the only trading they might do is meat today for meat tomorrow. Frequent attempts to steal another hunter's food lead to fighting, injuries, or even death (negative-sum).

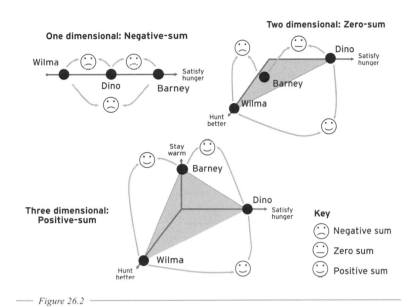

One dimensional: Negative-sum

Two dimensional: Zero-sum

Three dimensional: Positive-sum

— *Figure 26.2* —

Caveman economies.

When Wilma invents a trap to hunt rodents (upper right of figure 26.2), the economy has now expanded from a one-dimensional line to a two-dimensional "plane" that satisfies two human needs, hunger and hunting effectiveness. The three individuals now have some options: each one can hunt, make traps, trade meat and traps, or combinations thereof. Every point on the plane represents a possible combination of hunting and trap making that an individual might choose. If Wilma is passionate about making traps, and Dino about hunting, they might specialize in those areas and trade with each other (positive-sum). But even if they don't specialize and trade, they still have more freedom to pursue whatever combination of the two activities they prefer. Their livelihood options have increased. If Barney is not into making traps or hunting, he may still be stuck in zero- or negative-sum interactions with Dino and Wilma. Their world isn't very positive-sum (yet), but at least it is less negative-sum.

Now let's say that Barney discovers how to control fire and satisfy a third human need—staying warm (lower center of figure 26.2). The economy has expanded to a three-dimensional "space" that offers the individuals many more options than before: each one can hunt, make traps, control fire, trade one for the other, or combinations thereof. Every point in that 3-D space represents a possible combination of the three activities that an individual might choose. If each of the three is passionate about an activity, each may specialize in that activity— perhaps Wilma making traps, Barney controlling fire, and Dino hunting for meat—and trade with the others for the products and services they specialize in (positive-sum). But even if they don't specialize and everyone does some of each, they still have more freedom to pursue whichever activities they wish than they did in the one-dimensional and two-dimension cases. With just one additional innovation, Barney has provided many more livelihood options for everyone; simply surviving is now less of a concern. Each new dimension in the economy has let the participants "spread out," avoid competing directly (recall chapter 16 "Avoiding Competitors"), and engage in more positive-sum interactions.

Now fast-forward two million years to the present. Those three products and services (meat, trap, fire) have expanded into an estimated fifty billion[6]—many more than the number of people living on earth. Imagine the human needs space with not just three dimensions but billions of dimensions.[7] We can't visualize more than three dimensions in our 3-D world, so please just try to imagine it. Blows your mind, doesn't it? The combinations of those dimensions offer the seven billion people on earth today *quadrillions* of options for making a living, including those that provide us with the most personal fulfillment. Despite that huge number, each time an entrepreneur provides a new solution to a new customer need, it adds yet another dimension to this space.

ABUNDANCE AND SCARCITY

The familiar Maslow's hierarchy (figure 26.3) stacks human needs from basic at the bottom (e.g., food, clothing, and shelter) to high-level at the top (e.g., recognition, respect, and personal fulfillment).[8] As we have seen, more dimensions to the economy allow individuals to satisfy an increasing number of higher-level needs without putting lower-level, more basic needs at risk. I call that *abundance*. In contrast, if individuals increasingly have to trade off (give up satisfying) higher-level needs to satisfy lower-level needs, I call that *scarcity*.[9]

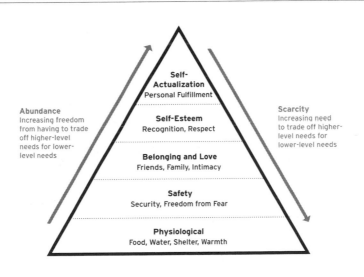

— *Figure 26.3* —

Abundance and scarcity in Maslow's hierarchy of needs.

Note: Maslow's hierarchy of needs proposed in 1943 A. H. Maslow, "A Theory of Human Motivation," *Psychological Review* 50 (4) 370–96.

Abundance arises when entrepreneurs are able to live and work under Adam Smith Rules for enough time to satisfy, thereby generate, and again satisfy more and more human (customer) needs. In earlier times, abundance might have meant not having to trade off food and warmth. Today, abundance is reflected in the ever-proliferating billions of options and opportunities available to us. For example, consider

- **Video:** 120 billion choices of videos—entertainment, education, hobbies, training, news and sports—on YouTube

- **Medical devices:** Over half a million types of medical devices worldwide[10]

- **Music:** Hundreds of types of popular music (e.g., forty-four genres of African, thirty-seven genres of country, twenty-nine genres of blues, etc.)[11]

- **Recreation:** Nine types of sports fishing, eight types of kayaking, seven types of archery . . .

When more and more people can enjoy or benefit from the ever increasing numbers of such options without putting satisfaction of more basic needs at risk, that is abundance.

In contrast, if today you have to give up stylish clothes (higher-level need) for home security (lower level); a new car (higher level) for an adequate secondary education for your child (lower level); precious time (higher level) to wait in line for hours to buy a half tank of gasoline (lower level) when previously you did not, that is scarcity.

The Nixon administration's wage and price controls of 1971–1974 were the period of greatest scarcity in the United States in recent decades. If you are under age forty, you missed it. Lucky you. In addition to waiting in line for hours to buy a half tank of gasoline, national shortages arose in such everyday staples as chicken and steak. The quality of products ranging from lumber to chewing gum was debased to match allowed prices. The controls artificially imposed scarcity. They did not stop inflation as intended; they merely postponed it until after the 1972 presidential election.

Of course, the privations Americans suffered then were nothing compared to those suffered by people in many parts of Africa, Latin America, and Asia every day. But just as during the Nixon era, many of the scarcities faced around the world today—of food, natural resources, energy, fresh water, wireless bandwidth, and health care—are either unnecessary or artificial.

Take food, for example. In 1870, 70 percent to 80 percent of the US population of about thirty-eight million was employed in agriculture. By 2008, we fed almost ten times the population with less than 2 percent directly employed in agriculture.[12] Millions of entrepreneurs living and working under the Adam Smith Rules and the resulting innovations large and small over the decades made this possible. So why are people in Africa, Latin America, and Asia still starving? You don't have to look far. In any country or on any continent you choose, see how many of the Adam Smith Rules are being followed, if any. During the scarcity-ridden years of the Nixon wage and price controls, the United States abandoned at least three of them.

Besides food, natural resources are often seen as scarce. In 1980, Julian Simon, author of *The Ultimate Resource* (Princeton University Press, 1981), and Paul Ehrlich, author of *The Population Bomb* (Ballantine, 1968), made a famous wager. The two noted public figures bet on prices of five commodity metals (copper, chromium, nickel, tin, and tungsten) and a time period (1980 to 1990), both chosen by Ehrlich. As supplies of these metals were depleted, Ehrlich was confident that their prices would rise. But just the opposite happened. Thanks to technology advances and substitutions such as fiber optics and plastics, all the metal prices declined. Again, entrepreneurs and the Adam Smith Rules were at work. Simon won the bet.[13]

Some say abundance destroys the environment, but actually the opposite is true. Haiti, the poorest country in the Western Hemisphere, shares the Caribbean island of Hispaniola with its wealthier neighbor, the Dominican Republic. Haiti's GDP per capita is about $1,300 per year; the Dominican Republic's is about $9,700 per year.[14] Lush green forests thrive on the Dominican Republic side of the border. In contrast, Haiti's side is a heavily deforested brown. According to *The New York Times*, Haiti has lost 98 percent of its forests to destructive land use, mainly from the clear-cutting of trees for firewood and making charcoal, the most commonly used cooking fuel in Haiti.[15] The Dominican Republic is wealthy enough to subsidize cleaner propane gas as a cooking fuel, and thus protect its forests. Sadly, Haitian firewood poachers are now making incursions into Dominican Republic forests. According to *The New York Times*, "brown patches are now spreading into the Dominican side."

The more expensive things are, the more we have to give up to enjoy them (scarcity). The cheaper they are, the less we have to give up (abundance). My MIT classmate and former Secretary of the US Treasury Larry Summers notes that costs in virtually all "nonpolitically inflected" product and service categories, as he calls them—for example, TVs, washing machines, software, computers, accounting and legal services—have fallen in the last decade. In contrast, the ones he calls "politically inflected"—for example, health care, food, and education—have risen. Resources become scarce and expensive when politics trump the Adam Smith Rules, thus discouraging or precluding entrepreneurship and innovation.

ETHICAL ENTREPRENEURS, LEADERS, AND INSTITUTIONS

I propose a new definition of *ethical*: that which shifts a relationship, community, or the world from zero-sum toward positive-sum. *Unethical* is the opposite, as shown in figure 26.4.

This definition does not capture all, but rather important aspects often overlooked, of what is ethical. The guidance it offers is very broad, like a compass, not a road map. Examples of shifting or helping shift a relationship, community, or the world from zero-sum to positive-sum are

- promoting freedom and free trade,

- creating, enforcing, and reinforcing property rights,

- alleviating constraints that don't protect life or property,

- sharing knowledge that helps eliminate constraints and scarcity,

- looking for and recognizing the good in others, thus helping build those qualities in others,

- fulfilling your commitments and thereby building trust, and

- innovating solutions that help accomplish any of the items in this list.

Zero-sum (or negative-sum)	Ethical → ← Unethical	Positive-sum
Constraint		Choice
Theft		Voluntary exchange
Regulation		Freedom
Stasis		Innovation
Trade barriers		Free trade
Scarcity		Abundance
Envy		Goodwill
War		Peace

—— *Figure 26.4* ——

Zero-sum (or negative-sum) versus positive-sum.

Given my definition, you can now see why I call entrepreneurs a uniquely ethical bunch: They create new solutions for new customer needs, making the world more positive-sum, creating abundance, and eliminating scarcity. Consider just two of the many ways entrepreneurs are alleviating constraints to convert zero-sum scarcity to positive-sum abundance today:

- **Sharing or renting online:** The growing "shared economy" eliminates the need to buy or own many items outright. Examples include cars (e.g., Zipcar, Getaround, and JustShareIt); taxis (Uber and Lyft); overnight lodging and vacation rentals (Airbnb and HomeAway); household tools and equipment (Rentalic and Rent-Instead); and online courses (Codecademy, Coursera, Udacity, and Udemy).

- **Converting goods and services from physical to virtual:** In changing from "rivalrous" (physical goods that can be used by only one person or group of people at a time) to "nonrivalrous" (online goods can be enjoyed simultaneously by an unlimited number of consumers).

As a result, these products and services (see table 26.1) are becoming more affordable to consumers everywhere, often regardless of geographical location, and often even free of charge. They are helping make the world more abundant.

Table 26.1. Moving from scarcity (zero-sum) to abundance (positive-sum).				
Information	City and university libraries		→ Home encyclopedias	→ -Google Search -Wikipedia
Communication	-Postal mail -Face-to-face meetings	→ Long-distance phone calls	→ Free texting and voice calls	→ Free long-distance video calls
Entertainment	Theatre movies		→ DVD movies sent by mail	→ Movies downloaded on demand
Transportation	Fixed itinerary and schedule railroads and buses		→ Flexible and intelligent shared vehicles (e.g., Getaround, Zipcar, Uber, Lyft)	→ Self-driving taxis and trucks
Higher education	Tuition, campuses, and residential lodging		→ Free online courses	
Health care	Human physicians; expensive, top-down clinical trials; proprietary pharmaceuticals		→ Video access to physicians, expert-system-based diagnoses, 3-D printed open-sourced pharmaceuticals	

Dark gray = sharing or renting online; light gray = shifting from physical to virtual.

As your start-up grows beyond a few team members, your most important job will become creating and maintaining a positive-sum organization, one that creates win-wins for your team members, customers, and all of your company's stakeholders, including you. That means communicating and demonstrating that the success of your organization and stakeholders reinforce each other (a positive feedback loop). Positive-sum environments uniquely allow team members to differentiate, collaborate, and excel, and thus attract and retain high-performance talent. Organizations falter and then nosedive when positive-sum collaboration gives way to zero-sum infighting. Helping others *see* positive-sum potential—on a team, in an organization, and in the world—is a first step to *realizing* that potential.[16]

Research university MIT is positive-sum in one sense and zero-sum in another. Its research and developments in aerospace, architecture, aviation, communications, biology, chemistry, computing, e-commerce, electronics, energy, finance, materials, mechanics, medicine, nutrition, packaging, robotics, and transportation since its founding in 1861 have far advanced human knowledge, spawned thousands of companies, and defined and satisfied many new dimensions of human needs. That is highly positive-sum. At the same time, like any elite university, is it zero-sum: The size of each freshman class is limited to about 1,050 and the number of applicants is over seventeen times that number, meaning for any freshman admitted, many others are turned away.

But MIT is shifting even education from zero-sum to positive-sum. Starting in 2002, OpenCourseWare (OCW) made lecture notes for most MIT courses free to anyone online. In 2011, MIT expanded OCW to full courses with MITx.[17] To convey the magnitude of its impact, when the first MITx course, Circuits and Electronics, went live in 2012, more than 154,000 enrolled and over 7,000 passed the course, as many as had taken and passed this core electrical engineering course in the preceding forty years at MIT. Later in 2012, MIT further expanded MITx by partnering with Harvard and forming edX. Today, edX is one of many free online learning resources that include Khan Academy, Coursera, Udacity, and Codecademy. These initiatives make MIT, Khan, and the others highly ethical institutions by my definition. A quality education—at least the noncampus experience part—no longer requires entrance qualification exams and thousands of dollars for tuition and expenses. Increasingly, today, all it requires is initiative, self-discipline, and willingness to work hard (requirements that will not go away).

It can be hard to determine if work or other activity is positive-sum or zero-sum. Consider the legal profession:

- Some lawyers are beneficial to society: they help draft and enforce agreements, resolve disputes, and help protect life and property. But having too many lawyers invites zero-sum litigation.

- If a lawyer's work is dividing a couple's assets in a divorce, that is generally either zero-sum (if you neglect the lawyer's fees) or negative-sum (if you deduct them). But if the same lawyer minimizes her fees and creates a bigger pie by helping couples assign each asset to the party who most values it, that is positive-sum. At the same time, if the other side is not behaving fairly or negotiating in good faith, protecting a client's property (generally positive-sum, but in a divorce case, zero-sum) may require the threat of a negative-sum outcome.

- Drafting regulations that force specific resolutions to disputes, with no options for the parties to find mutually beneficial resolutions, is clearly negative-sum. But helping the same parties—say, beekeepers and nearby seedless citrus growers, whose fruit loses value if cross-pollinated with fruit with seeds—explore, discover, and reach mutually beneficial resolutions out of court is positive-sum.[18]

It may be that no amount of cost-benefit analysis can determine whether you are making the world more or less positive-sum. At some point, only your conscience can tell you.

UNETHICAL: TURNING POSITIVE-SUM INTO ZERO-SUM

Examples of shifting or helping shift an environment from positive-sum to zero-sum are obstructing free trade; persuading officials or regulators to exclude competitors (protectionism); disregarding property rights, or redefining them so frequently as to create uncertainty and discourage preservation and investment; arousing fear or envy (e.g., pitting one segment of society against another); and eroding trust and thus cooperation.

Entrepreneurs and others who persuade officials or regulators to disallow competitors in their industries are almost certainly unethical, by my definition: Not only are consumers and businesses precluded from buying goods and services that may better fit their needs or budgets, but the disallowed businesses are denied access to willing customers. Both sides lose (negative-sum). Consumer safety or welfare may be disingenuously used as justification. *Examples*: conventional car dealers and manufacturers who band together to persuade state legislatures to disallow sales of Tesla, which doesn't use dealerships, and conventional cab companies that unite to persuade city councils to disallow ride-sharing services like Uber and Lyft.

Despots around the world pit one segment of society against another—Muslims, gays, blacks, the top 1 percent, Asians, Latinos, you name it—that purportedly takes more than its "fair share" of a supposed fixed pie of resources. Creating envy, the perception of scarcity, or both strengthens the power of the despot: He or she that promises to help constituents get their fair share of the pie.

But such zero-sum politics ultimately shrink and shrivel the pie. "Exhibit A" is the late President Hugo Chavez of Venezuela. In 1999, he and the 350 articles of his constitution nationalized oil and other "strategic" industries, flouting private property; obliged citizens to spy on each other; made promises of salaries and retirement benefits the state could not keep, thus eroding trust; and gave Chavez control of congress, judiciary, and the central bank. Fifteen years later, Venezuelans line up for necessities like baby formula, flour, milk, and toilet paper (now strictly rationed).[19] Critical shortages have led the government to put Venezuela's food distribution, including chicken and laundry detergent, under military protection.[20] Venezuela's current regime blames the recent falling price of oil for these problems, but in fact, they started years before and are much more pervasive than oil prices alone. In the words of Harvard's Steven Pinker,

> Countries with an abundance of non-renewable, easily monopolized resources have slower economic growth . . . and more violence . . . because [the resources] concentrate power and wealth in the hands of whoever monopolizes them, typically a governing elite but sometimes a regional warlord. The leader becomes obsessed with fending off rivals for his cash cow and has no incentive to foster the networks of commerce that enrich a society and knit it together with reciprocal obligations.[21]

MAKE THE WORLD MORE POSITIVE-SUM

Finally, where does most funding for philanthropy come from? You guessed it: current or former entrepreneurs. People who don't make money don't become philanthropists.

Steve Jobs, the late and great cofounder, chairman, and CEO of Apple, is sometimes called unethical because he didn't very actively engage in philanthropy. I emphatically disagree. Look how much good he brought to the world through the Macintosh, iPod, iPhone, iTunes, and iPad, enhancing the lives of millions worldwide. Personal computing. Entertainment. Education. Companionship for the elderly and lonely. Business productivity. Beyond that, Apple provides full-time employment for over ninety thousand employees and probably ten times that number including suppliers, manufacturers, and app developers. Apple is among the most widely held stocks in the world and at this moment, is both the most profitable and highly valued company in the world. Many Apple employees and investors have become millionaires. Few human beings have done as much good in the world as Steve Jobs. As much as anyone, he made the world a more positive-sum place.

You and I can do the same. You have made it all the way through this book. That demonstrates your passion and perseverance for unleashing your inner company. Now keep going and make it happen. You can do it—go for it! Good luck to you. And please keep in touch through www .unleashyourinnercompany.com.

ACKNOWLEDGMENTS

This book is dedicated to my friends and colleagues at four institutions who have most influenced my thinking and enabled my personal and professional growth over many years. MIT is a wellspring of innovation and entrepreneurship infused with a spirit of intellectual curiosity and generosity. Silicon Valley, my creative workplace and home, has provided me mentors, collaborators, role models, and inspiration for over three decades. Dale Carnegie & Associates, for whom I was privileged to serve as instructor early in my career, grandfathered much of today's human potential movement. Its leadership and human relations principles apply every day of your life. Despite being available to anyone at modest cost, its flagship course has been the most valuable training I have ever taken. The Santa Fe Institute, the world-leading research center in complex systems, has deeply influenced the way I understand entrepreneurship, economics, law, the environment, and the human mind. Its influence pervades *Unleash Your Inner Company*.

Individuals to whom I am indebted include Daron Acemoglu, Kare Anderson, Ken Arrow, Brian Arthur, Bill Aulet, Mike Beasley, Eric Beinhocker, Tom Bell, Nick Bertrand, Max Borders, Erik Brynjolfsson, Josh Calcott, Gabriel Calzada, Elizabeth Chenette, David Colander, Bob Colopy, Glenn Cripe, Jason Cunanan, Michael Curzo, Ervan Darnell, George Gilder, Monika Gruter, Gali Hagel, John Hagel, Stephen Hicks, Lee Hill, Giancarlo Ibarguen, Carlos Jimenez, Sampson Lee, Bob Metcalfe, Quee Nelson, Gerry Ohrstrom, Tom Palmer, Mike Parrish, Jim Petkas, Ben Powell, Howard Raiffa, Ed Roberts, Roy Rood, Art Schleifer, Michael Strong, Alton Sun, Nathan True, Alice Tse, Marshall Van Alstyne, and Rebeca Zuniga. Still others are my friends and colleagues at Pyze, CustomerSat, Decisive Technology, the University of Francisco Marroquin (where my 2011 TEDxUFM talk gave me the idea of writing this book), the Center for Ethics and Entrepreneurship at Rockford University, the Kauffman and Thiel Foundations, the Gruter Institute for Law and Behavioral Research, Liberty Fund, Singularity University, TED, the Institute for New Economic Thinking, the Harvard Kennedy School Center for International Development, the Clinton Global Initiative, and the Network for Teaching Entrepreneurship. Perhaps the greatest asset with which any individual can be endowed in life is loving and supportive parents, which I have enjoyed in spades. Most of all, I thank my parents.

Appendix A

UNLEASH YOUR INNER COMPANY: THE PROCESS

Unleash Your Inner Company is an iterative, organic process for creating and building your ideal business. In nature, organisms vary, and successful variations are selected based on their fitness, giving rise to the creation of new species. The process is bottom up, without top-down design. Similarly, *Unleash Your Inner Company* is a process of exploration, bottom-up variation, and selection.

You first explore terrain you know well—the areas you are passionate about—in search of unsatisfied customer needs. Then you propose solutions to these needs and test them on prospective customers. When you have one or more promising needs and possible solutions, you match each need and solution with your resources and passions to select the ones with the best fit. Wherever possible, you strengthen fit by acquiring or developing resources. You then look at others addressing the same customer need (your potential competitors) to determine which needs and solutions you have the strongest advantages for. From these you select your best opportunity (customer need and solution). Finally, you design, customer test, and scale up your delivery of that solution.

#	Step	Collect Data	Experiment		Build	Chapters
			Variation	Selection		
1	Identify/develop passions	✓				1, 2
2	Generate/refine customer needs in those areas	✓	✓	✓		2, 3, 4, 5
3	Generate/refine possible solutions to those needs	✓	✓	✓		3, 4, 5
4	Inventory your resources (STARS)	✓				6, 7, 8, 9, 12, 14
4a	Generate additional needs suggested by your resources	✓	✓			10, 11
5	Match needs and solutions with resources and passions			✓		13
6	Develop or acquire resources to strengthen fit				✓	15
7	Determine advantages relative to competitors for each need and solution	✓				16, 17, 18, 29
8	Choose your best opportunity (customer need and solution)			✓		20
9	Test and launch your minimum viable solution (MVS)			✓	✓	21, 22
10	Scale up				✓	23, 24
After-word	· Regulation: Hidden roadblocks to your success · The ethics of entrepreneurship					25 26

―――― Figure A.1 ――――――――――――――――――――――――――――

Unleash Your Inner Company: the ten-step process.

Appendix B

VISUALIZING NUMBERS OF COMBINATIONS

A handy tool for visualizing the number of combinations possible for multiple technologies—or skills, assets, other resources, and any items, for that matter—is Pascal's Triangle. Named after the French mathematician Blaise Pascal (1623–1662), the triangle starts with the number 1 in row 0. Below that, any number in the triangle is the sum of the two numbers above it (we assume diagonal rows of invisible zeroes extending down either side of the triangle). Figure B1 shows the first few rows of Pascal's Triangle; the real thing continues indefinitely.

Row									
0					1				
1				1		1			
2			1		2		1		
3		1		3		3		1	
4	1		4		6		4		1

Figure B.1

Pascal's triangle.

To find the number of combinations of N technologies taken M at a time, where $M = 0, 1, 2, 3 \ldots$ up to N, go to the Nth row and count over M numbers, starting with 0 for each of M and N. So for six technologies taken two at a time, for example, there are fifteen combinations (figure B2). Taken three at a time, there are twenty combinations.[1]

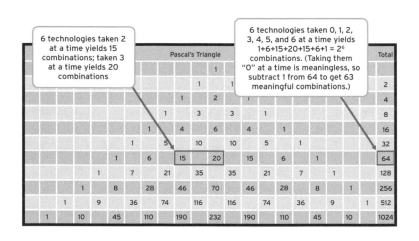

Figure B.2

Possible number of combinations of N technologies.

The *total* number of combinations of N technologies taken *any* number of times is the sum of the numbers in the Nth row, or 2^N. For $N = 6$, $2^N = 64$. One of these combinations is meaningless—taking the technologies "zero" at a time—so let's subtract one from the total. We get $2^N - 1$ meaningful combinations.

Pascal's Triangle shows us how rapidly the number of combinations of technologies grows as we add technologies. While the number of combinations of N technologies taken two at a time grows with N^2—the exact formula is $N(N - 1)/2$—the total number of combinations of N

technologies taken 1, 2, 3, or any other number of times up to N, grows much faster, by 2^N (figure B3).

For $N = 1000$, the total number of combinations is about 1 followed by 301 zeroes. Wow! You can see why the more technologies we have to work with, the number of possible new technologies grows even faster, and the faster technology advances.

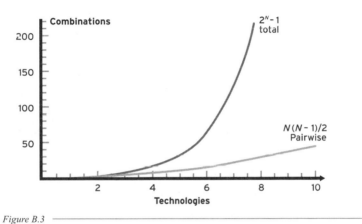

——— *Figure B.3* ———

Growing combinations.

Combinations show you the power of having a cofounder with advantages complementary to yours. For example, if you have nine advantages, they can be combined in a total of $2^9 = 512$ different ways (figure B2), or in $512 - 1 = 511$ meaningful ways. If your prospective cofounder has eleven advantages, her advantages can be combined in $2^{11} - 1 = 2,047$ meaningful ways. Let's say that her advantages are all different from your advantages. Separately, between the two of you are $511 + 2,047 = 2,558$ combinations. But if the two of you team up, you have $11 + 9 = 20$ different advantages that can be combined in $2^{20} - 1 = 1,048,575$ different ways. Together, the two of you have many more potential advantages and customer needs you could satisfy than you have separately—in this example, over 400 times as many.

This same effect applies on a global scale. Humanity's progress is limited today not by the number of combinations of existing technologies—far more than the number of atoms in the universe ("only" about 1 followed by 80 zeroes)—but by the number of entrepreneurs and innovators on earth exploring and developing those combinations and collaborating to satisfy human needs with them. Today, most of the people doing so are in higher-income countries. But thanks to advances in information, communications, and mobile commerce technologies and to the Adam Smith Rules becoming more widely adopted (see chapter 26 "The Ethics of Entrepreneurship"), lower-income countries are catching up. These include China, India, Indonesia, and Brazil. As a result, the number of entrepreneurs and innovators worldwide collaborating and building on each other's work is growing very rapidly. This growth benefits people in higher- and lower-income countries alike. It accelerates innovation and the satisfaction of human needs, enables ever more people to find personal fulfillment—to flourish—with less concern for mere survival, and creates a more abundant world for everyone.[2]

Appendix C

CREATING FINANCIAL MODELS OF YOUR BUSINESS: PROJECTING INCOME, CASH FLOW, AND BALANCE SHEET

In chapter 17 "Where Do Your STARS Shine Brightest?" and chapter 21 "Five Pricing Principles," we saw that creating a financial model of your business can let you better

- analyze the financial impact of decisions or actions on your business,

- choose between alternatives,

- generate and preserve cash, and

- explain or justify a decision to investors, partners, and others.

A comprehensive financial model of your business includes projections for income statement (profit and loss), cash flow (cash), and balance sheet (assets and liabilities). Here, we look at just income projection and briefly touch on projecting the two other financial statements.[1]

Table C1 is an income statement projection for your hypothetical Smart Bear Company that we saw in chapter 21. Your company's product is a stuffed toy bear that speaks to a child, understands its responses, and intelligently responds to many of the child's responses. You and your cofounder, an expert software developer in natural language processing, founded the company eighteen months ago. The first quarter shown in table C1 was your first full quarter of shipments of the bears, which you sell through a regional toys retailer. The table starts with actual income for your just-completed first quarter and projects income for the following three quarters.

What follows are the notes about each line item in table C1.

Actual vs. projection: As mentioned previously, the column headings show that your results for the first quarter (January through March) are actual figures and that those for the remaining three quarters of the year are projections. When you complete and have actual figures for that quarter, you will change "projection" to "actual" for the second quarter, and so on as you complete later quarters.

Units sold (Line 1): You and your retail channel together forecast that about half of your bears will be sold during the holiday season (fourth quarter in this case; i.e., October through December), and the other half sold off-season (first three quarters; i.e., the preceding nine months of the year). So of 6,000 units you expect to sell this year, 3,000 of them are during the fourth quarter. Beyond that, you believe that the first and third calendar quarters should be slightly weaker than the second quarter, due to families not needing to purchase toys immediately after the holidays and postponing toy purchases in the third quarter until the holidays. You also believe that, in addition to these seasonalities, a steady quarter-over-quarter growth underlies your sales, so that a quarter in the following year (not shown in the projection) would be 30%–40% higher than its corresponding quarter in the current year. Given all these factors, you arrive at the unit sales projection shown in Line 1.

Revenue (Lines 2 through 5): Your smart bear carries a list price of $99.50, a price you don't expect to change throughout the year (Line 2). Your distribution channel, the regional toys retail chain, receives a 30% discount from list price and you expect 5% of the bears you sell to be returned to you (Lines 3 and 4). Your net revenue is thus $99.50 × (1 − 30%) × (1 − 5%) = $66.17 per bear (Line 5).

Table C1. Smart Bear Company—income statement projection.

Line #	Item	1st quarter (actual)	2nd quarter (projected)	3rd quarter (projected)	4th quarter (projected)	Total (projected)
1	Units sold	900	1100	1000	3000	6000
	Revenue:					
2	Gross revenue/unit	$99.50	$99.50	$99.50	$99.50	$99.50
3	Less channel discount	30%	30%	30%	30%	30%
4	Less returns	5%	5%	5%	5%	5%
5	Net revenue	$59,551	$72,784	$66,168	$198,503	$397,005
	Cost of goods sold:					
6	Variable cost per bear	$26.50	$26.50	$27.00	$27.00	$26.83
7	Total cost of goods sold	$23,850	$29,150	$27,000	$81,000	$161,000
8	**Gross profit**	$35,701	$43,634	$39,168	$117,503	$236,005
	Operating costs:					
9	Salaries (nonfounders)	$18,000	$18,000	$20,000	$25,000	$81,000
10	Salaries (founders)	$0	$4,000	$4,000	$10,000	$18,000
11	Payroll taxes and benefits (20%)	$3,600	$4,400	$4,800	$7,000	$19,800
12	Marketing and advertising	$6,000	$8,000	$8,000	$12,000	$34,000
13	Office rent	$3,000	$3,000	$3,000	$3,000	$12,000
14	Other expenses (insurance, supplies, etc.)	$3,000	$3,000	$3,000	$3,000	$12,000
15	Total operating costs	$33,600	$40,400	$42,800	$60,000	$176,800
16	**Operating profit (EBITDA)**	$2,101	$3,234	($3,633)	$57,503	**$59,205**
17	Depreciation and amortization	$3,000	$3,000	$3,000	$3,000	$12,000
18	Earnings before interest and taxes (EBIT)	($899)	$234	($6,633)	$54,503	$47,205
19	Interest expense	$0	$0	$0	$0	$0
20	Profit before tax (PBT)	($899)	$234	($6,633)	$54,503	**$47,205**
21	Taxes (20% estimated)					$9,441
22	Profit after tax (PAT)	($899)	$234	($6,633)	$54,503	**$37,764**

Note: Numbers may not calculate exactly due to rounding.

Cost of goods sold (Lines 6 and 7): You expect the variable cost per bear (materials and labor) to stay roughly flat throughout the year (Line 6) as higher volume discounts for materials, production efficiencies, and rapidly declining costs of integrated circuits and memory offset higher costs of the more powerful processor and larger memory that you plan for your smart bear in the third quarter. Total cost of goods sold (Line 7) is simply variable cost per bear times the number of bears sold. In the far right total column, $26.83 is the average variable cost per bear (total cost of goods sold divided by total unit sales forecast) for the entire year.

Gross profit (Line 8): This is your net revenue (Line 5) minus total cost of goods sold (Line 7).

Salaries (Lines 9 and 10): The increase in Line 9 over the course of the year reflects both a raise in your employee's salary in the third quarter and the addition of a permanent part-time employee in the fourth quarter (whom you expect to convert to full-time next year). For the first time starting in the second quarter, you and your cofounder start paying yourselves modest salaries (Line 10). You plan to increase your own salaries gradually over the course of next year. Extending this forecast through the end of next year will help you determine to what extent that is feasible.

Payroll taxes and benefits (Line 11): You estimate the total of these to be a constant 20% of total salaries (Line 9 plus Line 10).

Marketing and advertising (Line 12): Your ramp up these expenses over the course of the year, and additionally increase them during the holiday season.

Operating profit (Line 16): EBITDA denotes earnings before interest, taxes, depreciation, and amortization. Operating profit is gross profit (Line 8) minus total operating costs (Line 15). Virtually all your profit comes in the fourth quarter. The modest salaries that you and your cofounder start to take in the second quarter contribute to a modest loss in the third quarter, but since you anticipate strong sales in the fourth quarter and continued growth next year, you are comfortable taking the risk.

Depreciation & amortization (Line 17): You have a grand total of $36,000 of tangible assets such as equipment that you depreciate (write off) over three years and intangible assets such as software that you amortize over three years. Your total depreciation and amortization is thus

$36,000 / (3 years × 4 quarters / year) = $3,000 per quarter.

EBIT (Line 18): This is earnings before interest and taxes.

Interest expense (Line 19): Since you have no debt, your interest expense is zero. But given the seasonality and growth of your business, next year you expect to take out a short-term "revolving" business loan (one that you pay off fully at least once per year) to help cover expenses in the first three quarters. When you create your projection for next year, you will have interest expense as a result of the loan. That expense will be deducted from EBIT to get earnings before taxes (or more commonly, profit before taxes [PBT]).

Taxes (Line 21): The taxes not yet subtracted from EBIT (the T in EBIT and EBITDA) are state and federal taxes. Here, we estimate them at 20% of PBT. Other taxes, such as real estate, payroll, and city and local taxes are subtracted before arriving at EBITDA, as we did with payroll taxes in Line 11. This will be the first year your business has made a taxable profit, so you show taxes for the year all being paid in the fourth quarter. (Taxes for the year would actually be due and payable in a later quarter, but your current business model only extends to the fourth quarter, so you show them there so as not to overlook them. In subsequent years, assuming your business remains profitable, you will need to make quarterly tax payments.)

Profit after tax (Line 22): Also called "net income" (though net income sometimes also refers to profit before tax).

Since you expect to need a business loan next year, you will want to prepare a similar projection for next year right away. Any commercial lending institution will require it as part of your application.

"WHAT-IF?" ANALYSIS

Your model lets you ask "what if?" questions, such as the following:

- What if you raised the price of the bear by 50% to $149? Presumably this would reduce sales somewhat, but by how much? Enter your revised pricing and unit sales estimates into your model to see their impact on your operating profit.

- What if you increased marketing and advertising in the fourth quarter by 50% from $12,000 to $18,000? Presumably that would increase sales, but by how much? Would the increased sales generate more than enough gross margin to cover the extra $6,000 in marketing and advertising?

- You currently give up approximately (6,000 bears per year)($100 per bear)(30%) = $180,000 per year in total discounts to your channel. Could these funds be better applied in other ways? For example, if most people learn about your bear through word of mouth and online rather than in-store displays, would you do better by selling the bear online through Amazon and your own website, letting Amazon handle the fulfillment, and applying some or all of $180,000 to marketing and advertising?

CASH FLOW (STATEMENT AND PROJECTION)

In many ways, cash flow is even more important than net income. Cash is needed for payroll, rent, utilities, and other essential expenses. If you cannot pay these in a timely fashion, your employees will quit, your service providers will discontinue service, and you will go out of business. Indeed, lack of cash is the most common reason that companies declare bankruptcy. If sales take an unexpected nosedive or unexpectedly long to collect, cash reserves enable your company to stay afloat.

Cash flow has three components: from operations (sales, fulfillment, and delivery of your product or service), from financing (capital raised less dividends paid to shareholders), and from investing (outflows and inflows resulting from purchase or sale of long-term investments). You can arrive at cash flow from operations by making adjustments to net income as follows:

Net Income (after taxes)
+ Depreciation + Amortization
– Increases (or + Decreases) in Accounts receivable
– Increases (or + Decreases) in Inventories
+ Increases (or – Decreases) in Accounts payable
+ Increases (or – Decreases) in Notes payable (bank loans)
= Cash flow from operations

If you use accrual rather than cash accounting, be especially attentive: Having revenue does not mean that you are getting paid. If your customers or partners are slow to pay or your sales channel is absorbing product that is at risk of being unsold and returned, your company may recognize substantial revenue but receive little cash in a particular time period.

BALANCE SHEETS (ACTUAL AND PROJECTED)

In addition to your income statement and cash flow projections, lending institutions will likely require a balance sheet of your business itemizing assets and liabilities. While your income and cash flow statements cover a period of time, such as a quarter or year, your balance sheet shows the state of your business at a single point in time. A balance sheet tells you many things about your business that the other statements do not:

- **What your company owns** (assets), both current assets (those convertible to cash within one year—cash, accounts receivable, and inventory), and long-term assets (furniture, equipment, and property)

- **What your company owes** (liabilities), both current (those due within one year—accounts payable, accrued taxes, and current portion of long-term debt), and long term (noncurrent portion of long-term debt)

- **What is left** after your liabilities are subtracted from your assets— owner's equity or book value of the company

Many free online resources can help you create a balance sheet, cash flow statement, and projections, for example, www.accountingcoach .com. If you are comfortable with accounting, consider creating a three-statement financial model combining projections of income statement, balance sheet, and cash flow statement.[2] Alternatively, hire an accountant to help you.

SCALING YOUR SMART BEAR BUSINESS

Adding intelligence to your toy bear significantly increases its value, the age range of children it appeals to, the size of the market it serves, and customer demand, yet adds little in variable and fixed costs, thus making your business more scalable. By upgrading a bear's central processing unit, memory, and programming, you can expand the vocabulary and increase the intelligence and memory of the bear.

Your first model of your bear is for children ages three to five years; your second model, with more intelligence, will be for ages six to eight; and your third model, with the most intelligence, will be for ages eight to twelve. As a child grows from the first to second age range, and later from the second to third age range, you plan to let parents order upgrades for their children's bears, so the bear will grow in intelligence but still remember previous interactions with and facts about each child. Eventually you will be able to perform these upgrades online. You incorporate these assumptions into your financial model and discover that you very much increase the margins in your business.

You further envision your bear being able to market itself by responding to such questions as "Where did you come from?" or "Where were you born?" The bear will explain that it came from Smart Bear Company and offer to email or text ordering information to those who provide their email addresses or phone numbers. Beyond that, your cofounder appears to have discovered a way to readily adapt the bears' speech and understanding to languages other than English, opening up the international market for you.

Marketing and delivering the software upgrades will require communicating with children's parents or guardians. Selling the bears online gives you a more direct link to your customers than does the regional toys retail chain you use. You begin to think of online as your strategic channel and the regional toy retailer as a secondary channel.

What previously appeared to be a business with modest growth and margins is shaping up to be a promising high-growth, high-margin business. Financial modeling has helped you see your business in a new light. You start to think about seeking outside investors to help fuel the growth of your business.

Appendix D

UNLEASH YOUR INNER COMPANY AND THE BUSINESS MODEL CANVAS

The Business Model Canvas[1] provides snapshots of nine key elements of your business: customer segments, value propositions, channels, customer relationships, revenue streams, key resources, key activities, key partnerships, and cost structure. As you follow the *Unleash Your Inner Company* process and consider or specify those aspects of your business, the Business Model Canvas captures them on a single sheet for discussion, analysis, and presentation. Figure D1 shows the nine key elements of the Business Model Canvas and table D1 offers a mapping of the chapters of *Unleash Your Inner Company* to the elements of the Business Model Canvas. A check mark (✔) indicates that the chapter can help specify that element of your business.

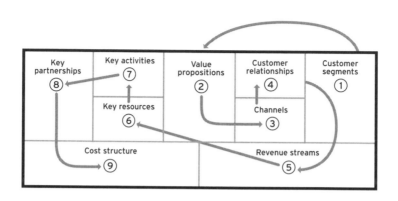

—— Figure D.1 ——————————————————————————

Nine key elements of the business model canvas.

	Business Model Canvas elements								
Unleash Your Inner Company chapter	Customer segments	Value propo-sitions	Channels	Customer relation-ships	Revenue streams	Key re-sources	Key activi-ties	Key partner-ships	Cost structure
1. Passion and Perse-verance (Step 1)	✔	✔	✔	✔	✔	✔	✔	✔	✔
2. All You Need Is a Need and Advantage: Roadmap to Creating Your Business	✔	✔	✔	✔	✔	✔	✔	✔	✔
3. Let a Thousand Needs Bloom (Steps 2 & 3)	✔	✔							
4. Don't Listen to Your Customers; Discover Their Goals	✔	✔		✔					
5. Think Big; Start Focused	✔								
6. The Future Is in Your STARS (Step 4)						✔			
7. Growing Your Mind from the Inside Out						✔			
8. You're a Technolo-gist. Know It.						✔			

Table D1. Unleash Your Inner Company chapters mapped to elements of the Business Model Canvas.

Unleash Your Inner Company chapter	Business Model Canvas elements								
	Customer segments	Value propositions	Channels	Customer relationships	Revenue streams	Key resources	Key activities	Key partnerships	Cost structure
9. Different Is Better than Better		✔							
10. Listen to Your Resources (Step 4a)	✔	✔				✔			
11. Look, Mom . . . I'm Inventing!	✔	✔				✔			
12. 1 + 1 = 3						✔	✔		
13. Matching Needs to Your Resources (Step 5)	✔	✔				✔			
14. The Freedom of Frugality						✔			✔
15. Mind the Gaps (Step 6)						✔			
16. Avoiding Competitors (Step 7)		✔							
17. Where Do Your STARS Shine Brightest?		✔							
18. Partnering, Right-sizing, and Upsizing			✔					✔	
19. Creating Positive Feedback Loops among Customers (Network Effects)				✔					
20. Choose Your Best Opportunity (Step 8)	✔	✔	✔	✔	✔	✔	✔	✔	✔
21. Five Pricing Principles					✔				✔
22. Designing, Customer Testing, and Launching Your Minimum Viable Solution (Step 9)		✔					✔		
23. Don't Waste Time Raising Money						✔			✔
24. Scaling Your Business (Step 10)					✔				✔
25. Regulations: Hidden Roadblocks to Your Success	✔	✔	✔	✔	✔	✔	✔	✔	✔
26. The Ethics of Entrepreneurship	✔	✔	✔	✔	✔	✔	✔	✔	✔

Appendix E

MAKING THE MODERN REGULATORY STATE MORE RESILIENT, HUMANE, AND FRIENDLY TO START-UPS AND INNOVATION

It will be of little avail to the people that the laws are made by men of their own choice if the laws be so voluminous that they cannot be read, or so incoherent that they cannot be understood; if they be repealed or revised before they are promulgated, or undergo such incessant changes that no man, who knows what the law is today, can guess what it will be tomorrow.
—*James Madison*

Modern societies and economies are not mechanical systems that are designed or can be controlled top-down. Their customs, practices, and innovations are emergent, dynamic, and self-organizing. They are much more akin to coral reefs than to machinery. Slight changes in chemistry and temperature can kill a reef. The same is true for regulation of an economy or society. Venture capitalist John Doerr remarked that, we can "bail out the economy, but we can't bail out the environment." The statement is half right. We can't bail out either one.

As was noted in chapter 25, hundreds of thousands of pages of statutes and regulations govern virtually every aspect of life around the globe. Which regulations most inhibit entrepreneurship and stifle innovation—not to mention personal freedom—depends on industry, technology, geography, and regime. Eliminating the most harmful imposed regulations in any jurisdiction would indeed be a positive step. But such regulations are manifold, intertwined, and cancerous: any one, no matter how small, can become a life-, company-, industry-, or society-threatening obstruction. There is no easy fix. For quality of life to advance and humanity to flourish, every single entrepreneur and innovator in the United States and around the world needs to speak out and take a stand:

- To help distinguish between good (organic) and bad (imposed) regulations, which are defined in chapter 25

- To raise awareness of the costs, both explicit (e.g., licenses and penalties) and hidden (e.g., disallowing life-saving drugs), of imposed regulations

- To fight to repeal thousands of imposed regulations

- To adopt new mindsets of extreme forbearance in imposing regulations

- To promote organic regulation as a better way

Given entrenched interests, the path forward is not easy. Entrepreneurs are competing not just with incumbent businesses with political clout but also with regulators themselves interested in preserving or growing their staff, tax revenues, and monopoly power. Here are seven proposals and recommendations.

MAKE EVERY REGULATION AND ITS OVERSIGHT AS LOCAL AS POSSIBLE

Small first steps are to *devolve* regulations—that is, transfer or delegate authority for them from more central to more local jurisdictions. Doing so

- empowers legislators and regulators who are closest to and most informed of local conditions and can best tailor regulations to those conditions,

- makes it easier to hold local legislators and regulators accountable, and

- enables jurisdictions to learn from one another's experiences and experiments.

The shale gas revolution has driven major reductions in natural gas costs and is transforming and lifting the US economy as a result.[1] Shale gas and drilling are regulated mostly by the states, less by the national Environmental Protection Agency (EPA). Individual states are more sensitive to intrastate variations in geology and hydrology of shale formations, in contrast to EPA one-size-fits-all regulations. Such local oversight has helped enable the shale gas revolution.

Do costs of complying with regulations exceed their benefits, whether real or purported? Local legislators and regulators are most readily held accountable for each regulation's benefits exceeding its disadvantages and held responsible for amending or repealing regulations when they don't.

More-local jurisdictions learn from and copy each other. Cities excel at this, adopting best practices from each other for such services as parks and recreation, road maintenance, public transportation, and police and fire protection. Online technologies today let networks of states, cities, and even private citizens coordinate joint efforts and adapt to dynamic circumstances better than federal authorities can. For example, the Harvard Kennedy School's Center for International Development finds that crowdsourcing volunteers with cell phones can gather and disseminate more timely and actionable earthquake and hurricane geographical and weather data than can official emergency response systems that gather and disseminate information centrally.[2]

Beyond greater accountability and adaptability and productivity, multiple decentralized authorities exploring different paths in parallel mean greater and faster learning that benefits everyone. The larger the jurisdictions, the fewer the real-world trials and opportunities for learning.

CAP THE NUMBER OF WORDS AND PAGES OF EACH LAW OR REGULATION AND OF TOTAL REGULATIONS

A brief regulation is not necessarily good, but long, complex regulations are bad. Period. If the number of pages of a law exceeds about a hundred, legislators will not readily absorb their contents, comprehend their probable consequences, or even read them. Unlimited words and pages hide special-interest provisions and invite lobbying and horse-trading to pass the legislation. Their complexity at once empowers regulatory agencies and disempowers the people that the agency serves.

In the United States, further cap the total number of words and pages of the Code of Federal Regulations where the total stands today. For every new number of words or pages approved, eliminate an equal number of words or pages.

CREATE STATE- AND FEDERAL-REGULATION-FREE ZONES

These zones determine their own regulations and taxes. Such zones may be partially or fully exempt from being taxed for or receiving state and federal funds.[3] Starting in 1978, China recognized the economic importance of local autonomy and created six Special Economic Zones (SEZs). The first of these, Shenzhen, has been among the fastest growing economies in the world. In the 1970s, Shenzhen was a fishing village; today it is a sprawling metropolis of approximately fifteen million people. A growing percentage of the world's newest technologies come from China, and Shenzhen in particular, thanks to SEZs.

Eight of the most economically depressed cities in the United States are Akron, Ohio; Cleveland, Ohio; Detroit, Michigan; Flint, Michigan; Gary, Indiana; Lansing, Michigan; Stockton, California; and Toledo, Ohio. To revitalize these and other depressed areas, turn them into state- and federal-regulation-free zones. Government commitments must be genuine and long term—on the order of decades, not merely years—to persuade entrepreneurs that they are not bait-and-switch gimmicks to get them to move and start businesses there. But if the commitments are genuine and long term, watch how quickly entrepreneurs and investors are attracted to and transform these blighted areas.

SEZs in the United States won't help the entire United States immediately, but such pockets of economic freedom and growth will make visible how much better life can be with less regulation. Expect other cities and regions of the United States to clamor for similar treatment.

REQUIRE INNOVATION IMPACT ASSESSMENTS (IIAs)

Before proposed regulations are enacted, require innovation impact assessments. IIAs are similar to environmental impact assessments, assessing how wildlife will coevolve over years with real estate developments and landscaping. Both innovation and the environment are complex systems with aspects that are chaotic, nonlinear, or both that simply cannot be predicted. But where a regulation's impact on innovation can be documented or reasonably predicted, it should be included in regulatory review and approval.

At the Neurogaming 2013 conference, panelists openly shared tips with entrepreneurs on how to avoid the Food and Drug Administration. If your game measures heart rate, don't advertise that fact; otherwise, the game may be considered a medical device and subject to FDA scrutiny. The detrimental impact of FDA regulations on such promising new industries would be highlighted in IIAs and cause regulators to either narrow the scope of regulations or exempt the industries.

The Americans with Disabilities Act requires ubiquitous wheelchair ramps in public places. Has this requirement discouraged investment in and development of smart, low-cost prosthetics that allow the disabled to comfortably negotiate stairs? If so, the ADA is not only hampering innovation but further disabling the disabled.

APPROVE NO STATE OR FEDERAL REGULATION THAT HAS NOT BEEN ENACTED, TESTED, AND PROVEN ON A SMALLER SCALE FIRST

If unexpected costs overwhelm, or unintended consequences circumvent, a regulation's objectives in a smaller jurisdiction, those costs and consequences will surely do so in a larger jurisdiction where the regulation's overall fit with customs, practices, and economic conditions is necessarily worse.

The US Affordable Care Act (ACA) perversely incentivizes business owners to convert formerly full-time employees to part-time status, bad for businesses and employees alike. Testing first on a smaller scale would have revealed this.

Thousands of common law cases provide the experimentation, variation, and selection needed to explore, reveal, and evolve the right laws for a complex society. Good imposed law builds on, and extends no further than, these secure, anti-fragile foundations.

INCLUDE A SUNSET CLAUSE IN EVERY STATUTE THAT SPECIFIES ITS AUTOMATIC EXPIRATION DATE

Technology is changing our lives at an ever-increasing rate, so the period of time a law goes unreviewed should systematically decline. My suggestion: let every regulation expire in no more than ten years, with the limit declining continuously by 10 percent every decade starting today. For any regulation enacted in 2015, its limit would be ten years. For a regulation enacted or reenacted in 2025, the limit would be nine years. If one enacted or reenacted in 2025 still made sense in 2035, its limit then would be approximately eight years.

RELY ON ORGANIC REGULATION

Common law. Supply and demand. Word of mouth. Private contracts. Common law is generally simple and comprehensible, reflects widely accepted norms and practices, and has the fewest unintended consequences. With online social networking, word of mouth is more powerful today than ever before. Private contracts enable self-organization. Further imposing regulations on top of organic regulation creates uncertainty, stifles entrepreneurship and innovation, raises costs and unemployment, and tilts the playing field toward those with the deepest pockets. As we saw in chapter 25, organic regulation fits the complex systems nature of society and best enables it, with minimal unintended consequences, to innovate, progress, and evolve.

NOTES

Chapter 1: Passion and Perseverance

1. A drop of this size is not unusual in a cyclical business with a strong fourth quarter. But not only was our recurring revenue model not particularly cyclical, we also had been enjoying secular (sustained over multiple years) growth of about 20 percent per quarter, or more than doubling each year. So despite its possibly modest sound, a 20 percent drop was very significant.

2. Mihaly Csikszentmihalyi popularized the term in his book *Flow* (Harper Perennial, 1991). Implicit in flow are a challenge, relevant skills, a goal, and feedback. He defines flow as the experience when one's skills are sufficient for a challenging activity, in the pursuit of a clear goal, with immediate feedback on progress toward the goal. In such, concentration is fully engaged in the moment, self-awareness disappears, and sense of time is distorted. Closely related is work by R. M. Ryan and E. L. Deci "Self-determination theory (SDT) and the facilitation of intrinsic motivation, social development, and well-being," *American Psychologist* 2000 Jan; 55(1): 68–78.

3. Opportunities abound for improving on or providing alternatives to government-run services, which, because they are largely insulated from market forces and competition, routinely lag behind privately run services in innovation, customer satisfaction, and efficiency. But regulation often raises obstacles to addressing these opportunities; see chapter 25.

4. Cal Newport, "Follow a Career Passion? Let it Follow You," Job Market Blog, *New York Times*, Sept. 29, 2012, http://www.nytimes.com/2012/09/30/jobs /follow-a-career-passion-let-it-follow-you.html?_r=0.

5. Raman Kumar Jha, *A Short History of Grameen Bank*, Scribd, http://www.scribd .com/doc/74392667/A-Short-History-of-Grameen-Bank#scribd.

6. See Junkin Video, "Underwater Scuba Golf: Par with the Fishes," published Jan. 7, 2014, https://www.youtube.com/watch?v=PSM7T3wIQf8.

Chapter 2: Your Road Map to Creating a New Business

1. You can use this approach not only for new businesses but also for new products, services, and processes within existing businesses and for new features of existing products and services.

Chapter 3: Let a Thousand Needs Bloom

1. See "A computer network based conditional voting system" (www.google.com/patents/US5400248), my first patent. It eventually became part of Google's patent portfolio, but was not incorporated into any Google product, to my knowledge.

2. See John Chisholm, "Decisive Survey for Windows" (1996), posted Nov. 10, 2013, https://www.youtube.com/watch?v=PP4ht52_Lxo.

3. Steve Blank and Bob Dorf, *The Startup Owner's Manual: The Step-by-Step Guide for Building a Great Company* (K&S Ranch, 2012), xxix.

Chapter 4: Discover Your Customers' Goals

1. We'll discover new techniques for thinking of and applying technologies in chapter 11.

2. I can confidently say this because the number of unsatisfied customer needs exceeds by many orders of magnitude the number of people in the world (about seven billion).

Chapter 5: Think Big; Start Focused

1. The "bowling pin" model of using a series of customer need segments to knock down successively larger segments was first widely disseminated by Geoffrey A. Moore in *Crossing the Chasm: Marketing and Selling High-Tech Products to Mainstream Customers* (HarperBusiness Essentials, 1991).

Chapter 6: The Future Is in Your STARS

1. Russell Conwell (1843–1925), founder and first president of Temple University in Philadelphia, popularized this story, "Acres of Diamonds," in early twentieth century speeches. AmericanRhetoric.com today hails them as among America's finest.

2. Stuart Anderson, "40 Percent of Fortune 500 Companies Founded by Immigrants or Their Children," *Forbes*, June 19, 2011, www.forbes.com /sites/stuartanderson/2011/06/19/40-percent-of-fortune-500-companies-founded -by-immigrants-or-their-children/.

3. Sigrid Folkestad, "Entrepreneurs with Little Capital Are Most Successful," *NHH Paraplyen*, March 15, 2012, http://paraplyen.imaker.no/paraplyen/paraplyen_/ english_ve/english_ve/entreprene/.

4. CustomerSat had two great corporate investors, NICE Systems and J.D. Power and Associates, but no venture capital firms as investors. Corporate investors are often more interested in strategic alliances that benefit their existing businesses than in growing start-up companies, and so often cannot or do not provide follow-on growth capital as do most VC firms. Of course, during the dot-com bust, VC firms also were unwilling or unable to provide additional capital for many of their investments.

5. *Entrepreneur* magazine currently ranks Harvard Business School as the #1 graduate program in entrepreneurship worldwide. See www.entrepreneur.com /slideshow/237323.

Chapter 7: Growing Your Mind from the Inside Out

1. "Randy Pausch's Last Lecture," Sept. 18, 2007, http://www.cmu.edu/randyslecture/.

2. The chance that at least one of these four start-ups is successful is 100 percent minus the chance that all of them fail, which is $1 - (1 - 30\%)(1 - 50\%)(1 - 70\%)(1 - 85\%) = 98.425\%$.

3. www.findagrave.com/cgi-bin/fg.cgi?page=pv&GRid=111931926&P lpi=81868608.

Chapter 8: You're a Technologist. Know It.

1. Using business rules, cases were automatically opened and assigned to a client response team when the businesses' high-value customers indicated dissatisfaction in surveys. This feature, called "action management," helped turn surveys into closed-loop processes.

Chapter 9: Different Is Better than Better

1. Interview with Paul Cook in 2012. Tyco International acquired Raychem in 1999.

Chapter 10: Listen to Your Resources

1. HowStuffWorks.com.

2. "Incorrect Predictions," Wikiquote, last modified Feb. 27, 2015, http://en.wikiquote.org/wiki/Incorrect_predictions.

Chapter 11: Look Mom . . . I'm Inventing!

1. See Hyejin Youn et al., Invention as a Combinatorial Process: Evidence from US Patents, June 2014.

2. Personal interview, Erik Brynjolfsson, Director of the MIT Center for Digital Business.

3. Natural language processing (NLP), a field of computer science, artificial intelligence, and linguistics, is concerned with enabling computers to understand and synthesize (generate) human (i.e., natural) language.

4. But with at least two significant differences: (a) a technology may have any number of "parents," and (b) its parents need not be "alive" (currently in use) when the offspring technology is conceived.

Chapter 12: 1 + 1 = 3

1. Dickey, Prabhjot Singh, and I have since cofounded Pyze, Inc. (www.pyze.com), a provider of intelligence solutions for mobile apps.

2. Or business partner. While a cofounder is understood to join a company early on, a business partner may join the company well after it is founded, contribute capital rather than labor, and increase the company's chances of success through relationships, experience, and other means.

3. Larry Reed, "The Deficit Americans Should Think Most About: Personal Character," Jewish World Review, Dec. 2, 2014, http://www.jewishworldreview .com/0611/character_deficit.php3#.VRCNcVrQmgE; Larry Reed, "Character: Nothing Is More Important," *Atlanta Business Chronicle*, May 4, 2012, http: //www.bizjournals.com/atlanta/print-edition/2012/05/04/character-nothing-is -more-important.html?page=all.

4. http://characterfirsteducation.com/c/about.php

5. Most definitions of character disregard this reinforcing feedback between values (attitudes) and actions (behaviors); instead, they see values influencing actions, but not vice versa. For example, CharacterFirst.com defines *character* as "inward values (attitudes) determining outward actions," and CharacterUnlimited.com defines it as "actions taken to carry out the values, ethics, and morals."

6. A different meaning of trust is simply that you can predict what the person will do (good, bad, or neutral), regardless of what they say or don't say they will do. For example, you can be confident (trust) that a person will dress or order her coffee a certain way, arrive at work at a certain time, be cheerful or dour, or be sober or drunk when she shows up at your house. Trust in this neutral sense of predictability has some value in any venture, but not as much as our definition in the chapter.

7. Naval Ravikant, "How to Pick a Co-Founder," Venture Hacks, Nov. 12, 2009, http://venturehacks.com/articles/pick-cofounder.

8. See, for example, Scott E. Page, *The Difference: How the Power of Diversity Creates Better Groups, Firms, Schools, and Societies* (Princeton University Press, 2007).

9. Ibid. Page also shows that physical or identity diversity is mainly valuable to the limited extent that it indicates cognitive diversity.

10. This is an example of a *Goldilocks* effect, in which the optimal value of a variable is intermediate between two extremes. The term comes from the fairy tale "The Three Bears" in which a little girl named Goldilocks enters a house owned by three bears and finds and samples three bowls of porridge. One is too hot, one is too cold, and one is "just right."

Chapter 13: Matching Needs to Your Resources and Passions

1. L. Pritchett & F. de Weijer *Fragile States: Stuck in a Capability Trap? Background Paper to the World Development Report 2011* (World Bank, 2010), http://siteresources. worldbank.org/EXTWDR2011/Resources/6406082-1283882418764/WDR _Background_Paper_Pritchett.pdf.

2. For example, how will the customer click-through rate change if we raise the discount from 10 percent to 20 percent?

3. Contextual data provides context for behaviors and attitudes, and may include demographics (e.g., age, gender, zip code), technographics (e.g., type of mobile device, speed of Internet access), and psychographics (e.g. risk aversion, inclination to judge versus perceive).

Chapter 14: The Freedom of Frugality

1. Nick's counting rules: exclude consumables like food and toiletries; exclude his wife Chloe's possessions; and count things that are always bundled together as one thing (like a first-aid kit or a bundle of pens). For more, see www.nickwinter.net /things.

2. This simple formula makes many assumptions, including that you could liquidate such assets as your home or a business for cash to live on within the time period calculated. It neglects such factors as interest on your investments, inflation, Social Security, any future inherited wealth, and the impact of selling assets on your annual spending. For example, selling a home that you own outright may mean incurring new expenses in rent. For a slightly more detailed calculator, see http: //www.calcxml.com/calculators/i-am-retired-how-long-will-my-savings-last.

3. The larger the number of years calculated, the more this formula understates the true number of years, since the formula ignores interest on your savings and investments.

4. See, for example, http://gosset.wharton.upenn.edu/mortality/perl/CalcForm.html.

Chapter 15: Mind the Gaps

1. *The Perpetual Calendar of Inspiration* (Spirit, 2010).

2. Besides developing and acquiring resources, the other way to improve the fit (close the gap) is to refine or downsize your customer need, as we saw in chapter 5, so that the need can be better satisfied by the resources you already have.

Chapter 16: Avoiding Competitors

1. Pew Research Center Internet and American Life Project 2013 Spring Tracking Survey.

2. Dealer Text Solutions, "Mobile Statistics," http://www.dealertext.com/news /mobile_statistics.html. Total messaging, including conventional short message service (SMS) messaging and Internet-based messaging applications, such as WhatsApp, Facebook Messenger, and Apple iMessage (also known as over-the-top or OTT messaging apps, which are themselves cannibalizing SMS), well exceeds 100 percent per year growth.

3. Greg Bensinger, "Talking Less, Paying More for Voice," *Wall Street Journal*, updated June 5, 2012, http://online.wsj.com/news/articles/SB1000142405270230 4065704577426760861602618.

Chapter 17: Where Do Your STARS Shine Brightest?

1. While the vendors in this example are real, the ratings are fictitious and serve only to illustrate our approach. Since these are established vendors, their resources include their solutions.

2. Not only do the *strengths* of your advantages vary, but also their importance *weightings* vary. If your service bundles full-length movies and video bandwidth, and if the market price for video bandwidth is substantially higher in Belize than in the United States, and if the market price for movies is lower in Belize than in the United States, then customers in Belize will likely weigh your video bandwidth more heavily, and your full-length movies less heavily in importance, than those same products in the United States.

3. Suman Chowdhury, "Some Landmark Innovations of the 21st Century," *Brac*, Feb. 13, 2014, http://learning.brac.net/index.php?option=com _k2&view=item&id=507:some-landmark-innovations-of-the-21st-century.

4. Christine Erickson, "A Brief History of Text Messaging," *Mashable*, Sept. 21, 2012, http://mashable.com/2012/09/21/text-messaging-history/. The iPhone was introduced in 2007.

Chapter 18: Partnering, Rightsizing, and Upsizing

1. These are in addition to your customers, which you may also refer to as partners when you codevelop, codeliver, or customize solutions with or for them.

2. The practice of manufacturing when customers place orders, typically to each customer's specifications, facilitated by advances in 3-D printing and reconfigurable robots and manufacturing systems, on-demand manufacturing reduces costs of inventory and eliminates need for shipping from manufacturing plant to warehouse.

3. Supply chain management (SCM) encompasses sourcing (identifying potential suppliers); procurement (negotiating with and purchasing from those suppliers); logistics (management of flows of materials, services, information, and payments for them); and more broadly, coordination and collaboration among a company's suppliers and channel partners. The loosely coupled, self-organizing network of businesses that make up a supply chain is sometimes called an *extended enterprise*. For more, see Council of Supply Chain Management Professionals (http://cscmp.org).

4. See, for example, Jeff Bercovici, "Amazon Vs. Book Publishers, By the Numbers," *Forbes*, Feb. 2, 2014, http://www.forbes.com/sites/jeffbercovici/2014/02/10/amazon-vs-book-publishers-by-the-numbers/.

5. See Amy Dusto, "60% of U.S. Retail Sales Will Involve the Web by 2017," *Internet Retailer*, Oct. 30, 2013, https://www.internetretailer.com/2013/10/30/60-us-retail-sales-will-involve-web-2017.

6. For "network" businesses—those in which more of one type of user attracts more of either a complementary type of user (e.g., credit card users and merchants that accept those cards, electronic device users and application developers for the device, buyers and sellers on eBay, men and women on Match.com, or drivers

and passengers on Uber and Lyft) or the same type of user (e.g., video callers on Apple FaceTime or friends on Facebook)—increasing the size of your market may strengthen your overall advantage. For more on this, see the next chapter, chapter 19 "Creating Positive Feedback Loops among Customers."

7. For more on how the economy is a complex adaptive system, see Eric Beinhocker, *The Origin of Wealth* (Harvard Business School Press, 2006); and Brian Arthur, *Complexity and the Economy* (Oxford University Press, 2015).

Chapter 19: Creating Positive Feedback Loops among Customers

1. I have taken the liberty of editing Darwin's original text to make it clearer to modern readers; the quote is Darwin describing the accelerating pace of pasture development due to the positive feedback loop between earthworms and plants: more earthworms → more feces → more mold → more fertile soil → more plants → more earthworms. *The Formation of Vegetable Mould, Through the Action of Worms, with Observations on their Habits* (1881).

2. A measure of the potential value of a network is the number of possible pair-wise connections among its N users, *viz.* $N(N-1)/2$, which is approximated by N^2 for large N. For the actual value of the network to equal the potential value using this measure, every user would have to connect with every other, and every connection would have to have equal value. Since only some users in a network are typically directly connected, some view $N \log N$ as a better measure of actual network value. Of course, $N(N-1)/2$ is also the number of pairs of N technologies we saw in chapter 11 "Look, Mom . . . I'm Inventing!" and in appendix B "Visualizing Numbers of Combinations." Most combinations of technologies are not useful, so possibly $N \log N$ also better approximates the actual value of a set of N technologies. In any event, the value of either network or set of technologies increases faster than linearly with N. For more, see Bob Briscoe, Andrew Odlyzko, and Benjamin Tilly, "Metcalfe's Law Is Wrong," *IEEE Spectrum*, posted July 1, 2006, http://spectrum.ieee.org/computing/networks/metcalfes-law-is-wrong, named after Ethernet coinventor Bob Metcalfe. I don't agree with the article's characterization of Metcalfe's Law as wrong, just that potential network value is frequently misstated as actual value.

3. FaceTime is actually part of a double network. Besides attracting more FaceTime users (one-sided network), FaceTime also makes the iPhone's iOS operating system more attractive to software developers, thus attracting more third-party apps that subsidize the costs of both FaceTime and iPhone (two-sided network).

4. The underlying dynamic is called preferential attachment and gives rise to networks whose numbers of nodes (in this case, users or customers) are approximated by power-law distributions. For more, see M. J. Newman, *Networks* (Oxford University Press, 2011), 247, 487.

5. Google speeds searching by suggesting possible completed search criteria and displaying possible results as the user types, both based in part on searches by millions of other users.

6. In contrast, most online dating sites charge men and women equally. At this writing, Tinder has no user fees, advertising, or revenue but has announced plans for premium subscriptions.

7. See the now-classic paper by Thomas R. Eisenmann, Geoffrey Parker, and Marshall W. Van Alstyne, "Strategies for Two-Sided Markets," *Harvard Business Review*, Oct. 2006.

8. See David Gelles, "Question-and-Answer Site Quora Raises $80 Million," DealBook, April 9, 2014, http://dealbook.nytimes.com/2014/04/09/question-and-answer-site-quora-raises-80-million/. The company was founded in 2009.

9. See Sangeet Paul Choudary, "How to Build a Two-Sided Marketplace with the Yelp Model," *Platform Thinking* blog, platformed.info/yelp-craigslist-padmapper-two-sided-marketplace/.

Chapter 20: Choose Your Best Opportunity

1. This approach is a variation on the venerable SWOT (strengths, weaknesses, opportunities, threats) matrix. Strengths and weaknesses are your STARS relative to competitors (advantages and disadvantages); opportunities and threats are your customer needs and external risks respectively. Broadly, strengths and weaknesses are internal to you and your organization; opportunities and threats are external. When presented as a 2 x 2 matrix, a SWOT analysis has Helpful-Harmful on one axis, and Internal-External on the other.

Chapter 21: Five Pricing Principles

1. See Mark Stiving, "Value-Based Pricing (VBP)," *Pragmatic Marketing*, May 4, 2010, pragmaticpricing.com/2010/05/04/value-based-pricing-vbp/.

2. Net revenue and net sales are distinguished from *gross revenue*, which is the revenue that a company receives in a specific period, before commissions and other discounts and deductions for returned units.

3. If customers returning units receive only partial refunds, and unit returned, if physical, can be resold with minimal cost or refurbishment, your gross margin can increase and your breakeven point decrease as a result. However, returned units may indicate customer dissatisfaction, a negative factor not reflected in gross margin or breakeven.

4. Although sales commissions vary with sales, they are usually treated as one of the deductions to sales (along with customer and trade discounts) to get net sales, rather than as a variable cost. This treatment of sales commissions does not affect contribution or contribution per unit, but it does affect gross margin. For example, if sales were $100, commissions were $10, and other variable costs were $40, so that contribution per unit was ($100 − $10) − $40 = $50, then gross margin would be contribution/net sales = $50/($100 − $10) = $50/$90 = 55.5%. If sales commissions were instead treated as variable costs rather than as a deduction to sales, contribution per unit would still be $100 − ($10 + $40) = $50 but gross margin would be $50/$100 = 50%.

5. If x is your breakeven units, then breakeven revenue = x(net sales per unit) = x(variable cost per unit) + fixed costs. That is, x is the number of units for which your total net sales equals your total variable costs plus fixed costs. Solving, x = (fixed costs)/(net sales per unit − variable cost per unit) = fixed costs/(contribution per unit).*

6. As we just saw, breakeven units = fixed costs/(contribution per unit). Also, since gross margin = contribution/net sales, it follows that (net sales per unit) = (contribution per unit)/gross margin. So using these two expressions for breakeven units and net sales per unit in the equation breakeven revenue = (breakeven units)(net sales per unit) and simplifying, we get: breakeven revenue = (fixed costs/[contribution per unit]) × ([contribution per unit]/gross margin). Simplifying, we get breakeven revenue = fixed costs/gross margin.*

7. If, as in our toy bear example, you sell to wholesalers, retailers, or resellers, and not directly to retail customers, and base breakeven revenue on your net sales into these channels rather than retail revenue, breakeven revenue may be referred to as *wholesale* breakeven revenue.*

---

*Accounting is not conceptually difficult, but the wide range of businesses and number of financial details it must address, and accounting terminologies in common use, make it complicated. You can see why modern civilization has evolved Certified Public Accountants (CPAs) and generally accepted accounting principles (GAAP).

8. As shown here, you can also express breakeven revenue in terms of retail revenue, rather than net sales, simply by multiplying breakeven units by retail sales price. The number of units that you must sell to reach breakeven is the same.*

9. A more complex but realistic model would recognize that a large percentage of toys are sold during the holiday season (October through December). It is not uncommon for two-thirds of a toy's annual sales to occur in the fourth calendar quarter. Appendix C builds a one-year financial model for your toy bear business that assumes that half of your annual sales will be in the fourth quarter.

10. From "free + premium." "Freemium" may be either a noun (the product or service offered for free) or an adjective (referring to such free products and services).

11. Erick Schonfeld, "Skype Files for IPO, Only 6 Percent of Users Pay, TechCrunch, posted Aug. 9, 2010, http://techcrunch.com/2010/08/09/skype-ipo/.

Chapter 22: Designing, Customer Testing, and Launching Your Minimum Viable Solution

1. "Minimum viable product" (MVP) is more widely used, but I prefer "minimum viable solution" (MVS) to include both products and services.

2. When Decisive Survey 1.0 was launched in 1995, virtually all email was text based. Few email users had access to the Web and HTML forms that would later become the standard for online surveys.

3. The term *gamma* test is also used to denote later stages of beta test. See also "Software Release Life Cycle," Wikipedia, last modified March 11, 2015, http://en.wikipedia.org/wiki/Software_release_life_cycle.

4. The workstation was the Xerox 6085, better known as the Xerox Star. It was the butt of such Silicon Valley jokes as, "What do you call Lassie, Rin-Tin-Tin, and the Xerox 6085? Two stars and a dog." In fairness to the Xerox Star, it was the hugely groundbreaking workstation whose pioneering graphical user interface was copied by the Apple Mac, Microsoft Windows, and others. Had Xerox targeted the Star at the outset narrowly for technical publishing (the positioning Xerox ultimately

---

*Accounting is not conceptually difficult, but the wide range of businesses and number of financial details it must address, and accounting terminologies in common use, make it complicated. You can see why modern civilization has evolved Certified Public Accountants (CPAs) and generally accepted accounting principles (GAAP).

arrived at for the Star) and expanded from there "bowling pin style" as we saw in chapter 5, rather than broadly for office automation, the Star would be remembered today as a commercial as well as technical success, in my view.

5. If your customers are consumers, you may also want to have a presence on YouTube, Instagram, and/or Pinterest. Most of the same content can be used on all these platforms, but every platform has unique requirements. Be cautious of spreading your marketing resources too thin.

6. Mike Blumenthal, "Hitwise: Google Maps Passes MapQuest," *Blumenthals Blog*, April 13, 2009, blumenthals.com/blog/2009/04/13/hitwise-google-maps-passes -mapquest/.

Chapter 23: Don't Waste Time Raising Money

1. The Jumpstart Our Business Startups (JOBS) Act, which provides rules for small businesses to raise funds from nonaccredited investors, is expected to take effect in late 2015 or early 2016.

Chapter 24: Scaling Your Business

1. Like profit, there are many definitions of cash flow. One common definition is the following:

   Cash flow (from operations, for a particular time period) = Net profit + depreciation − increases in accounts receivable − increases in Inventories + increases in accounts payable. Equivalently, cash flow is the difference between actual cash received from, and actual cash used for, the company's operations for the period. *Total* (as opposed to *operational*) cash flow includes changes in cash reserves resulting from investments (purchase or sale of long-term investments such as land, buildings, equipment, and vehicles) and financing activities (raising equity, issuing debt, paying off debt, or paying dividends).

2. Operating profit = net sales − variable costs − fixed costs.

3. Technographics segments consumers based on ownership, usage, and attitudes toward information, communication, and entertainment technologies; psychographics segments consumers based on personality, values, beliefs, and lifestyles.

Chapter 25: Regulations: Hidden Roadblocks to Your Success

1. Michael Snyder, "12 Ridiculous Government Regulations That Are Almost Too Bizarre to Believe," *Business Insider*, Nov. 12, 2010, http://www.businessinsider .com/ridiculous-regulations-big-government-2010-11?op=1.

2. See http://www.irs.gov/uac/Form-SS-8,-Determination-of-Worker-Status-for-Pur poses-of-Federal-Employment-Taxes-and-Income-Tax-Withholding. I am not sure if worker status is more onerous today than in 1992 because of changes to the reg- ulation, stricter enforcement, or a combination of the two. Form SS-8 was revised thirteen times between 1985 and 2014, both reflecting and contributing to the uncertainty of the regulatory environment.

3. In *Simple Rules for a Complex World* (Harvard University Press, 1995), author and law professor Richard Epstein says, "Never ask more from a legal system than covering 90–95 percent of the cases; the effort to clean up the last 5 percent leads to the system's unraveling." With worker status, the IRS appears to me to be trying to cover 99.9999999999 percent of the cases.

4. A tax lien is federal, state, or local government's right to keep possession of prop- erty to secure the payment of taxes. Tax liens are more enforcement mechanism than regulation.

5. I put "Affordable" in quotes because tens of millions of US citizens' insurance premiums have skyrocketed as a result of ACA.

6. See "Federal Register Document Pages Annual Percentage Change 1976–2013," https://www.federalregister.gov/uploads/2014/04/OFR-STATISTICS-CHARTS -ALL1-1-1-2013.pdf.

7. See Taxpayer Advocate Service, "The Complexity of the Tax Code," *2008 Annual Report to Congress*, vol. 1, http://www.irs.gov/pub/tas/08_tas_arc_msp_1.pdf.

8. Institute for Justice, "License to Work: A National Study of Burdens from Occupa- tional Licensing, Introduction," https://www.ij.org/l2w-intro.

9. "Braiding Freedom: A Project of the Institute for Justice," http://braidingfreedom .com/#report.

10. Source: Bob Luddy, founder and CEO of CaptiveAire.

11. Barry Lynn & Lina Khan, "Out of Business," *New America Foundation*, July 2012, http://newamerica.net/publications/policy/out_of_business.

12. *Small Business Administration and Job Creation*, Congressional Research Service, Jan. 30, 2013.

13. Ying Lowrey, "Estimating Entrepreneurial Jobs: Business Creation Is Job Creation" American Economic Association Annual Meeting, 2011, Jan. 8, 2011, http://papers.ssrn.com/sol3/papers.cfm?abstract_id=1759548.

14. Robert Pear, "Faster Approval of AIDS Drugs Is Urged," *New York Times*, Aug. 16, 1990, Late Edition—Final, Section B; Page 12, Column 4. The credit for the saved lives would (deservedly) go to the pharmaceutical innovators, not the FDA.

15. The CE marking (an acronym for the French *Conformité Européenne*), required to market many products in the European Union, certifies that a product has met EU health, safety, and environmental requirements.

16. Source: Fred Dotzler, De Novo Ventures.

17. See Simon Goodall and Jennifer Tom, "Regulation and Access to Innovative Medical Technologies," June 2012, http://www.eucomed.org/uploads/ModuleXtender /Newsroom/97/2012_bcg_report_regulation_and_access_to_innovative_medical _technologies.pdf. The BCG study also finds that, despite its much longer approval times, US PMA is no more of a safeguard than the EU CE mark.

18. See Alex Davies, "The UK Just Made Itself a Fantastic Place to Test Self-Driving Cars," *Wired*, Feb. 12, 2015, http://www.wired.com/2015/02 /uk-just-made-fantastic-place-test-self-driving-cars/.

19. Among Amtrak's many accountability problems is employee theft. See "Amtrak Losing Millions Each Year on Food Sales," *New York Times*, Aug. 2, 2012, http: //www.nytimes.com/2012/08/03/us/politics/amtrak-lost-834-million-on-food-in -last-decade-audit-finds.html?_r=0.

20. See Frederic Bastiat, *That Which Is Seen, and that Which Is Not Seen*, "The Broken Window," 1850, http://bastiat.org/en/twisatwins.html; and Jodi Beggs, "The Broken Window Fallacy," About Education, http://economics.about.com/od /output-income-prices/a/The-Broken-Window-Fallacy.htm.

21. For a discussion of how property rights and free trade can emerge spontaneously in society, see, for example, Economics Nobel prize winner Vernon Smith, *Rationality in Economics: Constructionist and Ecological Forms* (Cambridge University Press, 2008), 16–18, 192–194.

22. Other examples of complex systems are the environment and the human brain. For more, see Melanie Mitchell, *Complexity: A Guided Tour* (Oxford University Press, 2009).

23. Table A1 in appendix A shows how over half the steps of our ten-step process to discover your best business opportunity similarly involve variation or selection.

24. Nassim Nicholas Taleb, *Antifragile: Things That Gain from Disorder* (Random House, 2012); Taleb, *The Black Swan: The Impact of the Highly Improbable* (Random House, 2007).

25. Oliver Wendell Holmes Jr., *The Common Law* (1881).

26. See, for example, Paul G. Mahoney, "The Common Law and Economic Growth: Hayek Might Be Right," *The Journal of Legal Studies,* 30, no. 2 (June 2001), 503–52

27. Theodore F. T. Plucknett, *A Concise History of the Common Law*, 5th ed. (Lawbook Exchange, 2001).

28. Rafael La Porta, Florencio Lopez-de-Silanes, and Andrei Shleifer, "The Economic Consequences of Legal Origins," *National Bureau of Economic Research*, Working Paper 13608, Nov. 2007, http://www.nber.org/papers/w13608.

29. Gillian K. Hadfield, "The Quality of Law in Civil Code and Common Law Regimes: Judicial Incentives, Legal Human Capital and the Evolution of Law," University of Southern California Law School (March 2006).

30. See Federal Aviation Administration, "Unmanned Aircraft Systems," last modified March 12, 2015, https://www.faa.gov/uas/. In February 2015, the FAA proposed new rules that if approved will allow commercial use of UAVs within the other four constraints.

31. See A. Michael Froomkin and Zak Colangelo, "Self-Defense Against Robots," March 2014, http://works.bepress.com/amichael_froomkin/2.

32. See James M. Anderson et al., *Autonomous Vehicle Technology: A Guide for Policymakers* (Santa Monica, CA: Rand, 2014), http://www.rand.org/content/dam/rand/pubs/research_reports/RR400/RR443-1/RAND_RR443-1.pdf.

33. Andy Boxall, "2014 Is the Year of Health and Fitness Apps Says Google," *Digital Trends*, Dec. 11, 2014, http://www.digitaltrends.com/mobile/google-play-store-2014-most-downloaded-apps.

34. World Bank Group, "Doing Business: Economy Rankings," http://www.doing-business.org/rankings/; see also *Doing Business 2015: Going Beyond Efficiency, Economy Profile 2015 United States,* (Washington, DC: World Bank Group, 2014), http://www.doingbusiness.org/~/media/giawb/doing%20business/documents/profiles/country/USA.pdf.

35. Matthew Dolan, "To Outfox the Chicken Tax, Ford Strips Its Own Vans," *Wall Street Journal,* Sept. 23, 2009, http://www.wsj.com/articles/SB125357990638429655.

36. See Liz Alderman, "Au Revoir, Entrepreneurs," *New York Times,* March 22, 2014, www.nytimes.com/2014/03/23/business/international/some-french-entrepreneurs -say-au-revoir.html.

37. Caroline Bauman, "Kansas City Suburb to Allow 9-Year-Old's Little Free Library," *Wichita Eagle*, July 8, 2014, www.kansas.com/news/article1148033.html.

Chapter 26: The Ethics of Entrepreneurship

1. If a casino, or "house," keeps a share of each player's winnings, then gambling is negative-sum for the players.

2. Robert Wright makes the compelling case that the entire rise of civilization over the millennia is due to humanity turning zero-sum into positive-sum interactions. See Robert Wright, *Nonzero: The Logic of Human Destiny* (Pantheon Books, 2000).

3. See the timeless *The Theory of Moral Sentiments* (1759) and *The Wealth of Nations* (1776).

4. Wages and prices are the means by which information about demand and supply is conveyed throughout the economy. Inflation (increases in the money supply) affects different parts of the economy unevenly and with different time delays, causing wages and prices to rise and fall relative to each other for reasons other than changes in demand and supply. Unsound currency thus adds "noise" to wage and price "signals" and disrupts positive-sum exchanges. George Gilder describes how the economy is an information system in *Knowledge and Power: The Information Theory of Capitalism and How it Is Revolutionizing Our World* (Regnery, 2013).

5. If not implicit in free trade and protection of private property, a sixth Adam Smith Rule would be just enforcement of agreements (contracts).

6. In *The Origin of Wealth: Evolution, Complexity, and the Radical Remaking of Economics* (Harvard Business School Press, 2006), economist Eric Beinhocker estimates the number of stockkeeping units (SKUs) in the world to be about twelve billion. I estimate (conservatively) that that number has approximately quadrupled in the decade from 2006 to 2015 (about 15 percent growth per year).

7. The number of products and services in the world does not necessarily equal the number of dimensions of human needs served, because (1) some products and services satisfy the same human need (e.g., two identical competing products); (2) some satisfy different human needs (e.g., water is good for drinking, bathing, and swimming); and (3) some satisfy the same needs for different groups of humans (e.g., massage services in Australia versus Africa versus Asia).

8. Abraham Maslow, *Motivation and Personality* (Harper & Row, 1970).

9. Economists use "scarce" to describe any finite resource—for example, Pepsi, books, or clothes hangers—whether in short or ample supply. Common parlance, in contrast, uses it to mean in short supply. Here I use "scarcity" to mean *declining* availability of resources over time—i.e., trends—not their absolute availability. This is closer to common parlance: A good may be said to be scarce if it has recently become less available or affordable (its cost has gone up in terms of what one has to give up to get it). Using my definitions, scarcity and abundance may arise in any economy, no matter how primitive or advanced.

10. See "Medical Devices and Pharmaceuticals: Two Different Worlds in One Health Setting," Eucomed, http://www.eucomed.org/key-themes/medical-devices-directives/devices-pharmaceuticals.

11. "List of Popular Music Genres," Wikipedia, last modified on March 12, 2015, http://en.wikipedia.org/wiki/List_of_popular_music_genres.

12. "Agriculture in the United States," Wikipedia, last modified on March 11, 2015, http://en.wikipedia.org/wiki/Agriculture_in_the_United_States.

13. In *The Population Bomb* Ehrlich argued that mankind was facing a demographic catastrophe with population growth quickly outstripping growth in food supplies and resources. But the opposite happened: The percentage of people and land required to feed the growing world population has steadily declined, and growing wealth has caused birthrates to decline naturally.

14. "Haiti vs. Dominican Republic," Index Mundi (Source *CIA Factbook*), http://www.indexmundi.com/factbook/compare/haiti.dominican-republic.

15. Nathanial Gronewold, "Environmental Destruction, Chaos Bleeding Across Haitian Border," *New York Times*, Dec. 14, 2009, http://www.nytimes.com/gwire/2009/12/14/14greenwire-environmental-destruction-chaos-bleeding-acros-35779.html?pagewanted=all.

16. Thought leaders who are helping others see the world as positive-sum include Matt Ridley, author of *The Rational Optimist: How Prosperity Evolves* (HarperCollins, 2010), Peter Diamandis, cofounder of Singularity University and author of *Abundance: The Future Is Better than You Think* (Free Press, 2012); Ramez Naam, author of *The Infinite Resource: The Power of Ideas on a Finite Planet* (University Press of New England, 2013); Byron Reese, author of *Infinite Progress: How the Internet and Technology Will End Ignorance, Disease, Poverty, Hunger, and War* (Greenleaf Book Group, 2013); and Arnold Kling and Nick Schultz, *From Poverty to Prosperity: Intangible Assets, Hidden Liabilities and the Lasting Triumph over Scarcity* (Encounter Books, 2009).

17. "MITx" edX, https://www.edx.org/school/mitx.

18. See Terry L. Anderson, "If Hayek and Coase Were Environmentalists: Linking Economics and Ecology," The Ends of Capitalism conference, NYU School of Law, Feb. 25–27, 2015.

19. Peter Foster, "Venezuela's 'Socialist Paradise' Turns into a Nightmare: Medical Shortages Claim Lives as Oil Price Collapses," Feb. 3, 2015, http://www.telegraph.co.uk/news/worldnews/southamerica/venezuela/11385294/Venezuelas-socialist-paradise-turns-into-a-nightmare-medical-shortages-claim-lives-as-oil-price-collapses.html.

20. Andrew Rosati and Noris Soto,"Venezuelans Throng Grocery Stores under Military Protection, " Bloomberg Business, Jan. 9, 2015, http://www.bloomberg.com/news/articles/2015-01-09/venezuelans-throng-grocery-stores-on-military-protection-order.

21. Steven Pinker, *The Better Angels of Our Nature: Why Violence Has Declined* (Viking Penguin, 2011).

Appendix B: Visualizing Numbers of Combinations

1. In general, if you have N technologies taken M at a time, the number of combinations is $N!/(M!(N - M)!)$, where "!" is pronounced "factorial." $3! = 3 \times 2 \times 1 = 6$. So six technologies taken three at a time is $6!/(3! \times 3!) = 6 \times 5 \times 4 \times 3 \times 2 \times 1/(3 \times 2 \times 1) \times (3 \times 2 \times 1) = 20$ combinations.

2. Ricardo Hausmann of Harvard and Cesar Hidalgo of MIT show that a country's economic growth is driven and predicted by the number of combinations of its capabilities, ranging from technologies to raw materials. R. Hausmann and C. Hidalgo "The Network Structure of Economic Output," *Journal of Economic Growth,* (2011), 1–34.

Appendix C: Creating Financial Models of Your Business

1. Use any spreadsheet software such as Microsoft Excel (part of Office), Apple Numbers (part of iWork), or Apache OpenOffice to build your model and see the impact of different assumptions.

2. For a step-by-step guide to creating a financial model of all three financial statements, see http://www.streetofwalls.com/finance-training-courses/investment-banking-technical-training/three-statement-financial-modeling.

Appendix D: Unleash Your Inner Company and the Business Model Canvas

1. Alexander Osterwalder and Yves Pigneur, *Business Model Generation: A Handbook for Visionaries, Game Changers, and Challengers* (Wiley, 2010).

Appendix E: Making the Modern Regulatory State More Resilient, Humane, and Friendly to Start-Ups

1. See David Brooks, "Shale Gas Revolution," *New York Times,* Op-Ed Columnist, Nov. 3, 2011, http://www.nytimes.com/2011/11/04/opinion/brooks-the-shale-gas-revolution.html?_r=0.

2. Asim Ijaz Khwaja, "Natural Disasters Decentralized Responses," Evidence for Policy Design, Center for International Development, Oct. 2012, www.hks.harvard.edu/index.php/content/download/70466/1254674/version/1/file/Natural+DisastersAsim.pdf.

3. As one example, the autonomous Basque Country of Spain collects all of its own taxes and pays a fixed 7 percent to 8 percent of them to the Spanish federal government, which is generally lower than the rest of Spain. In a positive feedback look with this arrangement, the Basque region enjoys the highest per capita income in Spain.

ABOUT THE AUTHOR

John Chisholm has three decades of experience as entrepreneur, CEO, and investor. He founded and for five years served as Chairman/CEO of Decisive Technology (now part of Google), publisher of the first desktop and client-server software for online surveys. Later, he founded and for eleven years served as Chairman/CEO of CustomerSat (now part of Confirmit), a leading provider of enterprise feedback management systems. Earlier he served in marketing and management positions at General Electric, HP, Xerox, and Grid Systems. Today he serves as CEO of John Chisholm Ventures, an entrepreneurship advisory and investment firm, and chairman of Pyze, a mobile intelligence firm.

He is president of the worldwide MIT Alumni Association, a member of the MIT Corporation (board of directors), and a trustee of the Santa Fe Institute. He has served on the advisory boards of the Network for Teaching Entrepreneurship (NFTE), the Gruter Institute for Law and Behavioral Research, the Antigua Forum, and Spark Academy, a Khan Academy Partner School. He is a member of the Global Partners Council of the Institute for New Economic Thinking (INET) and advises entrepreneurs through the MIT Venture Mentoring Service, the Thiel Foundation 20under20 Fellowship, and the Plug and Play Tech Center. He has chaired the Stanford Institute for the Quantitative Study of Society, one of Stanford's independent laboratories and served on the visiting committee of the MIT math department.

He holds bachelors and masters degrees in electrical engineering and computer science from MIT and an MBA from Harvard Business School. An avid mountain climber, he has summited Mounts Rainier, Shasta, Whitney, St. Helens, and live volcanoes in Chile and Indonesia.

INDEX